D0077944

CLASSROOM DISCIPLINE

for Effective Teaching and Learning

LAUREL N. TANNER Temple University

**HOLT,
RINEHART
AND
WINSTON**

New York
Chicago
San Francisco
Atlanta
Dallas
Montreal
Toronto
London
Sydney

Mount Saint Mary's College
Emmitsburg, MD 21727

WITHDRAWN

FOR
Dan

Library of Congress Cataloging in Publication Data
Tanner, Laurel N.
    Classroom discipline for effective teaching and
learning.

    Includes bibliographical references.
    1. School discipline. 2. Educational psychology.
I. Title.
LB3011.T36   371.1'02   77-22595
ISBN 0-03-019446-6

Copyright © 1978 by Holt, Rinehart and Winston
All rights reserved
Printed in the United States of America
8 9 0 1   090   9 8 7 6 5 4 3 2 1

FOREWORD

Classroom discipline is a menacing term when voiced. Its paired sibilants give off a fork-tongued hiss. Equally menacing are the mental images it brings to mind: rapped knuckles, dunce caps, hickory sticks —those relics of pedagogical sadism long past—or more modern-day visions of frustrated teachers splintering pencils and rulers on the edges of desks as they rap vainly for order at the close of a trying day. Shouts and commands, reprimands and threats, denials and deprivations—harsh utterances all, and all a part of our collective memory of what the keeping of order in classrooms can entail. Such thoughts are better forgotten and with them the term that summons them forth: classroom discipline—hardly a topic to buoy the spirits, a dismal and oppressive sport.

In this book Laurel Tanner reveals how misguided and shortsighted such a view truly is. The subject, as she treats it, is far from dismal and oppressive. On the contrary, with her customary skill and grace she succeeds in doing what we have been told from childhood cannot be done: making a silk purse out of a sow's ear. Suddenly, instead of a door in our memory to be kept shut, classroom discipline becomes a window through which to view in a fresh light many persistent educational problems. Curriculum reform? The key to eliminating those fearful visions of unruly classes that keep young teachers awake at night. Moral development? No less than the goal toward which the teacher is moving when she raises her hand for silence. Classroom ecology? The floor-to-ceiling approach to disciplinary problems. And so it goes. The central topic remains our old friend, or enemy, classroom discipline, but by turning it upside down and inside out in a manner that comes close to legerdemain Tanner manages to trace its linkage to our most profound educational questions, all of which boil down to the single query: what is school all about? Classroom discipline is not the answer to that question, as Tanner clearly understands; but as she slowly unravels the complexity of her subject, we begin to suspect that the answer is not far afield.

I admit to being carried away with enthusiasm for this informative and down-to-earth treatment of the topic that heads the list of our pedagogical woes, but my reaction is at least understandable in the light of my initial expectations. For, triggered by the title alone, Dickensian visions of Mr. Gradgrind* twisting the ear of a hapless student danced in my head as I turned to the text. Given my prior acquaintance with the author's insight into educational affairs, I should have known better from the start. All readers lacking that acquaintance and all who suffer, as did I, from such outdated and negative associations to the term: classroom discipline, are in for a pleasant surprise.

Philip W. Jackson

University of Chicago
June 29, 1977

* Dickens: *Hard Times.*

PREFACE

This is a book for everyone who is interested in orderly classrooms, places where learning can take place. Classroom teachers, their college instructors, school administrators, and parents will find answers for their concern about school discipline in the body of knowledge and the set of guiding principles for classroom management presented here.

Classroom Discipline for Effective Teaching and Learning is a practical guide for those who will be or are practicing education. It is designed for use in courses that deal with methods of teaching and for the classroom teacher who may be experiencing disciplinary problems or may simply wish to enlarge his or her repertoire of disciplinary concepts and practices. It is my hope that the profession at large, as well as the general public, will find the book useful in extending their understanding of the theory and applications of school discipline.

Anyone who has lived through the 1960s and 1970s cannot help but be aware of the concern and controversy surrounding school discipline. The reform movement of the sixties was a revolt against the traditional school, conceived as an impersonal and dehumanizing institution. Doubtlessly, the movement awakened in many parents and teachers the hope that schools might play a more positive role in children's lives. Yet too many of the reform books were filled with fiery rhetoric and devoid of practical suggestions. Much of the polemic writing of the sixties was based on a premise that is both incorrect and dangerous—that our children's troubles are all the result of restrictions imposed on them by inhumane and demanding schools. The 1960s reform style was "do-your-own-thing." In too many classrooms pupils were left to their own unguided spontaneity. The idea of development was approached in an empty way—with predictably disappointing results.

The reckless radicalism of the 1960s led to widespread demands for a return to "the basics" in the 1970s. The obvious counterpart in school discipline was rigid control by external discipline—discipline for its own sake. In an effort to redress the excesses and correct the mistakes of one era, new excesses were created and new mistakes made.

Amid the educational battles and shifting stances about school discipline, the school's objective remains constant. Self-direction is the goal of discipline in a democratic society. In light of this objective, neither turning children loose in an unstructured environment nor autocratic control is acceptable. Most teachers would probably agree that these are dead ends for self-direction, but this still leaves them with the question of what to do next. Without a practical guide, "self-direction" bogs hopelessly into cliché. This is precisely the problem confronting teachers. Self-direction is the goal, but how does one help children move in that direction? Teachers are in the position of trying to build a house without blueprints. The specter of its falling apart is ever present. The applications contained in this book are intended to provide a blueprint for self-direction.

Oddly enough, while the foremost concern of both prospective teachers and the general public is school discipline, there *does* exist a body of knowledge for teachers. The problem is that this knowledge is usually presented in piecemeal fashion so that concepts and ideas appear in conflict and discipline is divorced from teaching and learning. Seldom are teachers provided with knowledge about models of discipline as alternative routes to classroom control. Rather they are presented with a single model. The consequence is that the model fails to meet all of the teacher's needs and is readily discarded in favor of another model, soon to suffer the same fate. Throughout this book emphasis is given to the need for teachers to have at their command alternative models of discipline, the need for following an ecological approach to discipline— identifying the factors which are within the teacher's power to control and influence, and the need for viewing classroom discipline, curriculum, and instruction relatedly.

In the twentieth century punitive methods of education and socialization have given way to a concept of helping an individual to develop. In recent years, psychology has made spectacular progress in describing the course of human development. However, only the most general educational aims can be located in developmental stages, and developmental psychology stops short of prescribing what to do about classroom discipline. Teachers need a developmental guide to discipline which they can use to determine the characteristics of pupil behavior at various stages and which defines the teacher's role in getting pupils to each stage. This book presents the developmental stages of discipline, a conceptual framework for the role of the teacher.

It is vitally important that short-range disciplinary measures be consonant with long-range developmental goals. The disciplinary techniques discussed throughout the book and particularly in Chapters 9 and 10 are examined in light of their consonance or conflict with long-range goals. Thus, the developmental stages provide an anchor or point of reference for teachers in deciding whether or not to use a given strategy.

Principles of classroom discipline are presented throughout all of the chapters. They are offered at the start of the book as a kind of preamble and reflect the nature of content covered in each chapter.

I am greatly indebted to my students and colleagues at Temple University who read and criticized the book during its conceptual stages. For helpful criticism of the manuscript, I am deeply in the debt of Bruce D. Cheney of Michigan State University, Richard H. Coop of the University of North Carolina, Donald R. Cruickshank of the Ohio State University, Norma M. Dimmitt of the University of Washington, Phil C. Lang of Teachers College, Columbia University, and Dorothy A. Moore of George Washington University. For contributions to my thinking on the personal-social growth model of discipline, I am most grateful to Lawrence Cremin of Teachers College, Columbia University. To E. Edmund Reutter, Jr., also of Teachers College, I owe a special word of thanks for his valuable suggestions on the chapter, "Dealing with Discipline Problems." Marion Ann Keller, who typed the manuscript, deserves special appreciation. Finally, my debt to my husband is reflected in the dedication.

Philadelphia, Pa. L. T.

CONTENTS

Foreword   iii

Preface   v

1   The Nature of Discipline   **1**
    Thinking Clearly about Discipline   2
    Models of Discipline   5
    Summary   16
    Problems and Activities   18

2   Discipline and Development   **19**
    Developmental Stages and Discipline   19
    Stages of Discipline   27
    Summary   39
    Problems and Activities   41

3   Discipline and the Curriculum   **43**
    Content and Class Control   44
    Interest and Discipline   51
    Social Attitudes   60
    Summary   62
    Problems and Activities   63

4   Discipline and Teaching   **65**
    Teacher Authority and How To Have It   66
    The Problem of Waiting   71
    Summary   80
    Problems and Activities   82

5   Lack of Attention and Teacher Expectation   **83**
    Attention and Development   83
    Interest and Attention   85
    Dealing with Task Inattentiveness   87
    Expectancy and Attention   89
    Summary   94
    Problems and Activities   95

6 Discipline in Special Settings   **97**
    Open Classrooms 98
    The Small Group Setting 110
    Independent Study 113
    Summary 114
    Problems and Activities 116

7 The Ecology of Classroom Discipline   **117**
    Ecological Factors Influenced by Teachers 118
    Ecological Factors Controlled by Teachers 133
    Summary 137
    Problems and Activities 138

8 Socializing the Unsocialized   **139**
    Socialization, The Necessary Objective 139
    Redirecting Negative Behavior 140
    Discipline-Developing Activities 143
    Criteria for Discipline-Developing Activities 150
    Summary 153
    Problems and Activities 154

9 Dealing with Discipline Problems   **155**
    Acceptable versus Unacceptable Behavior 156
    Dealing with Disruptive Behavior 156
    Punishment 172
    Summary 178
    Problems and Activities 180

10 Discipline and the Needs and Rights of Children   **181**
    The Realm of Feeling 182
    Basic Needs 184
    The Rights of Children 191
    Possibilities, Not Limitations 197
    Summary 198
    Problems and Activities 199

Selected References 201

PRINCIPLES OF CLASSROOM DISCIPLINE

First Principle: *The aims of education and classroom discipline are the same: to help children and youth become self-directing people.* (Chapter 1)

Second Principle: *Discipline should be dynamic, helping pupils channel their energies toward learning goals.* (Chapter 1)

Third Principle: *Discipline is inseparable from teaching.* (Chapter 1)

Fourth Principle: *Discipline should change with the child's stage of development and help him move to the next stage.* (Chapter 2)

Fifth Principle: *Appropriate behavior is determined by the rational demands of specific situations.* (Chapter 3)

Sixth Principle: *Teaching effectiveness, as perceived by pupils, invests the teacher with classroom authority.* (Chapter 4)

Seventh Principle: *Discipline is the ability to attend to a task.* (Chapter 5)

Eighth Principle: *No matter what the classroom design or how pupils are organized for instruction, the principles for effective teaching and discipline apply.* (Chapter 6)

Ninth Principle: *By identifying and dealing effectively with the factors under their control and influence, teachers can, in most cases, tip the ecological balance in favor of discipline.* (Chapter 7)

Tenth Principle (Principle of Redirection): *Socialization requires the redirection of destructive behavior into socially useful behavior.* (Chapter 8)

Eleventh Principle (Principle of Consonance): *Ways of dealing with misbehavior should be consonant with developmental goals.* (Chapter 9)

Twelfth Principle: *Basic discipline can be achieved only when basic needs, such as food and safety, are gratified.* (Chapter 10)

The Nature of Discipline

1

I first became interested in discipline some years ago as a beginning fifth-grade teacher in Columbus, Ohio. My interest was related to a desire to survive (both physically and on the job). I followed a Scheherazade-like approach, reading stories to my class of forty unmotivated, obstreperous nonreaders, in the instinctive hope that absorbed interest would replace the desire to create chaos. (Recall that Scheherazade, the fictitious narrator of the stories of the *Arabian Nights*, literally managed to keep her head by using this approach and even became Queen.)

This technique worked as well in a Columbus classroom as in Arabia. The children even branched out from listening to painting murals (about the stories) and to writing simple stories of their own. By Christmas they were taking a weekly trip to the neighborhood library (the school had no library), and doing arithmetic and social studies. What is more, I had come to love teaching. But I never forgot those terrible first weeks. The worst part had been that there was no one with whom I could discuss my problems of control, so they were never shared or examined with anyone's help. Nor had classroom management been a part of my professional preparation. In those days, discipline was swept under the pedagogical carpet. The young teacher who had trouble either "sank" or "swam" but in either case suffered in silence. Discipline was almost a taboo subject in colleges of education. Bringing this to attention, psychologist David Ausubel charged that they were maintaining "a conspiracy of silence about the existence of disciplinary problems in the schools."[1]

Although it is as true today as it ever was that when discipline is lost, all is lost, the teacher of today is better off than the teacher of fifteen years ago or even five years ago. For discipline (like sex) is no longer a taboo subject. Enlightened colleges of education are dealing with discipline in methods courses. University professors are conducting research on discipline problems commonly experienced in the public schools and there is a growing body of principles for teachers to apply in their classrooms. All this has been long overdue. For more than a half-century surveys have found discipline to be the primary concern of prospective and beginning teachers.[2] Moreover, time and time again discipline turns out to be the leading concern of the American public in opinion polls about the schools.

This book is based on the proposition that teachers can improve their effectiveness in three ways: (1) by understanding the models of discipline and their applications, (2) by following a developmental approach to discipline, and (3) by using approved practices in managing pupils. Approved practices, those practices on which recognized authorities agree, are found in the literature of the field. Approved practices may be research-based, or based upon techniques that are of demonstrable success in the field.[3]

THINKING CLEARLY ABOUT DISCIPLINE

Granted that teachers will inevitably fail without discipline, paradoxically, it seems to be something that we are more aware of when it is missing than when it is present. We know that teaching without discipline is exhausting, frustrating, demoralizing, and impossible. But what *is* this elusive quality that some teachers (the lucky ones) almost seem to take for granted?

Webster's Dictionary offers the following four common meanings of discipline: (1) training to develop self-control and orderly conduct, (2) the result of such training, (3) acceptance of or submission to authority

---

[1] David P. Ausubel, "A New Look at Classroom Discipline," *Phi Delta Kappan*, Vol. 63 (October 1961), p. 30.

[2] Frances F. Fuller, "Concerns of Teachers: A Developmental Conceptualization," *American Educational Research Journal*, Vol. 6 (March 1969), pp. 207-226; and Thomas J. Coates and Carl E. Thoresen, "Teacher Anxiety: A Review with Recommendations," *Review of Educational Research*, Vol. 46 (Spring 1976), p. 164.

[3] Daniel Tanner and Laurel N. Tanner, *Curriculum Development: Theory Into Practice* (New York: Macmillan, 1975), pp. 602-603.

and control, and (4) treatment that corrects or punishes. A dictionary is a guide to common usage. Logically, then, an army general, a prison warden, and an educator should all be able to use Webster in defining discipline. However, a school is not a military installation. Nor is it (hopefully) a prison. Discipline is not the same thing in an institution which seeks to develop people who can direct their own lives (the school) as it is in an institution which seeks acceptance of authority (the army) or an institution which seeks to correct or punish the inmates (a prison). Obviously for teachers the dictionary definition of discipline has limited usefulness.

There are crucial differences between Webster's definition of discipline and the concept of discipline as used in this book. To begin with, implied in the first and second definitions is that self-control and orderly behavior are the whole of discipline. While both are essential if teachers are to teach, there is much more to discipline if it is to be a force for learning rather than a force against learning.

Static Discipline

Discipline stressing only self-control and orderly conduct is static. The implication is that the children's energies should be used to control themselves and the teacher's energies should be used to train children to be orderly. There is something missing in dictionary definitions of discipline for there is more to schooling than being orderly. What is missing is the educational component of discipline. For discipline to be applicable to the classroom setting, it must be linked with the purposes of education. Let us see what happens to discipline when the educational component is added.

Dynamic Discipline

The aim of education in a democratic society is to help children and youth to be self-directing, to know how to act and how not to act in light of personal and social goals. It is interesting that when self-direction enters the picture, as opposed to self-control, the tone of discipline changes; it becomes dynamic rather than static. Children are responsibly directing their energy toward learning goals rather than turning their energy against themselves. And teachers are using methods that will facilitate and direct the flow of children's energy toward worthwhile goals instead of trying to turn it off. What we are seeking in our classrooms is dynamic discipline.

Two principles can be derived from these ideas.

First Principle: *The aims of education and classroom discipline are the same: to help children and youth become self-directing people.*

Second Principle: *Discipline should be dynamic, helping pupils to channel their energy toward learning goals.*

The purpose of discipline is to help teachers and children to achieve the goals of the school. This organization and behavior promote effective teaching and learning. Not an end in itself, discipline for its own sake creates an artificial distinction in minds of children (and in teachers' minds too) between goals sought and the behavior required to attain those goals. We want our pupils to understand that what one seeks and how one behaves are related. This is essential for dynamic discipline.

Submission versus Self-direction

Returning to Webster's Dictionary, discipline as submission to authority (in the third definition) is incompatible with the discipline we want. Submission is the diametrical opposite of self-direction. In a democratic society we do not want children and youth growing up to submit slavishly to a leader. We want actions to be based on principles, ideals, and a feeling for others. We want discipline which is based on understanding of a given goal and the behavior required to meet that goal. Acceptance of authority is, of course, required for the functioning of a school. To pretend otherwise would be delusory and dangerous. But, again, the purpose of the school *is not* to train children in obedience to strong people. It *is* to help each individual realize his or her potential and become a socialized person.

"Learnin' and Lickin' " and the Mind-Body Dualism

Finally, in the fourth definition, discipline is used as a synonym for punishment and correction. This probably dates back to the conception of human nature which dominated thinking during the colonial period in America, that people are innately evil due to the sins of their ancestors. In this view, because children are by nature totally depraved a constant guard must be kept to help them control their weaknesses. Education can help to "discipline" the mind and body by giving the child equal amounts of "learnin' and lickin'." This conception has been out of date for roughly 200 years. Eighteenth-century liberalism led to the view that misfortune and misbehavior are the result of environmental conditions and physical and mental disabilities, not human weakness.[4] Moreover, educators have long fought the notion that the mind and body are separate entities. The mind is the result of the total functioning of the person. Discipline will not be used as a name for punishment in this book. To do so would be both imprecise and a backward step in human progress. When punishment is discussed it will be called punishment.

MODELS OF DISCIPLINE

Robert Boguslaw, a systems-design engineer, distinguishes between *established* and *emergent* situations.[5] An *established* situation is one in which all action-relevant conditions are specifiable and predictable; whereas an *emergent* situation involves problems when the conditions are not perfectly specifiable and outcomes not predictable. The situations which we confront in our classrooms are either established or emergent. Established situations are cut and dried. All conditions are known and we are reasonably sure of the consequences of actions. A multiplication table is an established situation. Similarly, classroom routines are established situations.

However, in everyday living in and out of classrooms, problems crop up in which all conditions are not known, so there are no formulas to be "programmed" in advance. These are emergent situations. There are similar elements in some emergent situations and what we learn from one situation can be very helpful in dealing with another similar situation. But each situation must be dealt with individually. A small group in which some pupils are work-oriented but others are disruptive is an emergent situation. Models of discipline may be categorized as *established* or *emergent*.

Table 1-1 presents a synoptic view of several conflicting models of discipline representing conflicting viewpoints about education and human nature. The purpose here is to show briefly how these models serve as sources of ideals, aims, and methods in classroom discipline. Models of discipline are alternative routes to discipline. Teachers are so pressed with the need to develop on-the-spot classroom discipline that they seldom stop to think about the theories on which their methods are based. Although theory cannot give us the answer to such questions as "How can I make Henry stop bothering Eric?" it does provide a

---

[4] R. Freeman Butts and Lawrence A. Cremin, *A History of Education in American Culture* (New York: Holt, Rinehart and Winston, 1953), p. 62.

[5] Robert Boguslaw, *The New Utopians: A Study of Systems Design and Social Change* (Englewood Cliffs, N.J.: Prentice-Hall, 1965), pp. 7-8.

Table 1-1 Models of Discipline

Mode	Model	Controlling Aim	Method	Ideal of Learner	Ideal of Teacher
Established	Training	Automatic responses to specific stimuli; control through force of habit	Repetition and drill	Individual who responds automatically without accompanying thought	Trainer; drillmaster
	Behavior Modification	Automatic responses to specific stimuli; learner placed under control of situation	Behavior analyzed into constituent elements; pupil conditioned to make specific predestined responses	One whose behavior can be shaped at will and who responds mechanically to a predetermined program	Technician
Emergent	Psychodynamic	Control through understanding the individual child and the reasons for his or her behavior which have their roots in infancy and early childhood	Studying the emotional life of the child to find the causes of his or her behavior	Emotional being whose motivations, conflicts, and frustrations shape behavior	Psychoanalytically sophisticated person concerned with personal adjustment of pupils
	Group Dynamics	Control through classroom leadership based on a knowledge of group dynamics; group influence on individual behavior in desirable directions	Use of group dynamics to deal with whatever situation may arise; use of the instructional process	A member of an instructional group who contributes to the goals of the group and whose behavior is shaped by group expectations	Expert in group dynamics; one who can attain effective group behavior
	Personal-Social Growth	Pupil controls own behavior by thinking; sees his or her behavior in relation to goals and its effects on others	Pupil is provided with opportunities to choose appropriate behavior in terms of goals to be met and problems to be solved	Rational being who directs his or her own behavior and controls his or her environment (as opposed to being controlled by it)	Educator committed to helping pupils to develop effective self-direction

means for deciding whether our practices are in accord with our beliefs and for understanding the implications of alternative routes to discipline.

Training Model

Training Is Important.   The importance of training cannot be better illustrated than in a fire drill when children move out of the classroom in an orderly fashion instead of bolting for the door. Automatic behavior is appropriate, desirable, and necessary in established situations like a fire drill. Another established situation occurs when pupils raise their hands instead of calling out the answer to questions in the classroom. As noted, in an established situation all conditions are known and outcomes predictable. Baking a cake is an established situation. Similarly, there are recipes for some of the things that we do in classrooms but not for all things.

Clearly there is a place for training in school as in life. A proper learning atmosphere requires that pupils build up certain habits such as carrying their chairs instead of throwing them and talking instead of yelling. Most will already have formed these habits at home. But if they come to school without them, the school must provide training. Nor can we get by without habitual response outside our classroom doors. Who would cross a crowded thoroughfare without looking both ways? Training is required for survival both in and out of school.

Training and Education.   Although the importance of training cannot be discounted, it is only part of the discipline picture. The difference between training and education is relevant here. Children may be trained to respond a certain way in a given situation but they must guide their own behavior with thinking in order to be educated. Whereas training forms habits, education enables the learners to see their behavior in relation to their purposes and goals. Self-direction requires education as well as training.

Behavior Modification Model

The behavior modification model is based on the use of reinforcement procedures to shape pupil behavior in desired directions. Actually teachers have long used positive and negative reinforcers unsystematically. That is, they have rewarded desired behavior with praise and enjoyable prizes (games, parties, awards) and punished undesirable behavior by withholding these things. In so doing they have—sometimes—shaped pupils' behavior. But behavior modification is a *systematic way* to increase appropriate behavior and decrease inappropriate behavior and can be far more effective than the haphazard use of reinforcers. The process used in behavior modification is operant conditioning. As shown in Table 1-1, a target behavior—behavior that the teacher wants his or her pupils to engage in—is selected. This behavior is reinforced and increased while inappropriate behavior that is not reinforced decreases in frequency. For example, Susan Armstrong's target behavior is to have her fourth graders stay in their seats and raise their hands if they have a question instead of running up to her desk unnecessarily. (Susan counted 31 instances of the latter in one day.) Susan ignores all pupils who come to her desk, recognizing only those who raise hands at their seats. The occurrences of pupils at her desk have continually decreased to the point where it happens only occasionally.

Method.   Usually, teachers using behavior modification systems are instructed to ignore inappropriate behavior and reward appropriate behavior. The idea is that if undesirable behavior is ignored it is, thus, unrewarded by the teacher and can be expected to disappear. On the other hand, a desired behavior, encouraged by rewarding the child with attention, praise, or something tangible that the child values, is reinforced. A token-exchange system is often used in which the child earns tokens upon engaging in desirable behavior. The tokens are plastic discs which can be exchanged for a prize or a privilege. Generally, punishment is not used because disruptive behavior is ignored and attention is focused on pupils who are working well. However, some classroom behaviors cannot be ignored, such as behavior that might physically endanger the pupil or others (see Chapter 9). The point to be made here is that behavior modification systems have to bend to be usable in classrooms because of the emergent nature of classroom discipline. Therefore, in practice, many behaviors are not ignored.

In some programs, punishment is used, although called by another name. In an experiment involving disadvantaged inner-city elementary pupils in Atlanta, participating teachers ostensibly did not use punishment to control potentially dangerous behavior such as fights and tantrums. Instead they used a "time out procedure." Pupils were placed in a corner of the room or just outside the classroom door.[6] Clearly both of these are punishments. (Parenthetically, neither putting pupils in the corner nor the hall is an approved practice in classroom discipline. The former can stigmatize a pupil as a "dummy" and the latter may be regarded by pupils as a reward.) The problem may be that

[6] See Marion Thompson et al., "Contingency Management in the Schools: How Often and How Well Does it Work?" *American Educational Research Journal*, Vol. 11 (Winter 1974), pp. 19-28.

many teachers view punishment as synonymous with corporal punishment; they consider nothing else they do to control behavior as punishment. This semantic difficulty and its outcomes are discussed later.

Research Findings.   The study just mentioned found that twelve of fourteen experimental classrooms "improved dramatically" as a result of the behavior modification program with fewer disruptions and more task involvement. (There were no comparable changes in control classes.)[7] While the fact that not all disruptive behavior was ignored and teachers did actually use punishment may cast doubt on the validity of the experiment as a test of the behavior modification approach, this and similar studies point to the importance of using positive reinforcement procedures in the classroom. For while not all negative behavior is ignored in most behavior modification experiments, teachers do reinforce and strengthen positive behavior. (This is easier and more feasible than ignoring some types of negative behavior.) Whether or not teachers decide to use systematic behavior modification, the research on behavior modification seems to confirm the use of descriptive praise when a pupil works well or has substituted an appropriate for an inappropriate behavior.

Research on behavior modification finds this approach highly effective in residential schools for emotionally disturbed children.[8] Doubtless, this is because the environment in residential schools can be more completely controlled. A practical problem for teachers in using behavior modification is that the behaviors that they are trying to extinguish are often reinforced at home. Teachers can deal with this problem by enlisting the cooperation of parents. As Enzer points out, it is important that the goals of any intervention plan be clear to both parents and teacher and that, further, the goals should not be broad but limited to particular behaviors.[9] Disruptive behavior can be handled similarly at home and at school and both parents and teachers can discuss with the child their positive expectations and capitalize on the child's sense of pride by pointing out his or her achievements. Enzer stresses the importance of making children clearly aware of what is expected. He states that parents and teachers often say "Don't do that" but can be much more effective by saying "Let's do this."[10] Behavior modification

---

[7] Ibid.

[8] Frank M. Hewett and Phillip R. Blake, "Teaching the Emotionally Disturbed," in Robert M. W. Travers (ed.), *Second Handbook of Research on Teaching* (Chicago: Rand McNally, 1973), p. 673.

[9] See Norman B. Enzer, "Parents as Partners in Behavior Modification," *Journal of Research and Development in Education*, Vol. 8 (Winter 1975), pp. 31-32.

[10] Ibid., p. 24.

procedures are firmly based on the principle that pupils must be given positive direction.

While there is no clear evidence that the results of behavior modification "carry over" when the use of tangible rewards is discontinued, some investigators report that using such rewards *temporarily* "does not doom children to dependence on them" and that "such rewards may be extremely useful in launching children with behavior and learning problems in successful learning in school."[11]

Problems with the Method.   A common procedure in behavior modification programs is to have an "earning time" of an hour or so when the youngster can earn tokens through "good" behavior, followed by a "spending time" when the tokens may be exchanged for a prize. A problem commonly reported by teachers is that children frequently resume their misbehavior during "spending time." The problem may be that the rewards of learning are not tied to learning but rather to a release from the learning situation. Behavior modification is not a substitute for motivation. Attention is likely to be short-lived and superficial when the child is untouched by the assigned work and there is no interest. Whatever approach to discipline is used, there is the ever-present need to motivate pupils. Another problem is the unknown effect of isolation on some pupils, since ignoring is a form of isolation.[12]

Urban versus Suburban Discipline: Social Policy Issues.   Behavior modification has gained its widest acceptance in urban schools. This is understandable because of the critical nature of learning and behavioral problems in inner-city classrooms. However, methods for controlling the behavior of children from more advantaged segments of society are reasonable rather than mechanical. The consequences of behavior are emphasized, tending toward self-direction rather than external control. There is every evidence that classroom methodology is polarized in the same manner as society. As Brookover points out, the practice of perpetuating social segregation through differentiated educational approaches conflicts with the ideal of equality of opportunity.[12] This is

[11] See Frank M. Hewett, Frank D. Taylor, and Alfred A. Artuso, "The Santa Monica Project: Evaluation of an Engineered Classroom Design with Emotionally Disturbed Children," *Exceptional Children*, Vol. 35 (March 1969), pp. 523-529.

[12] Frances M. Culbertson, "An Effective Low Cost Approach to the Treatment of Disruptive School Children," *Psychology in the Schools*, Vol. 11 (April 1974), p. 184.

[13] Wilbur Brookover et al., "Quality of Educational Attainment, Standardized Testing, Assessment, and Accountability," in *Uses of the Sociology of Education,* Seventy-third Yearbook, Part II, National Society for the Study of Education (Chicago: The University of Chicago Press, 1974), p. 162.

an important issue for the public at large as well as for teachers. Classroom discipline should not perpetuate internal control for a more privileged group and external control for the disadvantaged.

Similarities and Differences with Training.   Behavior modification is similar to training in some respects. For example, the desired outcome in both is an automatic response (see Table 1-1). However there are some striking differences between the two models. First, explanations about approved standards are a part of training. Second, inappropriate behavior is pointed out in training. Finally, training need not involve extrinsic rewards and punishments. Teachers who feel that training is necessary in situations in which an automatic response is called for (established situations) do not necessarily subscribe to behavior modification theories. However, the point of importance is that both training and behavior modification are building blocks for education and self-direction.

Psychodynamic Model

The psychodynamic model of discipline is based on the idea that "understanding the child" is the solution for disciplinary problems. This is a child-centered model of discipline because the result of understanding is supposed to be a teacher response in terms of the child's "dynamics." The history of the psychodynamic model shows it to be rooted in child-centeredness.[14] The model developed in the 1920s as a result of a great national interest (bordering on a passion) in psychoanalytic theory, particularly that of Sigmund Freud. The Freudians saw as the primary educational goal the freeing of the child from "fixations" caused by repressive authority figures (adults). They believed that this freedom could only be achieved by activities which brought out into the open the ideas buried in the child's subconscious—emotional conflicts. Freudian pedagogy was practiced in only a few private schools in the 1920s and rarely if at all in the public schools.[15]

By midcentury the Freudian model had been considerably modified so that its main thrust lay in the need for teachers to be cognizant of the emotional factors which affect children's behavior. Rather than freeing youngsters from fixations, the emphasis shifted to the importance of mental health in education and personal adjustment. But for the teacher this still meant that "understanding the child" was supposed to be the

[14] Tanner and Tanner, op. cit., p. 254.
[15] See Lawrence A. Cremin, *The Transformation of the School* (New York: Knopf, 1961), pp. 209-215.

key to solving behavioral problems. In all fairness to this model, not enough teachers do try to search for the emotional reasons for problem behavior, probably because, as Philip Jackson has pointed out, teachers are primarily concerned with normality, not with pathology.[16]

"Understanding" and Classroom Discipline.   On the other hand, many teachers who do try to understand behavioral problem children are perplexed and frustrated because "understanding" does not automatically generate solutions. One may understand why Johnny behaves as he does but, more likely than not, Johnny and his teacher will still be left with Johnny's problem. Generations of teachers have been puzzled and disappointed by the failure of "understanding" to pay off in the lush benefits promised by theorists. The difficulty lies with the model which is still individualistic and rooted in psychoanalytic theory. According to this theory, understanding the emotions of the child should lead to nothing except ridding the child of emotional conflicts. According to Hewett, Taylor, and Artuso the preoccupation of psychoanalytic theory and psychodynamic psychology "with therapeutic goals to the almost complete exclusion of concern with educational methodology has restricted their acceptance and effectiveness in public school programs."[17] Teachers need concrete ways to deal with discipline problems, ways that are commensurate with their primary charge which is education. This book is an attempt to provide teachers with disciplinary methods that are in keeping with their educational charge.

Teachers should search for the reasons for children's behavior. They do so all too seldom. But it is cautioned that the reasons for misbehavior often transcend the emotional realm (the curriculum could be at fault, for example) and teachers are not, in any case, amateur psychiatrists. The point is that understanding the child should not be expected to lead automatically to his or her control, although it may provide valuable leads for selecting a disciplinary approach.

Group Dynamics Model

At the heart of the teacher's concern about discipline lies the classroom group. Most of what we do in classrooms is undertaken to promote the achievement of the classroom group. The group dynamics model is concerned with the authority and influence of the teacher in

---

[16] Philip W. Jackson, *Life in Classrooms* (New York: Holt, Rinehart and Winston, 1968), p. 170.

[17] Hewett, Taylor, and Artuso, op. cit., p. 523.

the classroom and how teachers can create effective working conditions. The model also focuses on how relationships between the group and individual class members affect disruptive behavior.

In this model, discipline is not something separate from teaching but is part of the instructional process. Problem behavior can be handled by directions, questions, explanations, clarification, giving cues, correcting mistakes, and the like. This leads to our third principle for effective discipline.

Third Principle: *Discipline is inseparable from teaching.*

Disciplinary methods relate not only to control but to learning. Successful discipline simply cannot be separated from what the disciplinarian does as a teacher. Recent research bears this out. In his investigations, Jacob Kounin identified two teacher characteristics associated with successful classroom management which he labeled *withitness* and *overlapping*.[18]

Withitness.   Kounin's first characteristic, withitness, could be translated as "eyes on back of head" and means knowing what is going on in the classroom. But in his studies Kounin found that it is not enough for a teacher to know what children are doing but the teacher also has to communicate to the children that he or she knows. To illustrate, Mrs. A is working with an arithmetic group and listening to Anthony recite his multiplication tables. In another part of the room Susan and Shirley are giggling over something written on a small piece of paper instead of doing their arithmetic seatwork. Mrs. A says, "Please go on with your tables, Anthony." Then she walks over to Shirley and Susan and says firmly, "I want this silliness stopped, girls. Now, finish your arithmetic. Susan! You haven't even gotten started. Better hurry, both of you." She then returns calmly to the small group and says, "Thank you, Anthony. Now, Mark, how about you? Let's try your 12's."

This teacher has withitness. She knows what the children are doing or not doing and by her actions has communicated that she knows. Although she physically absented herself from the arithmetic group for a few moments, she was still in contact. There was no mistaking the message that her actions conveyed: "I know what is going on." It would

---

[18] Jacob S. Kounin, *Discipline and Group Management in Classrooms* (New York: Holt, Rinehart and Winston, 1970), p. 79.

be impossible to separate Mrs. A's discipline from her teaching. Discipline was part of the directions she gave for work.

Overlapping.   Kounin's second characteristic means the ability to tend to two things at once. Like withitness, overlapping is an orchestral quality—leading the violins and toning down the trombones at the same time. Mrs. A was in an overlapping situation. Effective classroom management requires the ability to orchestrate. Timing is of the essence, just as it is in the orchestra pit. Mrs. A knew when to leave the small group and go over to Shirley and Susan. Had she waited too long the misbehavior might have spread to other children.

Comparison with the Psychodynamic Model.   As shown in Table 1-1, both group dynamics and psychodynamic models are emergent models of discipline. That is, they are concerned with helping teachers to deal with the behavior problems that arise as they work with children. Since each problem (whether a group or an individual problem) involves different circumstances it must be dealt with individually. Thus in the group dynamics model the strategies we use will depend on our problems in creating effective working conditions. These problems are not specifiable in advance but vary as teacher and pupil personalities and needs vary.

But there are striking differences between the two models. The group dynamics model is an action model. Knowledge about the power and authority of teachers and how individuals behave in groups is translated into strategies for preventing and dealing with discipline problems. It is easy to see how the group dynamics model is far more practical for teachers than the psychodynamic model which stops with "understanding."

There is another important difference between this model and the psychodynamic model. In addition to being based on the reality that teachers work with classroom groups, the group dynamics model is also based on the idea that learning is a social process. What we know and how we behave are largely outcomes of our interaction with others. Moreover the school is a social situation. It is here that the psychodynamic model (and all individual psychology) has been most wanting. Individual psychology neglects the reality of the classroom learning situation which is a social setting where people interact with each other, sometimes corrosively, sometimes constructively, but always interacting. Of all the models of discipline, the group dynamics model is most concerned with classroom management. While this is a decided advantage, it can also be a drawback. For discipline is more than "managing" others. The goal of discipline is *self*-management or *self*-direction.

Personal-Social Growth Model

A third emergent model of discipline is the personal-social growth model. Unlike the other models, the goal is to enable individuals to manage their own behavior. This ability comes from experience. To develop self-direction in pupils is to provide them with opportunities to choose appropriate behavior for meeting a goal or solving a problem.

Locus of Control.   Children must be helped to develop a feeling of cause-and-effect about their own actions. This is a part of personal growth and important for classroom discipline. Writers from Dewey to Coleman to Rotter have described this feeling of self-responsibility variously as environmental control, fate control, and locus of control.[19] According to Rotter, the perception by individuals that what happens to them is a result of forces outside themselves (luck, fate, or powerful others) is a belief in *external control.* If the individuals perceive a causal relationship between what happens to them and their own behavior and characteristics, this is a belief in *internal control.*[20] Recently, Rotter's construct has attracted great educational interest.

The following will serve to illustrate this construct. John says about a peer: "Terry's lucky. He always knows his spelling words. But I'm not lucky. So I never get A's." In truth, Terry takes his words home and studies them diligently but John never does. This difference must be pointed out to John, along with encouragement that he can do better if he tries.

The ability to manage one's own behavior requires the feeling that one is internally controlled rather than externally controlled. Teachers can help pupils develop this feeling by pointing out when they have successfully completed a task by their own efforts. They can foster internal locus of control in unsocialized pupils by redirecting negative behavior into socially useful behavior. (See Chapter 8.)

Means as Behavior.   A central idea in the personal-social growth model is that means and goals are related. How one behaves (the means for reaching a goal) is determined by the goal. Unfortunately, in many classrooms goals remain mysterious and obscure. The work of the school is presented to pupils as an obstacle course to be run, a series of

---

[19] John Dewey, "The Democratic Conception in Education," Chapter 7 in *Democracy and Education* (New York: Macmillan, 1916), pp. 81-99; James S. Coleman et al., *Equality of Educational Opportunity* (Washington, D.C.: Office of Education, U.S. Department of Health, Education and Welfare, 1966); Julian B. Rotter, "Generalized Expectancies for Internal versus External Control of Reinforcement," *Psychological Monographs*, Vol. 80, No. 1 (1966).

[20] Rotter, op. cit., p. 1.

meaningless tasks to get over. There is little or no attempt to help children understand the value of what they are doing. Behavior is separate from the goal because the goal is a chore to be finished with as quickly as possible. It is tempting to misbehave when there is no objective except to finish. On the other hand, when pupils understand the value of a task, they are more likely to want to master it. Behavior then becomes *what* one does when one is learning (or trying to learn). This is what is meant by ends and means being contiguous. Of course, behavior varies in accord with the work. Different learning tasks demand different kinds of order.

Choosing Appropriate Behavior.   Implicit in this model is the idea of children learning to choose their behavior. There are many opportunities in teaching for developing the ability to choose appropriate behavior. For example, groups ranging in size from two to eight children can be given a goal to achieve, but how group members accomplish the goal is entirely up to them. This helps children learn to interact socially and be independent in making decisions. Pupils should also study the problems of living together in their school and community and whenever possible plan and test solutions.

The Educational Side of Discipline.   It is important for children to deal with situations in which there are no ready recipes for behavior, which call upon intelligence for solutions rather than an automatic response. Most problems in life are emergent rather than established. We hope that the rising generation will be able to solve the problems of the future, problems that we cannot even envision. If they are to do so, they must have opportunities to practice problem solving in school. The personal-social growth model is the educational side of discipline. The objective is to enable individuals to control their surroundings. (This is the diametrical opposite of seeking external control of the individual by the situation.)

The group dynamics and personal-social growth models view discipline as a part of instruction rather than as something outside of instruction.

SUMMARY

Teachers can increase their effectiveness and decrease their problems of classroom control in three ways: (1) by understanding the models of discipline and their applications, (2) by following a developmental approach to discipline, and (3) by using approved practices (those practices found by authorities to be successful).

The goals of classroom discipline and education are the same—to help pupils become self-directing. Older conceptions of discipline stressed the use of pupils' energy to control themselves; discipline was divorced from educational goals. This was *static discipline*. What we are seeking is *dynamic discipline* in which pupils are responsibly directing their energy toward learning goals.

In our classrooms we confront *established* situations, in which all conditions are specifiable and the outcomes of actions are predictable, and *emergent* situations in which all conditions are not known so there are no formulas for solutions. Changing classes (transition) and other routines are established situations. Lack of attention, on the other hand, is an emergent situation. The conditions in problems of inattention vary, thus the approaches used must also vary.

Models of discipline are either established or emergent. Training is an established model of discipline in which repetition and drill are used to develop habits and approved standards. Inappropriate behavior is corrected. A second established model is the behavior modification model which advises the teacher to use approval and ignoring (an operant conditioning process) in controlling behavior. Inappropriate behavior is ignored and appropriate behavior rewarded. The controlling aim of both models is an automatic response.

Emergent models of discipline are the psychodynamic model, the group dynamics model and the personal-social growth model. The psychodynamic model advises teachers to search for the emotional reasons for children's behavior. This model has proven disappointing in the past, perhaps because its goals are mainly therapeutic. Teachers must deal with groups as well as individuals. Thus an enormously useful model is the group dynamics model which views classroom control as a part of instruction. In giving directions, explaining, questioning, and correcting mistakes we are managing our classrooms and teaching at the same time. To be successful managers, teachers have to know what is going on in their classrooms and communicate this knowledge to pupils (Kounin's "withitness") and be able to tend to two things at once (Kounin's "overlapping").

The goal of the personal-social growth model is self-management. Pupils who are self-responsible believe that they are internally controlled; that is, they perceive a relationship between what they do and what happens to them. Developing feelings of internal (as opposed to external) control is part of personal growth and extremely important for classroom discipline. Actually, the very nature of the teacher's job makes personal-social growth his or her overriding objective. Models of discipline are building blocks for self-direction and education.

Problems and Activities

1. Do you think that the principle of discipline being inseparable from teaching is valid? Why? Test the principle by observation. Visit a classroom and record the instances when directions, explanations, clarification, correcting mistakes, and giving cues are part of both discipline and teaching.
2. Draw up a list of established classroom situations in which training is important for good discipline.
3. Discuss the advantages of involving parents in a behavior modification program.
4. What advice would you give to a teacher who is using behavior modification and having difficulty getting pupils back to work after they have received their reinforcers?
5. Which models of discipline do you think teachers tend to use most often and which least often? Make classroom observations to test your hypothesis.
6. Which models of discipline are most closely identified with dynamic discipline? Why?
7. Which model of discipline is most in accord with the goal of discipline and education as set forth in this chapter? Why?
8. Should schools help children learn to deal with emergent situations? Explain. Give an example of an activity which you would use to help youngsters at a given grade level gain experience in problem solving.
9. Do you think that an understanding of the models of discipline and their applications can help teachers become more effective? Support your answer.
10. In this chapter it was pointed out that training and behavior modification are building block preliminaries for the self-direction of the personal-social growth model. In view of the difference in controlling aims between the training and behavior modification models on the one hand, and the personal-social growth model on the other hand, would you agree? Why? (Use Table 1-1 in framing your answer.)

Discipline
and Development

2

Obviously discipline is not the same thing in elementary school as it is in high school. Nor, for that matter, is it the same in first grade as it is in fifth or sixth grade. Discipline must be tailored to the developmental level of the child and the requirements of the curriculum. Equally important, the disciplinary methods that we use should advance, not retard, development. For instance, telling thirteen-year-olds that they should not cheat because "the one you copy from might have it wrong" is dealing with them at a level below their comprehension and ignores the interest of thirteen-year-olds in learning to make moral choices. How does a teacher bring about an appropriate match between discipline and development? A number of researchers in psychology and education have concentrated their energies on this problem and have come up with some ideas of practical use for teachers. It is to these ideas that we turn now.

DEVELOPMENTAL STAGES AND DISCIPLINE

Probably no fact of educational life has evoked more comment, and despair, from teachers than differences in the manageability of lower and upper grade pupils. "Until this year I taught first grade and the children were so anxious to please me—my word was law. But this year with the fourth grade it's so different—they don't hang on to every word I say and it's harder to get them interested," mourns Mrs. P to fellow teachers in the lunchroom. "I know," commiserates Mrs. Q who teaches the sixth grade in the room next door. "When they're little they seem so interested in school and the work, but when they get older the novelty wears off and they don't treat you like God any more. Something happens—I think it's in the third grade." The other teachers are at one with Mrs. Q in this judgment. "Yes, it's in the third grade that they change," they nod vigorously. "But isn't there something we can do? *What* is it that happens in the third grade?" puzzles Mr. R who teaches grade five. The others look surprised at this question and turn their attention to other matters. Mr. R was asking about what seemed to them to be an unfortunate but inevitable fact of classroom life. The fact that older children are often more difficult to handle because "they don't take your word as law" is regarded by most teachers as something to be lived with rather than as a developmental cue for the successful handling of children. Yet if development is ignored, discipline is bound to go wrong and, equally important, teachers are failing to help children move to the next stage of development. One should build on development, not ignore it. This principle is just as important in discipline as it is in teaching. The learner is an important source for determining classroom methods, and knowledge about development is an important kind of information about learners. Good teachers put this information to work for them rather than shrugging it off as a problem to be endured. This gives us our fourth principle of discipline.

Fourth Principle: *Discipline should change with the child's stage of development and help him or her move to the next stage.*

This experience of teachers, that little children regard the word of adults as something sacred, to be obeyed to the letter, but that with increasing age children tend to become less likely to accept the word of adults as right simply because it emanates from adults, is well supported by the work of developmental psychologists. According to Piaget and Kohlberg, the desirable direction of growth is away from obeying in order to please the teacher or avoid punishment and toward a sense of right or wrong that is based on situational factors, feelings of justice, and the child's individual principles.[1] In other words, if children are developing properly they are growing out of the habit of judging an

---

[1] Jean Piaget, *The Moral Judgment of the Child* (London: Routledge and Kegan Paul, 1932); Lawrence Kohlberg, "Education for Justice," in *Moral Education* (Cambridge, Mass.: Harvard University Press, 1970), pp. 57-65.

action as right simply because the teacher does it (because teachers can do no wrong) and are growing in the capacity to judge a situation by the particular circumstances (in which teachers like anyone else may sometimes be wrong). To illustrate, while first graders might think that it is all right for a teacher to keep the entire class in for recess when one youngster has misbehaved, fifth graders are likely to consider punishing all for the trangressions of one an injustice.

The point is that instead of lamenting the fact that older children need reasons other than adult authority for what they do, we should consider it a development in a desirable direction—an opportunity, not a loss. The problems that we experience when we deal with all children as though they were at the same developmental level lie with ourselves, not the children. In a very real sense we are flying in the face of growth and have only ourselves to blame when children lose interest in their schoolwork and classroom behavior deteriorates. A poor match between discipline and development can cause many problems. The alternative to treating eleven-year-olds as though they were seven-year-olds and then being shocked when they refuse to respond like seven-year-olds is a good one—to treat eleven-year-olds like eleven-year-olds, thereby convincing them of the sincerity of our efforts to help them learn. When youngsters sense that the teacher is really there to help, not to demean them, negative behaviors like yelling and fighting often drop off dramatically. (On the other hand treating older pupils like first or second graders is to demean them and convince them that we think very little of their ability to learn.)

Even if our eleven-year-olds should happen to be on the same achievement level as seven-year-olds they are no longer at the docile and anxious-to-please stage and are more likely to resent being treated like babies than are eleven-year-olds who are achieving at grade level. (Children who are achieving usually have the ego strength needed to tolerate being dealt with below their maturity but for those with learning problems this is adding insult to injury.) The work of Piaget suggests that a group of eleven-year-olds are more likely to judge appropriate behavior on situational factors and the needs of the group than on the need to obey adults, whereas for six-year-olds the reverse is true.[2] This would suggest that teachers of eleven-year-olds would be well-advised to help pupils learn to set behavioral standards that are in tune to the work to be done rather than to set arbitrary standards that seem external to the task and tuned to adult convenience. A number of other useful ideas proceed from the work of Piaget as will be seen in the next section.

[2] Piaget, op. cit.

Piagetian Theory

The research of Piaget points to the existence of important qualitative differences between the mental structure of the child and that of the adult. Piaget's research over several decades led him to theorize that intelligence undergoes qualitative changes linked with the child's maturation and experience. Piaget's general theory of intelligence is as important to us as his theory on the development of moral judgment because his theory of intelligence is actually a theory of behavior from the standpoint of intelligence. For Piaget, doing cannot be separated from knowing; developmental changes in the child's mental structure are inferred from developmental changes in behavior. Piaget identifies four stages of development: (1) the *sensory-motor* stage (approximately to age two), during which the child learns to control perception and motor responses in dealing with objects and language; (2) the *preoperational* stage (to about age seven), in which the child learns to form concepts from experience, and make perceptual and intuitive judgments; (3) the stage of *concrete operations* (from about age seven to eleven), in which the child learns to solve physical problems by anticipating consequences perceptually; and (4) the stage of *formal operations* (late childhood and early adolescence), when the child learns to think hypothetically—to think not only of relationships that he has experienced but to theorize about relationships and events that might take place.[3]

The last three stages are of the greatest interest for teachers. These stages have enormous implications for discipline as well as for learning, particularly since, according to Piaget, each developmental stage is a necessary condition for subsequent development (although there is some overlapping).

Preoperational Stage.   Looking first at the preoperational stage, we find that the predominant characteristic of this stage is *egocentrism*. By this Piaget does not mean self-centeredness in the usual sense but that the child perceives the world from his own point of view and is unable to understand that there are other perspectives. Since the child cannot conceive that from someone else's standpoint a situation might look different, he is incapable of true cooperation with others. And because he cannot conceive that there are other points of view besides his own, he seems oblivious of the possibility that he might be misunderstood by others in a social situation (such as a classroom).

As Piaget points out in his book, *The Moral Judgment of the Child,*

[3] Jean Piaget, *The Psychology of Intelligence* (New York: Harcourt, 1950), pp. 87-158.

obedience to adults is the moral philosophy of the child from the age of four until about seven. Thus through the second grade, for many children, "being good" is synonymous with obeying the teacher and "being bad" means disobeying the teacher. (For some children, however, this stage ends earlier and for others it may continue until adulthood.)

Piaget calls this stage of morality *moral realism*. For the child in this stage rules are rooted in adult authority and obedience is synonymous with virtue. When third graders start to see a situation from different perspectives instead of just one (the teacher's) this is a sign that they are moving out of the stage of moral realism. The point is that the change teachers often notice in children's behavior, particularly when children want to know the "why" of what is expected of them rather than just the "what," is explained by the theory of Piaget and is normal. Indeed it is desirable from the standpoint of the goal of discipline (self-direction) for children to move out of the stage of moral realism.

Concrete Operations Stage.   By the time children are in the third grade (earlier for some youngsters), they have developed the understanding that teachers' rules vary and there are inconsistencies even in the same teacher's rules. This understanding has grown from experience and may result in a blithe disregard of classroom rules that the youngsters once held as sacred. We may even find ourselves in a head-on conflict with a youngster who challenges a rule that seems to her to be unreasonable. For example, eight-year-old Nancy may argue, "I don't see why Susie and I can't talk quietly. We're not bothering anyone." The child is now in the stage of concrete operations. Piaget stresses that the predominant characteristic of this stage is the youngster's desire to know which means can accomplish which ends. In other words, the child is preoccupied with trying to relate behavior to its consequences.

As mentioned, teachers can build upon this knowledge about children in the concrete operations stage by emphasizing that how one acts in the classroom should be determined by the learning task. Put another way, the end (learning objective) determines the means (behavior). This suggestion is discussed in detail in the next chapter. It also pertains to the example of Nancy, just given. If Nancy understands that acceptable behavior is determined by the nature of the classroom activity, there should be no question about whether her talking quietly with Susie is appropriate. (If talking is necessary for attaining the objective of the lesson, then talking is certainly permissible. Otherwise, it is probably inappropriate.) How much better for children's development when they learn that we must have reasons for behaving the way we do than for them to feel subject to the arbitrary whims of an adult. Teachers should explain their reasons if they expect children to learn that concern for others matters. The teacher who explains rules by "because I said so" not only encourages blind obedience to authority but also stultifies language development and intellectual growth. Furthermore, this teacher is showing that concern for others is of little importance.

Should teachers of children below the age of seven or eight refrain from explaining which behavior can accomplish which ends on the basis that these youngsters have not yet entered the concrete operations stage and will be unable to understand? The answer is negative for several reasons. First, teachers should always stress the relationship between means and ends because their goal should be to move children to the next stage of development. By helping children understand how means and ends are related teachers are helping them to move to a higher stage of development. Second, in any classroom group of first and second graders (and even in kindergarten) there are always some children at the concrete operations stage who should not be dealt with at a lower level. Third, children are emergent creatures; their development is a continuous process. Because they are always growing and changing we cannot regard any stage of development as a finished product. We cannot treat children as established when they are emergent. Fourth, development is not an automatic, unfolding process. Development requires the proper environmental conditions *including skilled teaching.* The kind of teaching the children get at home and in school is part of their experience and is of crucial importance for their development (and their behavior—the manifestation of development).

In the concrete operations stage children are able to recognize that other points of view beside their own exist. Because they are able to exchange ideas with others they are capable of cooperation. Unlike the children in the preoperational stage who tend to see rules as inflexible and believe that people who violate rules should suffer for their offenses (the greater the suffering the better), the older children tend to view punishment as a means for deterring the offender in the future and for putting things right (restitution). Thus a child who has broken a toy belonging to another youngster should have to give the youngster one of his own toys or pay to have the broken toy repaired. This is clearly a more advanced kind of morality than the idea that punishment must take the form of inflicting pain on the offender. Also important in this stage is the question of intent.

According to Piaget, beginning around the age of nine or ten children are concerned about whether a misdeed was deliberate or unintended. Intention ("subjective responsibility") is considered rather than the consequences of an act. Piaget labels this level of morality the morality of *cooperation* or *reciprocity*. Important elements in this level of morality are the ability to work with others to improve a situation, sympathy for individuals, and awareness of others' points of view. These are also components in the socialization process. Until children have developed reciprocity they are socially insensitive and are therefore unsocialized. Reciprocity, or being able to understand the point of view of the other person and act upon this understanding, results from a combination of experience and maturation. Since reciprocity is required for socialization it must be consciously and conscientiously taught.

One of the best ways that teachers can teach reciprocity is by following the principle of restitution rather than retribution in dealing with discipline problems. The teacher is a role model and pupils are quick to adopt the teacher's code of behavior. A teacher who uses retribution (reprisal) in managing children is operating at the level of retributive justice, an immature level of morality (which is supposed to end around the age of eight). Teachers who follow the principle of retributive justice often rationalize their behavior by saying, "this is all they [the children] understand." If this is indeed the case, that the children only respect the adult who inflicts pain, this is all the more reason why they must be helped by their teacher to move to a higher level of morality.

Clearly, restitution is positive and constructive whereas retribution is negative and destructive, and may create sadists and bullies. If the teacher's idea of justice is that of retaliation (getting even with the child), he or she will be able to contribute little to the development of more sophisticated moral judgments in pupils.

Piaget's concept of reciprocity is a useful tool for teachers to use in determining whether or not children are ready to participate in the development of classroom rules. Two important characteristics of reciprocity are the ability to exchange ideas with others and the understanding that rules are means of achieving mutually valued goals. The second characterisic is harder to assess than the first but children should show an understanding that desirable behavior is a means for achieving classroom goals rather than a matter of obeying the teacher or principal.

Piaget's research suggests that reciprocity develops around the age of nine or ten. However, the subjects of Piaget's study on moral development were children from "the poorer part of Geneva." The generalizability of his findings to children from other social environments can therefore be questioned. Thus advantaged (middle-class) children might develop reciprocity at an earlier age than nine or ten and desperately disadvantaged children might develop it later, or not at all, depending on the kind of teaching they get at home and at school. Like other components of socialization, reciprocity must be taught diligently by the school if it is not taught at home or otherwise it may not be learned at all.

Formal Operations Stage.   According to Piaget's description of the development of moral judgment, in late childhood or early adolescence the individual's thinking goes beyond his or her immediate social situation. The child or youth reflects on human relationships in general and has the capability to work out his or her own ideals and principles for dealing with them. This is the stage of formal operations at which thinking is no longer confined to the concrete but can be abstract and hypothetical. Autonomy (self-direction) is the pervasive moral characteristic of this stage. Obviously, arriving at this stage is not an automatic maturational process and requires the proper environment at home and in school. Skilled teaching is an important part of the proper conditions for learning self-direction and developing a code of values.

Using Piaget:
Advantages and Limitations

Knowing the desirable direction of growth and being able to establish pupils' placement in the developmental sequence described by Piaget is helpful for teachers in planning classroom procedures. For example, children starting school at the age of five or six are usually in the preoperational stage and the predominant characteristic of this stage is egocentrism: the children are unable to think about their world in an interpersonal sense, only a personal sense. At the same time, they regard adults as omnipotent and rules, seen as emanating from adults, are to be accepted as a matter of course. Using Piaget's theories to guide practice, the teacher of children just being initiated into the school will provide an adult-structured atmosphere: rules and procedures will "descend" from the teacher. At the same time, however, the teacher will have in mind the objective of moving children to the next stage which means that situations covered by rules should be discussed in terms of the effects of actions on others and the work to be done. The teacher who is faithful to Piaget will hope that ultimately the children can understand that "A rule is therefore nothing but the condition for the existence of a social group."[4] This understanding may not (probably will not) develop for most youngsters before the fourth or fifth grade but the kindergarten and primary teacher should be working toward it nonetheless.

Understanding the course of development can help us meet the child

---

[4] Piaget, *The Moral Judgment of the Child,* op. cit., p. 101.

in terms of "where he is." However, developmental theories tempt us to look upon the changes that take place with increasing age as part of an automatic unfolding process. This way of thinking is a dangerous trap for teachers and should be studiously avoided. Children do not automatically become self-directing as they grow older. Nor do they necessarily develop the ability to cooperate with others. These changes are powerfully influenced by learning in and out of school. Cooperation and inner direction must be consciously taught the same as any other educational objective.

A limitation of Piaget's account of the stages of children's moral development is that it is based on children's moral judgments rather than on their actual behavior. As any experienced teacher knows there is often a striking disparity between what children espouse as proper behavior and the way they behave.

Another limitation of developmental psychology is that, at best, it can guide the teacher only in general ways. To be sure, general aims for teaching moral *judgment* can be found in the hierarchy of stages. But these aims do not concern classroom discipline itself. Indeed, the characteristics of developmental stages, although of great theoretical interest, are actually of limited practical value for teachers. This is in no way meant to disparage developmental psychology because it was never intended to do more than describe the course of human development. But to attempt to use it as a precise program for teachers is to misuse it and to defraud teachers and children. Teachers need a developmental guide to discipline which they can use to determine the characteristics of pupils' behavior in various stages and which defines the teacher's role in getting pupils to each stage. While developmental psychology stops short at the point of what to do, a developmental guide to classroom discipline should indicate to teachers what they need to emphasize or provide in their classrooms. It is with this crucial need of teachers in mind that the developmental stages of discipline are offered. (See Table 2-1.)

STAGES OF DISCIPLINE

Table 2-1 presents a developmental sequence of three stages in discipline. The table represents an extension of the foundational ideas of developmental psychology and is also based on approved practices in education. Under the model proposed here, both pupils and teachers have specific responsibilities in each stage of discipline. The purpose of the model is not to present an exhaustive list of pupil and teacher roles and responsibilities for each stage but to provide examples. Pupil

Table 2-1 Disciplinary Stages

Stages	Pupil Responsibility (Examples)	Teacher Role
Stage I (Basic Disciplinary Stage)	Listens to teacher and to other members of class; follows directions; asks questions when failing to understand concepts, procedures, etc.; knows how to share materials and resources.	Teaches effectively so that pupils understand concepts, procedures, etc.; encourages pupils to ask questions when they do not understand; helps pupils to judge behavior in terms of the work to be done; is a good role model.
Stage II (Constructive Stage)	Takes the role of the other person (reciprocity); recognizes the needs and rights of others; works cooperatively with others; understands the basis for all reasonable organizational rules and procedures; can select and develop procedures for accomplishing an objective; understands the concept of justice.	Explains bases for organizational rules and procedures; involves pupils in socially constructive activities; gives pupils opportunities to participate in planning and to work cooperatively together; uses incidents of daily life and the curriculum to develop the concept of justice; is a good role model.
Stage III (Generative Stage)	Autonomously behaving, socially responsible, leadership; upholds the concept of justice; conceptualizes a problem, generates and tests solutions; makes choices on his or her own responsibility in situations which have no rules.	Provides leadership opportunities; encourages the development of moral principles and values; helps students to conceptualize social problems and develop plans of action; provides students with the ego strength needed for autonomous, principled action; is a good role model.

responsibilities are matched with teacher functions at each stage of development. This answers an important teacher need because knowledge of what to do to foster development in discipline is one of the most difficult problems for teachers. Furthermore, teachers are often unsure about the direction of growth in discipline. What constitutes beginning competence in classroom behavior for a youngster and what constitutes fully developed competence? Unless the teacher understands the course of the development of discipline he or she may be unable to facilitate development except in a hit-or-miss fashion and may even cause fixation of pupils at the beginning stage, if indeed they get that far.

As seen in Table 2-1, the three stages in the developmental sequence are the *basic disciplinary* stage, the *constructive* stage, and the *generative* stage.

Stage I: Basic Disciplinary Stage

Listening and Following Directions.   Basic discipline is critical for school learning. Children must be able to listen and follow directions if they are to meet the requirements of the school. Moreover, they must ask questions if they do not understand how to do their work. As shown in Table 2-1, pupils are at the basic disciplinary stage if they can listen, follow directions and ask questions when they need help. These pupil responsibilities are not only crucial for learning but for living in classrooms. The reason is all too obvious: the child who is not listening or following directions is usually doing something else. That something else (playing, chair pushing, teasing, throwing objects, wandering aimlessly around the room) can make life miserable for teachers and other learners. Not only that, it can make other learners lose interest in their work.

An Environment in Which Learning Can Take Place.   The probability that children at the basic disciplinary stage are learning is high. This is in no small way because they are living in a classroom environment where learning *can* take place. Some children come to school at the basic disciplinary stage (or beyond) as the result of home training. Others do not. It is the business of the school to begin where the home leaves off (or never started) in discipline. This is a part of the school's induction of children into society and our obligation to each of them as a person. For unless they can channel their energies and direct their powers constructively, the children will be in a state of arrested development and their life options will be few indeed. (It will be noted that the emphasis in each stage of discipline is positive—*doing and growing*

—not restrictive. For example, in Stage I the child listens so that he may learn and give others a chance to learn.)

Sharing.   Another example of a pupil responsibility in Stage I is sharing. Children at the basic stage must be able to share materials and resources. Sharing the teacher's time (waiting for one's turn to talk to the teacher) is a related pupil responsibility in Stage I.

Asking Questions.   Whether the pupil carries out his responsibilities depends greatly on the teacher. Pupils will not ask questions if discouraged from doing so by teachers. In fact, pupils need to be actively *encouraged* to ask questions. Many youngsters will keep silent rather than admit that they do not understand a concept or procedure. One reason why children are reluctant to ask for help is cultural. In our culture approved ways of behaving tend to emphasize self-reliance and deny feelings of dependence on others.[5]

Another reason may be the learner's past experience: what happened the last time he asked a question. When the child who says "I don't understand how to do this problem" is told "You see what happens when you don't listen," she is hardly emboldened to ask more questions. Actually, she may have been listening when the procedure was being explained. On the other hand, she may not have been listening but the teacher still has a chance to build on her interest and meet the goal of the lesson. Building on children's questions rather than squelching interest is just common sense if we expect children to learn. Good teachers seem to do it automatically. Yet for many this skill was self-consciously practiced until it became part of their teaching behavior.

Training.   Pupils at Stage I are able to listen to their teacher and other pupils as well as ask questions. Neither is possible in any useful sense unless order is maintained. Certain procedures must be followed such as raising hands to speak and not talking when someone else is talking. When youngsters are volatile or impulsive learning not to call out may take a great deal of practice (and patience on the part of their teacher). In teaching children to raise their hands and not to interrupt when others are speaking we are using the training model discussed in Chapter 1. More than training is involved here, however, for what we hope for transcends mechanical behavior. What we are trying to develop is a sense of responsibility and consideration for others

---

[5] Paul Mussen, *The Psychological Development of the Child* (Englewood Cliffs, N.J.: Prentice-Hall, 1973), p. 55.

coupled with the understanding that rules are for the purpose of making classroom life pleasant, productive—and possible.

Pupils will be most likely to reach the basic disciplinary stage if teachers can keep in mind the following:

1. Those children who are having trouble listening should not be talked to at length. Work for all children should be varied from individual to group (and vice versa) and from reading and writing to manipulative.
2. Directions should be given clearly. What may appear understandable to the teacher may be difficult for learners. Learning should be broken up into small steps and teachers should ask pupils what the steps are to make certain of mastery.
3. Pupils who have sight and hearing problems should sit where they will have the least possible difficulty seeing and hearing what is going on in the classroom. The teacher should see to it that health services are obtained for the child who needs them. Many behavior problems which seemingly defy solution have been found to stem from a visual or auditory problem.
4. *How* pupils are to share materials should be made clear and definite. Materials should be ready because waiting for them can cause loss of class control.
5. Related to point 4, a definite place should be assigned for each material and supply closets should be kept in good order. This facilitates the distribution of materials and sharing can then be systematic. Some teachers maintain that there is yet another reason for keeping the room orderly: a disorderly room in which pupils can take little pride has a tendency to make them disorderly. Since there may be more than a grain of truth to this, teachers striving to make their pupils reach Stage I would be well advised to keep the room orderly, attractive, and interesting.

Routines as Means.   Although we want children to form habits of listening and following directions, the purpose of these habits is control over their environment (making it a place where learning and growing are possible), not the reverse. Never should routine deter development. The teacher must create the kind of environment where inquiry can exist. This means that pupils will feel that their teacher is hospitable to their questions about things that interest them.

Teachers Must Also Listen.   As noted, the teacher is a powerful model for pupil emulation. As shown in Table 2-1, part of the teacher's responsibility in getting pupils to Stage I is being a good model. Granted this, if teachers want pupils to listen to them and to each other they would be well advised to listen to each individual. When teachers do not really listen, children are discouraged from listening to each other and, not incidentally, from listening to the teacher. Listening to learners is essential if teachers are to help them reach the highest stage of discipline (Stage III). For only if they listen can the teachers encourage learners to support positions they feel are right.

The "Why" of Learning.   Although children must be able to follow directions to reach Stage I, they must not be encouraged to do so blindly but with a purpose that is shared with them by their teacher. With a rationale for learning, children are more likely to evaluate their behavior in terms of the work to be done.

Only the Beginning.   Finally, some teachers will heave a sigh of relief when pupils reach the basic disciplinary stage. Now this is understandable because so many youngsters come to school without the competencies implicit in basic discipline. These teachers are to be congratulated for what often represents brilliant teaching and always represents patience. Granted this, a word of caution is in order. Basic discipline is important and many teachers would wish for no more. "If they could only listen and follow directions," are words on the lips of thousands of teachers. But being able to listen and follow directions is not the end of discipline. These competencies are *turning points* in discipline, *not end points*. Basic discipline must be just the beginning in a democratic society.

Stage II: Constructive Stage

As implied by the name, children in the constructive stage are contributors to the social good of the classroom rather than beings who simply abide by the rules. They are able to work cooperatively with others (an advance over just being able to share materials with them). This means, of course, that they are able to exchange ideas with other children and work with them toward a mutually understood goal. And, as shown in Table 2-1, they understand the basis for reasonable rules and procedures. They have developed the concept of reciprocal obligation.

Pupils at this stage can participate in curriculum planning. They can help the teacher decide what projects should be given to various topics. As Table 2-1 indicates they can develop the procedures for reaching a goal. Obviously the children have moved to a more advanced stage of intellectual development as well as socialization. Planning the steps in a project is, after all, nothing more or less than problem solving, or thinking. Constructive discipline requires higher level cognitive processes than does basic discipline. (In basic discipline the emphasis is on following procedures already developed by someone else—the teacher.)

As might be expected, empathy is a part of the social insight of children in the constructive disciplinary stage. They recognize the needs and rights of others and the effects of their actions on others. Related to this is an understanding of the concept of justice and our national ideal of respect for every individual.

If children are to learn how to work together cooperatively, teachers must provide them with opportunities to do so. Socialization is as important as individualization. Recently, in our usual process of swinging from one philosophical extreme to another we have put individual values over the social. But social values can be an invaluable aid to the self-expression of the individual. Moreover, the balanced development of the individual depends on opportunities to practice social values. It cannot be stated too strongly that the child must assume the responsibility of self-direction in *group as well as individual situations* if he or she is to be a functioning member of a democratic society.

What is forgotten by those who stress the importance of "self-development" (individuality) is that people do not develop in a vacuum but with others. Moreover, unless the individual has a basic rapport with society and its goals, personal development cannot begin.[6] The development of children in our society depends on their relationships with others in our society. Whether they are able to cooperate for the common good—a fundamental principle in a democratic society—depends enormously on teachers. Although it is far easier for us to make all the decisions in the classroom than to teach children how to direct themselves, if children are always under the autocratic control of an adult they will be prepared only for submission to authority later. The main thrust of the constructive stage is social responsibility. An important part of social responsibility is self-direction in group situations (cooperation). Only when children and youth reach the constructive stage has the school realized its social function of preparing citizens for a democracy. (This is why teachers cannot rest when they have brought children to the basic disciplinary stage.)

The democratic ideal is that each contribute according to his ability. This is cooperation for the common good. How can this ideal be made operational in the classroom?

Small Group Activity.   Probably the suggestion most often made to teachers is to have children work in small groups (usually on social studies projects). As more children come to school unsocialized, this

---

[6] Gordon W. Allport, *Becoming: Basic Considerations for a Psychology of Personality* (New Haven, Conn.: Yale University Press, 1955), p. 32.

suggestion meets with less enthusiasm from teachers—particularly in urban classrooms. This is understandable. Many children in inner-city schools (and elsewhere) lack the skills to work together on their own in a small group situation. What may begin with seemingly good intentions on the part of group members may result in horseplay and a free-for-all. Before he or she knows it the teacher has lost control. The mere thought of this nightmare makes many teachers steer clear of small group activity. As one researcher into the problem points out, "the variability and inability of (group) members to respond to one another for more than a few minutes are factors that probably contribute to the loss of control."[7] But she goes on to report an experiment in which a group of low-income fifth- and sixth-graders in an urban elementary school were trained to be good leaders by being shown video tapes of good and poor leadership behavior. The trained student leaders were better able than teachers to increase participation of passive group members! (The teachers had volunteered to lead small groups for the experiment.)[8]

Working in small groups is a skill requiring practice. The foregoing experiment indicates that leaders and participants *can* be trained. Thus children *can* learn how to share different points of view in the process of cooperative problem solving. Although this takes work on the part of the teacher, it must be done if children are to cope with emergent situations. The model of discipline we are discussing here is the personal-social growth model. (See Chapter 1.)

Real Social Responsibility.   While some cooperative activities fail because learners lack the necessary skills and attitudes, others fail for a different reason: the nature of the activity. If children are to learn to work together on a common problem, it must be a real problem which gives them real social responsibility. Children learn by taking part in what is going on according to their developing abilities. Many small group activities fail because the problems given to children are contrived and the children know it. (Even role playing and simulations sometimes fail for this reason.) The curriculum must allow the children to function in real situations, not just discuss them. They must *act* for the sake of an objective which they have arrived at in concert with others.

Moral Education.   What is being suggested here is moral (or character) education in its fullest sense. If children participate in the life of our society and contribute to its improvement at their level of ability,

---

[7] Mary A. Wilcox, "When Children Discuss: A Study of Learning in Small Groups," *The Elementary School Journal*, Vol. 76 (February 1976), p. 304.
[8] Ibid.

they are learning to act morally. Needless to say, the best way to learn how to do something is to do it, not talk about it. Recently there has been renewed interest in moral education as a separate school subject. Unfortunately most of the programs developed to date are heavy on pupil discussion of moral dilemmas and light on providing youngsters with real situations in which they can function morally through social responsibility. For example, although Lawrence Kohlberg recognizes the futility of teaching moral behavior through preaching or moralizing, his model for moral education remains largely a discussion program.[9] It does not resolve the problem of the need for pupil experience. Kohlberg is aware, and rightly so, of the relation between moral judgment and action. But a weakness of his model is that it mainly takes the form of discussion; it is skimpy in examples of action. To illustrate, considerable attention is given by Kohlberg and an associate, Elliot Turiel, to the need for encouraging students to engage in political activity consistent with democratic principles.[10] Encouraging students to engage in an activity is simply not the same thing as providing them with practice. Moreover, political activity is just one kind of social function. Children and youth can and must participate in many other social functions and responsibilities if the school is to realize its moral education function. Even if situations and moral dilemmas are carefully described, as they are in the Kohlberg model, classroom moral discussion is of little value without practice. The model presented in Table 2-1, on the other hand, stresses the importance of providing situations in which the child is socially (and therefore morally) responsible. A number of concrete examples of social responsibilities are offered in Chapter 8. Others are suggested here.

There can be little question about whether moral education *should* be included in the curriculum; like it or not, it is. Public schools are committed to teach the deepest moral values of our society—liberty, justice, and respect for the individual. Moreover, if the schools are closely related to the society in which they function they must face up to society's most demanding moral problems. Educating individuals to control their environment and make it better is a moral task. Thus if we as teachers are realizing our commitment to society, whether or not to "have" moral education is an invalid argument.

Moreover, the nature of the teaching situation can result in moral learning. An example provided by Bidwell is the use of laboratory work in teaching science which can produce in students a commitment to the

[9] Kohlberg, op. cit.

[10] Lawrence Kohlberg and Elliot Turiel, "Moral Development and Moral Education," in *Psychology and Educational Practice* (Glenview, Ill.: Scott, Foresman, 1971), p. 464.

value of empirical investigation (while "blackboard science does not").[11]

What is at issue is whether moral education should be included in the curriculum as a separate subject. If the curriculum as a whole and in the ecological interaction of its parts is to provide control over environment and circumstance, then moral education should be the objective of all subjects. If moral education is the objective of the curriculum as a whole, children are more likely to see moral behavior in the holistic sense, as a part of their lives. If moral education is a separate subject the moral aspects of other subjects—social studies, for example—might go by the board. (In the case of the social studies this would indeed be tragic because the social studies concern the functions of human life in the community, nation, and world; deliberation over ethical values; and the implications of national and international decisions.) Further, if moral judgment and action are divorced from the other parts of the curriculum, it is less likely that pupils can develop integrity of personal outlook. In other words, the school could fail in its moral obligation to children and society simply by treating moral education as something separate from the rest of learning.

These ideas are not original with the writer but flow through the writings of John Dewey. Dewey's conception of moral education was education that enabled people to control their environment and provided them with the insight needed to make choices that go beyond past experience. But he felt that this must be the objective of the curriculum as a whole, not taught as a separate subject.[12]

Cooperative Experiences. To return to the problem of providing opportunities for children to work cooperatively, the following ideas are approved practices in education that have met with demonstrable success in schools for many years. Often, however, they have been allowed to lapse or have been forgotten. (The potential of older approved practices for socialization is frequently overlooked.)

1. Music is a means of helping children to learn to work together cooperatively. Through participation in orchestras or choruses children develop the cooperative skills and attitudes that are necessary for the success of these common efforts. Also, music can be a socially useful activity through the pleasure it affords others. By their playing and singing, pupils can provide a service to those who are old or ill. Every school should have an orchestra and a chorus.

[11] Charles E. Bidwell, "The Social Psychology of Teaching," in Robert M. W. Travers (ed.), *Second Handbook of Research on Teaching* (Chicago: Rand McNally, 1973), pp. 435-436.

[12] See in particular, John Dewey, *Moral Principles in Education* (Carbondale, Ill.: Southern Illinois University Press, 1975; originally published by Houghton Mifflin, 1909).

2. Drama is another means for providing pupils with cooperative experiences. Planning, directing, and performing a play can develop cooperation and responsibility as well as individual creativity.

3. The school assembly is used all too seldom as a socializing mechanism. Here children can share experiences of music and dramatics or report on mutually interesting ideas for the school or community. The assembly can be an effective means for developing common aims and purposes and creating a feeling of belonging among pupils. Both are of the utmost importance in socialization.

4. A classroom government is another infrequently used mechanism for teaching pupils how to be members of a democratic community. Through participation, children can learn to advance arguments, listen to the arguments of others, and reach decisions—in other words, to cooperate with one another.

5. In connection with suggestion 4, each school might organize a council composed of pupils and teachers which has real responsibilities and deals with real problems. Representatives may be elected at the classroom level or by the school at large.

6. A persistent area of concern of teachers and administrators is the lack of concern evidenced by pupils for the school building. Vandalism is a problem that grows increasingly more serious each year in many schools. The key to the problem may lie in giving pupils a role in the repair, upkeep, and decoration of the school. If the responsibility for its appearance is in their hands, pupils will more likely feel that the school is theirs. This is important from the standpoint of effect on moral character. Needless to say a plan must be worked out cooperatively among the building custodian, children, and teachers.

Finally, it is not easy for children to learn to work together when they have been working all through their school careers by themselves. Yet teachers must create situations in which youngsters can work together if children are to reach the constructive stage of discipline. Stage II is the minimum level of competence for effective functioning in a democratic society. But minimum does not mean optimum. Our goal must be to help each child develop to his or her optimum level, to full potential.

Stage III: Generative Stage

The most striking fact about individuals in the generative stage of discipline is that they are self-directing. Since this is the goal of discipline it might be said that they have fully developed competence. The differences between pupil responsibilities in the constructive and generative stages are in degree rather than in kind. Both engage in constructive action. But while an individual in the constructive stage recognizes the needs of others and is able to work cooperatively with others in the solution of problems, the individual in the generative stage is oriented toward the improvement of society to the point of taking the initiative. As shown in Table 2-1, the learners who have reached the highest stage of disciplinary development act on their own responsibility in emergent situations. Since how they act is based on a consideration of the values of society and the consequences of the act for themselves and others they are socially responsible. As a brief illustration, a thirteen-year-old boy in a slum neighborhood organized the tenants in his apartment house when the landlord refused to provide heat. The fact that he did this and no adult did is of striking interest. But the point is that leadership is involved in generative discipline.

While children at the constructive stage have the ability to solve a problem when it is presented to them, at the generative stage they can conceptualize a problem. The latter ability obviously requires higher level cognitive processes than the former. It is also clear that the role of intelligence becomes more central in the developmental progression from basic to generative discipline.

Yet while intelligence is important, generative discipline is also a matter of feeling. A person at this stage will be kind to others, serve the community, and uphold justice, perhaps to the point of sacrifice. These behaviors require more than intelligence. This is obvious since many intelligent people who seem committed to moral goals lack the moral courage to uphold them. Knowledge alone will not result in a better society. Courageous and competent action is also needed. As Dewey said, "The individual must have the power to stand up and count for something in the actual conflicts of life."[13]

Can what Dewey calls "force of character" be taught? Can even the most socially conscious school bring children and youth to the generative stage of discipline? We know that the family, community, and peer group figure so powerfully in the development of character that the influence of the school may be negligible by comparison. Nevertheless, the school has a responsibility to help each child develop as fully as possible. Therefore, it is incumbent upon us to approach the problem positively. The question with which we must concern ourselves is, what can teachers do to help children reach the generative stage?

Examples of teacher responsibilities are given in Table 2-1. The outlook of the teacher toward society is of great importance. Children can learn social optimism or social pessimism from their teachers. A good role model for developing generative discipline should be socially optimistic and oriented toward the improvement of society. He or she should value generosity and uphold the concept of justice in school and in the community.

Models are of great importance in encouraging social responsibility.

[13] Ibid., p. 50.

Granted this, conscious practice in assuming social responsibility is also apparently very important. If children and youth are involved in projects which serve society, they probably will be more likely to develop an active interest in social welfare.[14]

The following additional suggestions are offered for teachers:

1. Literature, history, science, and art can provide models of autonomous, principled action for pupils of all ages.
2. Children and youth should be taught the values of our society including justice and the responsibility of each individual for contributing to the welfare and progress of all. They should learn to analyze their own behavior in light of these values.
3. In social studies, history, and literature, older students can critically analyze men, women, and institutions in their fidelity to social ideals. Was Abraham Lincoln a responsible leader for the values of democracy? Did Jane Addams act in accord with the values of our society? Was Lyndon Johnson a good man in the social sense? To what extent are trade unions socially responsible institutions?
4. The curriculum should provide learners—particularly upper elementary, junior, and senior high schoolers—with opportunities to analyze the performance of the leaders of our society in terms of the values of our society.
5. The curriculum should make learners aware of the life about them in which they have to play a part and the contribution they can make.
6. Teachers should strive to help each child realize his or her potential. Generative discipline depends on the development of individual capacities and talents.

Finally, and perhaps most important if we expect children to move upward through the developmental stages of discipline, our emphasis must always be on the positive (what to do and how to do it) rather than on the negative (what not to do, what cannot be changed, what cannot be accomplished in the world). What we are trying to do is to help children develop their powers for constructive ends. This goal pervades all three stages of discipline. Development is, in itself, a positive concept. It is, after all, synonymous with growth. Personal and social growth should be never-ending.

SUMMARY

At the center of the teacher's concern for classroom discipline is the concept of development. Disciplinary methods should be matched to the developmental level of the child and help him move to the next

[14] Robert J. Havighurst, *Developmental Tasks and Education* (New York: McKay 1972), p. 79.

stage. When children need reasons other than adult authority for what they do they are developing properly. The desirable direction of growth is away from the need to obey adults and toward judging appropriate behavior by the situation. We can build on this developmental change by helping pupils learn to set behavioral standards that are tuned to the work to be done rather than to adult omnipotence.

Piaget's developmental stages have implications for classroom discipline as well as learning. The predominant characteristic of the *pre-operational* stage(ages two to seven) is *egocentrism;* children perceive the world from only one vantage point—their own—and are incapable of true cooperation. From the age of four until about seven children egocentrically accept the adult's point of view as their own and rules are rooted in adult authority. This is the stage of *moral realism.* Teachers can help children transfer from egocentric thinking to operational thinking by explaining the "why" as well as the "what" of behavior. In so doing they are helping pupils to enter the stage of *concrete operations.* When pupils are able to exchange thoughts with others, feel sympathy for others, and work with others cooperatively on a common problem they have developed the morality of *reciprocity.* These are also components of socialization.

Development is not automatic. Reciprocity depends on quality of relationships and teaching. (The development of reciprocity can be retarded by a teacher who sets an example of bullying, rudeness to others, and injustice.)

The final stage of development comes in late childhood or early adolescence with the attainment of formal operations. The child is able to reflect on human relationships and work out principles for dealing with them. Self-direction is the pervasive characteristic of this stage.

Developmental psychology can only guide teachers in general ways. Teachers need a developmental guide to discipline which indicates the characteristics of pupils' behavior at each stage and the teacher's role in getting pupils to each stage. With this need in mind, the developmental stages of discipline are offered. Pupils are at Stage I (Basic Disciplinary Stage) when they can listen, follow directions, and ask questions when they need help. Stage I is crucial for school learning but is only a turning point in discipline. Pupils at Stage II (Constructive Stage) can work cooperatively with others and contribute to the common good when given real social responsibility. (This is moral education in its true sense.) When presented with a problem they can make judgments concerning the proper course of action to be pursued. Learners at Stage III (Generative Stage) have achieved fully developed competence in self-direction and will take the initiative in the solution of social problems. Models are of great importance in encouraging social responsibility.

Problems and Activities

1. According to Piaget, the desirable direction of development is away from regarding rules as sacred because they come from adults and toward judging appropriate behavior based on situational factors. In view of this, how should the teacher's approach to discipline differ in working with primary and upper elementary school pupils?

2. Many teachers mourn the fact that beginning in the third grade, children often end the stage where "being good" means "minding" the teacher and enter a new stage. In your opinion, is this an appropriate attitude for teachers? Do you think that teachers should do everything possible to keep children in the stage at which appropriate behavior is synonymous with obedience to authority? Why?

3. Is development an automatic process? Support your answer.

4. In what ways can developmental psychology help teachers? What are its limitations?

5. What are the characteristics of Piaget's concept of reciprocity? Is this concept useful for teachers? Explain.

6. Should teachers be content when pupils reach the basic disciplinary stage? Why or why not?

7. What stage of discipline must children and youth reach if the school is to meet its obligation to society? Give reasons for your answer.

8. Draw up a list of suggestions for teachers to follow in teaching pupils cooperative skills and attitudes.

9. Do you think that moral education should be taught as a separate subject? Support your response.

10. In your opinion is classroom discussion an adequate approach to moral education? Why? If your response was negative propose an alternative.

11. Compile a list of contemporary persons who are making positive contributions to society and, in your opinion, are leading lives that can serve as models for children and youth. Give reasons for each entry.

12. Ms. Jones, a fourth-grade teacher at the Emerson School, does not get along well with the other teachers at Emerson. She refuses to share ideas and materials with them and is a carping critic of their methods, classroom control, grading, and so on. They deeply resent the fact that she is continually praising herself to get recognition and never praises their good work. Although disliked by her colleagues, Ms. Jones is a dedicated teacher. All of her pupils have reached the basic disciplinary stage and she is anxious to have them progress to the constructive stage. Do you think that she will encounter difficulties? If so, what are they and how can they be overcome?

13. What values should teachers demonstrate as good role models for the generative stage of discipline?
14. Compare and contrast the role of the teacher in the constructive and generative stages of discipline.

Discipline
and the Curriculum

3

At the heart of many discipline problems lies the curriculum: what is taught and how it is taught. Work that is too hard can cause discipline problems as can work that is too easy. (But the former is far more likely to happen than the latter.) Another frequent cause of discipline problems is error-oriented teaching, focusing on learners' mistakes without giving encouragement or making good work seem possible. Although errors have to be pointed out if children are to learn, errors can loom out of proportion to the goal, which is to do the work successfully. Errors are incidents on the way to learning and should be treated as such. Failure-oriented teaching is likely to have negative results for motivation and perseverance and can create discipline problems. On the other hand, a good teacher-disciplinarian keeps the learning goal foremost on everyone's mind by pointing out the steps needed to get there.

The curriculum can be a positive force in classroom control. As a matter of fact the most constructive approach to discipline is through the curriculum. Learning that is interesting and provides a sense of growing power and accomplishment is the best means of classroom control. Attaining discipline through the curriculum is the subject of this chapter.

CONTENT AND CLASS CONTROL

How can the curriculum bring about good discipline? We can begin to answer the question by looking at the nature of the curriculum itself.

Nature of the Curriculum

As seen in Figure 3–1, the curriculum consists of four interrelating parts: Formal Subject Matter, Skills and Concepts, Attitudes and Values, and Behaviors. Formal subject matter, and skills and concepts have always been considered part of the curriculum. The problem is that some people consider them to be the entire curriculum. This is dangerous for discipline. If we leave out attitudes, values, and behaviors from the curriculum we cannot expect children to grow in the ability to act responsibly.

The personal-social growth model of discipline presented in Chapter 1 is based on this holistic concept of the curriculum. Self-direction, the goal of education and discipline, means that the learner's behavior is guided by appropriate attitudes, values, and abilities (skills, concepts, and formal knowledge). Academic knowledge alone will not suffice. It

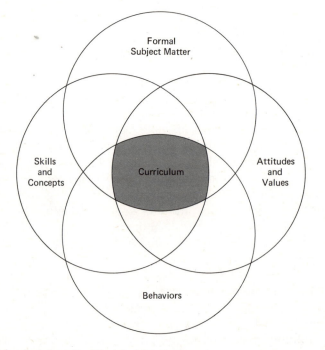

FIGURE 3-1   An Interactive Model of Curriculum

will not give youngsters the motives for behaving correctly. They need to develop a constructive attitude toward society and habits of considering others. These attitudes and behaviors are a part of the curriculum and must be consciously taught.

Many teachers depend on the home for instilling in children habits of considering others and positive attitudes toward learning. This is a strategic mistake. While it is true that some parents do send us models of industry, perseverance, and consideration for others, there are other parents who fall down miserably on the job. One should not blame the parents because fixing the blame is unproductive. Rather we should judge the situation and what it means for our job, which is simply that the school must teach these habits and attitudes.

Moreover, although habits of responsibility and respect for the rights of others taught by the family *do* transfer to the school, discipline is not the same thing in the family as it is in the classroom. The family is a small group who know each other intimately and rules can be more flexible than in classrooms. In the school, people are brought together by society for one purpose—education. Hence our willingness as teachers to bend to the individual is necessarily limited by our obligation to society. Durkheim pointed out that the classroom society resembles the larger society with its demands on individuals much more than it resembles the family and, further, that all children are initiated into serious social life by the school.[1]

The curriculum should consist of whatever is needed to make children competent, self-directing people. This would include both the academic and social-skills areas. In the following sections, we will be looking at how the academic and social-skills areas relate to class control.

Reading and Discipline

While it is true that education should not consist merely of textbook learning, reading constitutes the heart of the curriculum. The child who cannot read is tied hand and foot, pedagogically speaking, because in virtually every school subject the materials of instruction involve reading. Youngsters are unable to avail themselves of opportunities provided by the school unless they can read. Whether the subject is science or auto mechanics, the door of opportunity is slammed in the face of the nonreader. Children who cannot read cannot look up information in books. Self-education, self-direction, and even *following* directions

---

[1] Émile Durkheim, *Moral Education* (New York: The Free Press, 1973), pp. 147-149.

are impossible. Much of the time the children who cannot read have nothing to do. They fidget, make noise, and bother others. These children have not reached the basic stage of discipline.

Helping the Nonreader: Pay-off for Discipline. The best help that a teacher can give to these youngsters (and for everyone around them) is to teach them to read as soon as possible. Although learning to read usually does not happen overnight, the act of being taught to read can have an immediate effect on their behavior. They may begin to regard the teacher as a friend (particularly if the instruction has been on a one-to-one basis) and try harder to behave in ways valued by the teacher. Since working individually with children very often has an immediate pay-off for discipline, teachers should make every effort to work in this way with problem learners.

Additional suggestions for helping problem readers are as follows:

1. If you as the teacher are unable to give the individual help that the child needs find someone who can. Ideally this person should be specially trained, but student teachers, community volunteers, high school students, older children, and classmates can make real inroads on reading problems. Many schools have the services of remedial reading teachers. It cannot be overstressed that remedial teachers or tutors and classroom teachers should coordinate planning and that the classroom teacher should still read individually with the child whenever possible (to show the continuing interest that pays off in improved discipline and learning).

2. If you really want nonreaders or retarded readers to improve, expect that they will improve. Although research has not confirmed clearly that the expectations of teachers affect achievement, a number of studies lend convincing support to this hypothesis.[2]

3. With each gain inform the problem reader that he or she has made progress. However, concrete evidence that personal efforts have paid off in improved competence is best. Some teachers make a tape recording of oral reading and hold it. After a few weeks of special help another recording is made and the pupil compares the tapes. Evidence of overcoming the handicap can mark a new era in the life of the pupil. He or she may no longer feel uneducable and may even come to excel in several subjects of the curriculum by using the most important tool—reading. Discipline problems are less likely because destructive energies have been diverted into constructive channels.

4. Parents can teach their children to read if teachers work out an instruc-

---

[2] See, for example, W. B. Seaver, "Effects of Naturally Induced Teacher Expectancies," *Journal of Personality and Social Psychology*, Vol. 28 (December 1973), pp. 333-342; and Catherine Cornbleth, O. L. Davis, Jr., and Christine Button, "Expectations for Pupil Achievement and Teacher-Pupil Interaction," *Social Education*, Vol. 38 (January 1974), pp. 54-58.

tional program for the parent to follow. Simply asking the parent to "help" is not enough. It should be clear to the parent that progress hinges on a positive attitude. (If he or she seems unconvinced of the child's ability to learn it is better to find someone else to do the tutoring.)

5. Continued improvement in reading should not be left to chance in the secondary school. A growing number of junior and senior high schools are adopting developmental reading programs. Improving the ability of students to read is as much a factor in overcoming behavior problems at the secondary school level as it is in the elementary schools.

Power and Pleasure.   Space does not permit discussion on methods of teaching reading. But any method used should give learners a sense of the power and pleasure that come from reading. Phonics alone cannot do this. Many teachers report success with the language experience approach in which reading materials and stories are based on pupils' own language and experiences. Finally, it is noteworthy that nothing facilitates consciousness of achievement in reading more than reading. Children need to read from books to develop an emotional tie between themselves and reading. Children should hold books, use books, and love books as early as possible. They come to school eager to learn to read storybooks, readers, and books filled with the world's secrets. They should not be disappointed.

Purposeful Activity

At one time the ideal of good discipline was to have pupils sitting absolutely motionless without making a sound. ("So quiet that I can hear a pin drop" was the standard set by teachers.) Hand in hand with this ideal went an education consisting of meaningless repetition, drearisome drill, and parroting memorized responses to teachers' questions. But there came a day when objection to this view of education and discipline created a revolution in education. John Dewey was the central figure in this revolution. According to Dewey, learning was an active process in which the learner shared. In the words of Dewey, "The problem of instruction is thus that of finding materials which will engage a person in specific activities having a purpose of interest to him."[3] Dewey also said that doing (the activity) should require thinking for real learning to result.[4] What Dewey was suggesting was purposeful activity.

Unfortunately many of Dewey's followers interpreted activity as overt movement and left out the thinking part. Many of the activities

---

[3] John Dewey, *Democracy and Education* (New York: Macmillan, 1916), p. 132.
[4] Ibid., p. 154.

in the early decades of this century seemed to be intended only to get pupils up and moving around. This was a natural reaction to the form of education that was being reformed in which pupils could not move a muscle without being reproved or punished. Today neither pointless formalism nor activity for its own sake without a learning goal has a place in our schools. But the point is that Dewey's idea about learners being actively involved in their own learning still lives in the curriculum and has important implications for discipline.[5] First, learning is an active, not a passive process. Activity may be overt movement but this is not necessarily the case. For example, active learning can occur when the learner is quietly reading in the library. Learning in and of itself is an active process. Be that as it may, activity, when it is tied to a learning goal, is very much a part of Dewey's legacy. Learning can be facilitated by active experience as well as (and sometimes better than) reading. Firsthand experience is considered desirable in almost every area of the curriculum. Science, for example, must involve firsthand experiences. In an effective science program pupils are observing, investigating, exploring, experimenting, working together on projects, and sharing their ideas with others. This means that children are expected to move around and be active but theirs is *purposeful activity*—activity that is shaped and limited by a purpose.

Children (and teachers) must learn that behavior should be governed by the nature of the task. This is when classroom discipline comes in. Talking is allowed when pupils are working together on a project but it should have to do with the project. Similarly, the classroom must be organized so that pupils can experiment but their actions should be determined by the experiment. This leads to an important principle regarding pupil behavior in various areas of the curriculum.

> **Fifth Principle:** *Appropriate behavior is determined by rational demands of specific situations.*

This principle applies to all areas of the curriculum. It is easy for children to comprehend because from a very early age they are aware that people are expected to behave differently in different situations. One walks on tiptoe in the kitchen if there is a cake in the oven so that the cake will not "fall." But when the cake is out of the oven, one can

[5] Daniel Tanner and Laurel N. Tanner, "The Curriculum Legacy," Chapter 8 in *Curriculum Development: Theory Into Practice* (New York: Macmillan, 1975), pp. 351-395.

walk normally. To tell a child to walk on tiptoe in the kitchen without giving a reason would be ridiculous. Some of our school rules are as arbitrary and as senseless as this and recall the mindlessness which Charles Silberman saw as the central problem of public schools.[6]

Following the Principle. So that pupils can understand what is considered appropriate behavior in a given learning situation they must first know what the goals are. If the lesson is planned cooperatively they will know since they helped to develop the goal. Equally important, they will be cognizant of the steps that they are going to take to reach the goal.

Teacher-pupil planning is an approved practice in education. However, not every lesson can be planned cooperatively and some children are unable to even follow directions without close supervision, much less plan their activities. In such cases, the activity is planned by the teacher alone. The following steps are suggested for conveying to pupils that what they are trying to do at that particular time in the classroom should determine how they must behave at that time.

1. Explain the goal and the steps that pupils must take to accomplish it successfully.
2. Ask pupils what they are trying to learn or find out (or what the teacher is trying to find out if it is a testing situation), and what the things are that they must do to accomplish the goal.

What they are to do determines the right conduct for that situation.

Teachers will find the principle that behavior is determined by the objectives of the activity helpful for three reasons: (1) children and youth are more likely to follow a guide for behavior that makes sense to them than they are to follow arbitrary rules that may seem external to the task at hand; (2) the principle connects their behavior with the objective of the lesson and helps keep their minds on the work; and (3) teachers can know whether learners really are behaving the way they should. Sometimes teachers feel apprehensive when pupils are talking and moving about because they are afraid that the situation will get out of control. The rule of thumb is that if the activity and sounds are clearly directed to the goal of the task, then the children probably are behaving appropriately. We say "probably" because they could be making more noise than they need to, disturbing others (unintentionally), or operating at too high a peak of excitement. But generally, if activity is work-oriented we can relax and enjoy our pupils. One thing that we do

---

[6] Charles E. Silberman, *Crisis in the Classroom* (New York: Random House, 1970), p. 11.

know for certain is that chaotic activity (movement unguided by thought) is never appropriate behavior.

It is also clear that a quiet classroom is absolutely no evidence that the class has a repressive teacher who has them cowed into silence and does not regard learning as an active process. It may simply mean that pupils are so interested in their work that they do not want to talk or disturb others.

Discipline through Pupil Responsibility

At the beginning of this chapter it was stated that the most constructive approach to discipline is through the curriculum. A good way to use the curriculum itself to achieve good discipline is to give learners responsibility for some part of a lesson or activity. Sometimes this comes about naturally. The following case is illustrative.

Mr. McKim only learned that he was teaching seventh-grade science a week before the semester started. To his dismay, he was assigned room 2A which was not a laboratory. On checking he found that the science laboratory had been assigned to another class. In looking at the list of pupils, Bill McKim became even more glum. He had all the incorrigibles. It was probably just as well, he thought, that he would not be teaching a laboratory course to *this* bunch. A week after the semester began, Bill was approached by three of the youngsters, books in hand. "This chapter you assigned has experiments. Why can't we do the experiments?" asked Sally Maclure (probably the wildest seventh-grade girl in the school, if not the entire county). "Yeah, we wanna do the experiments," nodded the other two, Dick Perry and Bob Jones. Bill began to explain about the laboratory not being available that hour. Then he had an idea. "If you want to pick up the equipment from the lab, set up the experiments, clean up afterward, store the stuff in your lockers until after school and return the equipment to the lab before you get on the bus, you can have experiments," he said. The idea worked out better than he could have dreamed. The seventh graders had lunch before science and could use part of their lunch hour to set up equipment. Bill used part of class time to plan the experiments with the students but they conducted the experiments and explained the principles involved. They assumed part of the responsibility of teaching and in so doing became deeply involved in the science curriculum. Discipline problems with the seventh-grade science class that semester were at a minimum.

In following this approach, Bill McKim was not only using the curriculum as a positive force in class control but he was following two other principles. First, self-direction is learned when children are helped to deal with emergent situations (the desire to do experiments in an unequipped classroom was the emergent situation); and second, socialization is promoted through social responsibility. Teachers should not wait for the kind of situation described above. Youngsters should be given responsibility for teaching principles or procedures to the class at every opportunity. It deeply involves them in the work, clarifies concepts about which they may previously have given little thought, and instills confidence.

The teacher who is having discipline problems should look to the curriculum. It may be that it does not give children enough to think about or to plan for. The youngsters who come to class full of plans for their role in the school program have no time for misbehavior. Over and over again we have seen children without enough to do get into trouble. This is as true of adolescents as it is of children and as true out of school as in school. Not long ago in a nationally televised hearing on crime and violence, a youth told the investigating committee: "I was violent because I had nothing else to do." Work of real value and the satisfaction that derives from doing it can prevent discipline problems in the classroom and crimes of violence in the larger society.

To return to the idea of giving learners responsibility for classroom work, children and youth take pleasure in activities identified with the social good. Planning and conducting an activity which involves the curriculum is doing something of value that helps the progress of others. A teacher who asks, "Will you be in charge of this?" *when the responsibility involves a significant aspect of the curriculum,* is leading toward deeper pupil involvement with the subject and helping pupils progress through the stages of discipline.

INTEREST AND DISCIPLINE

The ideal in the elementary school is to have a room of lively youngsters busily at work on problems of interest to them. In the secondary school the ideal is similar: adaptation of the curriculum to students' varying needs and interests. When youngsters are deeply immersed in their work, problems of control are at a minimum or seem to disappear completely. But when youngsters are only superficially engaged (or not engaged at all), behavior problems erupt with distressing frequency. We all prefer the first situation in which children are absorbed in the schoolwork. Naturally we want to know the secret of making them absorbed (if there is a secret). First we ask, is engagement in work the same as interest?

This question is crucial for discipline. The answer is no. Learners may be involved in the work simply because they feel that learning the new skill will make them a better person or because their parents have told them that one goes to school to learn. On the other hand, they may have a genuine interest in the work itself. Perhaps they are indeed following their own interests. When the schoolwork and children's existing interests coincide, we have an ideal situation for discipline and learning. In fact, however, not all of the schoolwork coincides with childrens' present interests, nor should it if we want to broaden interests and abilities. The case of Harold B is not at all unusual.

> Harold B, a sixth grader, has a single-minded and consuming interest in the Civil War. This was fine in the fifth grade when the class studied the United States but this year they are studying Europe. Harold is completely bored with social studies this year although the rest of the class is interested (particularly in the imaginary trip that they are planning to Europe). Harold keeps asking his teacher, Mrs. Harris, for permission to go to the library to read about the Civil War. Mrs. Harris believes that the school should provide children with opportunities to follow their own interests. Some childhood interests do develop into lifelong interests. Perhaps someday Harold may even become a renowned Civil War historian, who knows! But in the meantime, there is Europe and the prescribed curriculum. What should she do? She finally decides to have an individual conference with Harold in which it is decided that Harold may spend time in the library continuing his own research on the Civil War. But he will also become involved in European history, starting with the Spanish Civil War, and will report on his findings of the causes and outcomes to the class. (Since Spain is on their "itinerary," he will be making a contribution to the class project.)

In this instance, the teacher used a child's existing interests as a bridge to new interests but also let him "follow his own interest." However, if Harold had absolutely *no* interest in social studies the problem would have required a different approach. Lack of interest in the curriculum is discussed shortly.

Behind the Ideal

The teacher's ideal of children busily at work on problems of interest to them need not depend on children following their own individual interests. It is more often realized when teachers make the curriculum interesting and in so doing develop new interests. The children in the example above had developed a new interest in Europe, sparked by the idea of planning a trip to Europe. Collecting travel folders, reading about the art and geography of western Europe, and consulting time tables was an exciting business for them. The development of new interests is a purpose of education. It is also a key to good discipline.

The tendency among the best teachers is to try to bring about a "fit" between the child and the curriculum. This means making sure that the work is challenging but within the learner's comprehension and that the materials used are of interest.

The Interested. There is absolutely no guarantee that the class will be interested in the prescribed curriculum. Some children are interested, simply because they love school and are avid consumers of whatever happens to be in the curriculum. These youngsters seldom cause problems.

The Willing but Unable. In almost every classroom there is a second group of children (perhaps only one or two in number but maybe nearly the entire class) who would *like* to do the work—if they knew how. But the teacher passes out books that they cannot read and assigns work that they cannot do. It is the work prescribed for the grade but the curriculum is as painful for these children as shoes that do not fit. They get farther and farther behind and because there is nothing to do for long stretches of time they become bored and their behavior deteriorates. Teachers have only one recourse with these youngsters: to identify their learning problems and to develop a program matched to their needs. This does not mean that the goals of the curriculum should not be the same for these children as they are for all children. Probably the children who appear to be slow learners can profit from the regular curriculum if activities are planned that give them a chance to practice their skills in reading (in which they are so often deficient) while they learn new content in the various subject areas.[7]

The Uninterested. A third group of children is seldom if ever interested in anything taught by the school. They rarely do any work and are unable to be quiet. These youngsters have not attained basic discipline. Although they usually have learning problems, their main problem appears to be lack of interest. Our main problem is to get them started. We turn now to this group.

Developing Interest in Work

Not infrequently a teacher finds herself (or himself) facing a class in which the handful who are motivated to learn are outnumbered several

[7] William J. Younie, *Instructional Approaches to Slow Learners* (New York: Teachers College Press, 1967), pp. 59-73.

times over by the undisciplined and the unmotivated. It is hard to get everyone to sit down at the same time. John is always getting up, poking someone and wandering around the room. His reading worksheet remains undone. Mark has junk in his pocket that he pulls out and plays with on his desk. Someone (who knows who) has just opened a bottle of very strong perfume. In an era in which one hears exciting talk about children choosing their own activities, one observes while ducking a paper airplane that this is precisely what these children are doing. (Only not in the way that the methods books mean.) One only hopes for the best, for survival.

The problem with these children and many thousands like them is to get them started with learning. It is plain that this will require adjustments in what is taught and how it is taught, but what kind of adjustments? What must be done is to make learning so interesting that they would rather do their work than bother others. This is our purpose as far as school discipline is concerned. As far as learning is concerned our goal is to have them so interested in acquiring new skills, concepts, and formal knowledge that learning will be like a snowball running down a hill or like a forest fire burning out of control—impossible to stop. Our objective will only be achieved when our pupils persist in doing their work and finding out what they want to know even in the face of difficulty. This is what is meant by disciplined learning. It is the exact opposite of finding every possible distraction and every excuse in the world not to learn.

Keeping our minds on the objective, which is to create in pupils an absorbing interest in the school curriculum, we turn our attention to the curriculum itself. One can without difficulty identify several common practices that "turn off" all but those whose motivation stems from sources outside the work itself. (Interestingly, included among the "turned off" are some teachers who may be as bored as the children but are following a curriculum prescribed by others or believe in all sincerity that they are helping children the best way possible.) A curriculum consisting largely of worksheets is one such practice. There is nothing interesting in blank-filling except for the little games that children sometimes devise (in self defense) to make the pastime tolerable. But worksheets do not make reading exciting. Books that children cannot read and books that are obviously intended for slow learners and seem "babyish" also shut off motivation. Endless hours of phonetic analysis also takes the joy out of reading and throws a pall on school as does a teacher who is grimly determined to "teach them their skills and nothing else this year." This last may mean that the children are cheated out of art, music, science, social studies, field trips, and physical education and get no chances to apply their skills in reading and writing. Included in this list are the most interesting things that children can do in school.

Reading to Pupils.   How does one interest children who are undisciplined and cannot read in the work of the school? One of the most obvious ways is to read to them. This idea is so obvious and simple that it is often overlooked. The writer did it in an instinctive effort to survive (see page 1). The idea is seldom mentioned in the literature on getting children started in learning, yet is an approved practice in education. As Hilda Taba and Deborah Elkins said some years ago in their book on working with "educationally disadvantaged" junior high school pupils, "students who cannot read well enough on their own must be read to."[8] Taba and Elkins pointed out that "to be capable of engaging these students emotionally, the content must be mature and engaging, rather than diluted and didactic," and that "stories, novels, and biographies that meet these criteria are not too easy to find."[9]

Granted this, the content *is* available and the results of following this strategy can be both welcome and exciting.

Carla T's sixth grade class fought easily, lacked academic skills, and never (or hardly ever) listened. None could read with ease and eleven out of the thirty-seven were nonreaders. All were accustomed to years of failure in school and felt that they had been put in "a dumb class." Carla tried to get them interested in reading stories, but the books she got from the storeroom were decidedly unpopular. One boy said that his brother had used the same book in the fourth grade. This led to a chorus of "I'm not using no baby book" followed by a slamming of books on desks. Recognizing the futility of teaching with these materials, Carla said, "All right, we won't use these books. I'll read to you from a book written for adults, for *grown-ups*, starting first thing tomorrow." The book that Carla selected later in a bookstore about a block from the school was a paperback copy of John Steinbeck's *The Pearl*. The simply written story had a theme of universal interest and appeal; changes in the way of life of a poor Indian family brought about by wealth in the form of a giant pearl. The first morning when she read, the children listened quietly for the most part, although one girl expressed skepticism about whether the story was really for adults. However, when Carla closed the book, the same girl asked, disappointedly, "that's all?" The second morning when she began to read, Carla was startled to see at least a half dozen youngsters reach into their desks and take out paperback copies of *The Pearl*. The third day there were even more. These children followed along silently.

[8] Hilda Taba and Deborah Elkins, *Teaching Strategies for the Culturally Disadvantaged* (Chicago: Rand McNally, 1966), p. 78.

[9] Ibid.

Discussion.   Reading of stories should be followed by discussion so that children can share their perceptions and insights about the meaning of the story. Teachers will find it useful to begin with open-ended questions to which all youngsters can respond without feeling threatened. Examples are "What would you have done differently if you were the father?" or "What do you wish had happened in the end?" These questions have no right or wrong answers; interpretation of literature is a highly individual matter. This is a boon for youngsters who all their lives have given the wrong answer to the teacher's questions.

In addition to allowing pupils to express feelings and encouraging them to ask questions of each other and their teacher, the discussion should develop respect for the opinions of others and a willingness to listen to others. These are social skills as well as ways of developing new insights and understanding. Freedom of expression for everyone is not possible, however, unless the teacher controls the discussion (by this we mean control of the sequence of discussion and not content). A rash of nonsequential remarks and unrelated side comments can result in chaos rather than developing insights and habits of considering the opinions of others. Therefore controlling the discussion is absolutely essential. This is not easy when youngsters are not used to the freedom of expressing their own ideas and are easily sidetracked, forgetting that even in free discussions the points that one makes should be related to the question being asked.

Discussion of literature can help children learn to express them themselves clearly and concisely. The direct personal interest in a good story (like *The Pearl*) can transfer to other forms of creative expression and other areas of the curriculum (not to mention motivating children to learn how to read). Carla T, the teacher in the foregoing illustration, was asked by several pupils if they could write a play about *The Pearl*. Since these pupils had little command of the skills of communication, this was a major undertaking. But because the youngsters had the incentive to write (and to read what they had written), fundamental skills were developed in the most meaningful way possible—through application. The children practiced the play over and over and finally gave it before the entire school in an assembly program. This experience was of social value as well as a milestone in their intellectual growth.

Understanding and Using
Children's Interests

The emotional power of good literature can get children started in learning. Another way is through children's interests. As in the use of literature, the intention is to lead from direct personal interest to the command of fundamental intellectual and social skills. The first thing that a teacher must do in using children's interests is to find out what interests the children. Recently the tide of ideas on interest and motivation has run strongly in the direction of the child's own environment. It is believed by many theorists that content and materials for unmotivated learners should utilize the youngster's immediate environment to spark interest. Thus some publishers of basal readers have developed reading programs for disadvantaged children that contain stories set in the inner city. It is believed that inner-city children will be more interested in learning to read when the stories take place in a neighborhood that resembles their own than in an unfamiliar or suburban neighborhood. Some teachers report that their pupils are making real progress with these materials. But how much, if any, of this progress can be attributed to the setting of the stories is unknown. (It may be that the teacher's belief that children will learn better with these materials is the most powerful factor.)

In any event the idea that content should reflect the child's neighborhood to spark learning is reminiscent of the expanding environment principle for teaching social studies which is based on the notion that young children's interest in their environment begins with the family and expands outward. From the 1930s until the 1960s most school systems based their social studies curricula on this principle and some of them still do. This curriculum is an ordered progression beginning with study of the family in kindergarten and grade one and moving on to the neighborhood, the city, the state, the nation, and the world in successive years. This curriculum and its underlying principle were almost unquestioned until the 1960s when some observers found an element of incongruity with children's real interests and experiences. Children who watched television had a window to the world and were no longer tied to the concentric circles of the expanding environment principle (if indeed they ever had been, because before television children listened to the radio, went to the movies, and read books about places far away in time and space).

Children's Interests Are Wide.   Children have many interests: happenings from the dawn of history, faraway lands, and nearby surroundings. A teacher attempting to spark the excitement of learning by engaging children in something of interest to them must be aware of the surprising breadth and sophistication of children's interests.[10]

[10] Dorothy Kirsch, "From Athletes to Zebras—Young Children Want To Read about Them," *Elementary English*, Vol. 52 (January 1975), pp. 73-78.

Interest and Experience.   The problem may be that interest is being confused with experience by some educators. These are two different concepts in education. Both are important in engaging pupils with the work of the school and in school discipline. A good teacher tries to relate the content of the curriculum to the learner's *experience* because this makes the work more meaningful and interesting, and learning easier. However, the conclusion that the only thing that can *interest* the unmotivated learners is their immediate neighborhood because this is the sum total of their experience is without foundation in fact. Unmotivated learners (like many motivated learners)[11] are interested in the era of the caveman and dinosaurs, distant places like Africa and South America, earthquakes, robots, explorations in space, and famous people. This list is only the beginning. But the point is that many of the things that interest children, and therefore can influence class control, are not identical with their real life experiences.

Personal and General Interests.   It is helpful to view children's interests as being of two kinds, *personal* and *general*. Children's personal interests are not easily known, particularly at the beginning of the school year. However, general interests may serve just as well as a spur to learning, as the following case illustrates.

> After only one week of teaching the fourth grade that year, Mrs. Burks felt that she was failing miserably with Charles Clark. Unless she could get him to stop annoying the children around him and become interested in his work, there was no way that his retardation in reading, language, and arithmetic could be eliminated. Mrs. Burks decided to try a general interest with Charles—the prehistoric age. She taught an emotion-packed lesson on the trials of living in that age and asked for volunteers to make a mural depicting the points made in the lesson. Charles and another boy made an extraordinarily creative mural showing a cave dweller in hand-to-hand combat with a cave bear. They used books and encyclopedias from the school library for authenticity and wrote a story (experience chart) to go with the mural. The art work that Charles did was powerful and mysterious and attracted the attention of everyone on the school faculty (and their husbands and wives). Charles was invited to talk about the mural on Parents' Night. The general interest in prehistoric people became a personal interest for Charles and led to concept development in history, geography, and science, and improvement in fundamental skills. As his interest grew more important to him, he had less inclination (and time) to annoy others. The general interest had had a self-propelling effect on learning and socialization.

[11] Ibid.

A point communicated by this case is that children's interests do transcend their immediate environment, even in the instance of the "educationally disadvantaged." (Charles lived in an urban slum.) Mythology would have it that classroom learning experiences for disadvantaged children should only concern their immediate environment. But by following the myth, the teacher is cutting down the number of options for reaching them and teaching them.

In sum, the objective of using literature or general interests as motivational devices is to get pupils started in the learning process and keep them learning. In so doing we are helping pupils come up to the basic discipline level.

Identifying Children's Interests.   Teachers are often told in their preparation programs that the best way to motivate children to learn is to let them "follow their interests." This vague directive is of little help to teachers and may cause further heartaches for the teacher who is experiencing problems in class control. In the first place, there are the practical problems involved. How does one ascertain children's interests? Asking them sounds like the best way and for this reason some teachers administer "interest inventories" to children. But the answers that the children give us can be very misleading. Children are usually anxious to say what they think their teachers would like to hear. Or they may respond without giving the question more than momentary attention and would probably answer differently tomorrow.

In 1934, Dewey became concerned about the problem of identifying children's interests and made a suggestion for teachers that continues to be a very good guide. Dewey was troubled because "interests" had come to mean choices expressed orally by the child.[12] Children usually snatched at transient interests when asked what they would like to do. For this reason and because children had many developing interests, it was the teacher's responsibility to identify those interests that are prized by the community and lead in the direction that the demands of society would take.

What Dewey was saying was that not all interests are of equal value and that it was the teacher's job, not the child's, to identify the child's interests and that, further, those interests should be valued by the community and help the youngster to meet the demands of society. An interest that engages children in learning activities would help them to

---

[12] John Dewey, "Comments and Criticisms by Some Educational Leaders in Our Universities," Chapter 5 in *The Activity Movement*, Thirty-third Yearbook of the National Society for the Study of Education, Part II (Bloomington, Ill.: Public School Publishing Company, 1934), p. 85.

meet the requirements of society. Similarly an interest in art, music, discovering new knowledge, or contributing to the welfare of society would be valued by the community.

By getting to know their pupils, teachers can identify their interests and decide which ones will promote individual development and positive social attitudes. Unfortunately some children do not have many personal interests. The schools should provide these and all children with opportunities to develop new interests. This is one reason in favor of using literature and general interests for getting pupils started in learning. A second reason is that these approaches are eminently practical because they can be used with an entire class. Each youngster can respond to the story or lesson in terms of its personal meaning.

SOCIAL ATTITUDES

If our objective is self-direction, social attitudes and social skills cannot be separated from the rest of the curriculum. As was mentioned earlier, pupils' behavior (like adult behavior) should be guided by what they know and can do as well as their attitudes and values. As shown, attitudes toward learning and the learning process itself are inextricably interwoven. We want the children in our classrooms to be engaged in learning activities for two reasons. First, learning is the goal of the school, and second, engagement in work makes discipline easier. Therefore we are interested in promoting positive attitudes toward learning.

This is one kind of attitude but is not the sum total of all the attitudes that the school should teach, any more than the so-called fundamental skills are the sum total of all the skills that children should be taught. Another kind of attitude that should be taught is social attitudes, a positive and constructive attitude toward society. Social attitudes are best taught functionally, that is by giving pupils opportunities to contribute to the welfare of the microsociety that is the school and to the larger society.

Developing Social Attitudes and Skills

It has already been suggested that giving children responsibility for part of the curriculum can create good social attitudes. Giving children responsibility is one of the best ways of developing and strengthening social attitudes because it gives the child the sense of belonging and worth that comes with being needed and being depended upon.

Positive social attitudes can also result from the mastery of fundamental skills, concepts, and academic knowledge. Mastery of the curriculum leads to the feeling that one is in control of a situation instead of being controlled by the situation. (Actually this is what the term *mastery* means: to be in control.) This feeling of power and control can extend to other areas. The pupils are more likely to feel that their actions can and do affect the lives of others. On the other hand the externally controlled child is like a puppet on a string. Since others control his behavior he does not see a relationship between his actions and the welfare of others.

Attitudes of Respect

Another crucially important attitude for classroom discipline is the attitude of respect for others. Although there is much talk about teaching respect, there is very little action. This is truly unfortunate because respect for others, although stated as an ideal, has some very practical implications for getting along in classrooms. For instance, without courtesy (a concomitant of respect), a schoolroom can become a mob scene—making teaching and learning impossible. All it takes is for one child to shove another instead of saying "excuse me" and a fight will result in many classrooms. Shouting and talking out of turn, which also make a teacher's life (and everyone else's) miserable, are caused when rules of courtesy fail to operate.

A Commonly Held Value.   One of the reasons why attitudes of respect are not taught in some schools is the confusion caused by those who argue that to cultivate respect for others is to impose middle-class values on children, many of whom are not from the middle class. The absurdity of this assertion is only outweighed by the damaging effects on classroom discipline. Those teachers who are afraid to teach respect for others because they are afraid of imposing their values on others are operating under a misconception. Many of the values which are taught by schools are not the exclusive property of any single social class but are the commonly held values of American society. Respect for others is a commonly held value of American society and therefore a legitimate concern of the school.

Teaching Courtesy.   Respect for others is not only concern for the rights of others and the effects of one's actions on others but simple courtesy. Courtesy and consideration can transform schools from places where no one (including teachers) wants to be to places where people enjoy coming and working. The basic components of courtesy are *established* (as opposed to *emergent*) learning. What we are seeking to develop are habits of courtesy. Here teachers must use the training model of discipline.

Respect as a Value.   Although habits are the foundation of respect, they are only the foundation. Respect for others must become a part of the children's developing value system so that these values influence their dealings with others and approaches to social problems. Attitudes of respect can, in part, be taught. One way is to teach about the contributions of others from various races and nationalities as well as their hopes, fears, and aspirations. Finally, respect is best taught when it is lived. Respect is not a one-way street; teachers must be respectful of children as well as the reverse.

Teaching respect for others is a social task which is of critical importance not only for the functioning of our classrooms but for the health and progress of our society.

SUMMARY

The curriculum is a key to classroom discipline and includes attitudes, values, and behaviors as well as formal subject matter, skills, and concepts. A "fit" between the child and the curriculum (work that is challenging but comprehensible and materials which are of interest) can reduce behavior problems. Helping the problem reader aids classroom discipline.

Classroom behavior is determined by the objectives of an activity. Generally, when activity is directed toward the goals of the task, pupils are behaving appropriately. Discipline problems may mean that the curriculum does not give learners enough to think about or plan for. Giving pupils responsibilities for classroom work involves them in the work and helps them progress through the stages of discipline.

General as well as *personal* interests can be a spur to learning. Children's interests are surprisingly broad and sophisticated. Many of the activities that interest learners (and can influence class control) are not identical with their real life experiences. Literature and general interests are a practical way of getting the whole class started in learning. Positive social attitudes can result from mastery of the curriculum.

Respect for others is a commonly held value of society and a legitimate concern of the school. By teaching courtesy and respect for others, teachers can positively affect the functioning of their classrooms and the welfare of the community. The training model is used in helping children acquire the basic learning necessary for courtesy.

Problems and Activities

1. In your opinion, does reading to children who have learning and behavior problems serve a legitimate purpose in the learning process? If so, what is it?

2. According to Taba and Elkins, "the very act of reading brings the teachers and students, as well as the peers, together emotionally." [Hilda Taba and Deborah Elkins, Teaching Strategies for the Culturally Disadvantaged (Chicago: Rand McNally, 1966), p. 77.] Do you agree with Taba and Elkins? Why or why not? If so, would you say that this emotional "togetherness" is favorable for classroom discipline? Explain.

3. Develop criteria for selecting literature for use with seventh graders who are problem readers and also problem behavers. Would you seek books and stories with content that is on a lower level of maturity than usual for a seventh grade since these children obviously have severe academic deficits? Why or why not?

4. Draw up a list of books and stories that you could use as Carla T did (see p. 55) to engage the emotions of sixth graders with defective reading skills. Preface the list with the criteria that you employed in selecting this literature.

5. Would you have dealt with the problem of Harold B the way Mrs. Harris did? (See p. 52) Why or why not?

6. Do you think that the principle that how pupils should act depends on the goals of the particular learning situation, is helpful for discipline and learning? Support your answer.

7. What positive outcomes for discipline can result from pupil participation in the planning of learning experiences?

8. In 1893 the Boston Daily Advertiser had this to say about education in Boston and elsewhere: "There is far too much of the mechanical in the existing system, especially in the 'busy work,' which here, as almost everywhere else, means a hindrance rather than a help to child education." [As quoted in Lawrence A. Cremin, The Transformation of the School (New York: Knopf, 1961), p. 6.] Busy work has as its primary objective keeping children busy and therefore out of trouble. Do you think that the problem described in the quotation is still prevalent in schools today? If so, give examples. In your opinion, what is the difference between busy work and a worthwhile task?

9. Do you believe that the attention of the unmotivated child can be attracted and held best through interests that concern familiar experiences instead of past and distant times and places? Explain.

10. Do you think that teaching children to respect the feelings of others is an imposition of middle-class values on all children and youth? Why?

Discipline and Teaching 4

Most teaching takes place in a room filled with children (thirty is the average number in a public school classroom) and one teacher. As indicated earlier, teaching tends to be an isolated affair. Principals may give directives, supervisors (in school systems that have them) may give advice, but when all is said and done they expect the teacher to run the class alone. Obviously, success or failure in teaching depends enormously on the teacher's ability to establish and maintain order in the classroom.

A good teacher endeavors to provide maximal educational opportunities for every pupil. It hardly seems necessary to say that this requires working with individuals in the class as well as with the classroom group. Yet even when we are working with individuals, and however much we individualize our teaching, we never stop being concerned with the class as a whole. It is the class to whom we have been assigned and with whom we are sharing time and a relatively crowded space. Moreover, the class seems (oddly enough) to have a personality, just as an individual does. Granted that this personality will differ from class to class (sometimes to our great relief), there are circumstances that characterize classrooms in general. Among these are a fairly dense population of children or adolescents, a teacher, a program of instruction planned by the teacher, pupil-teacher interaction concerning the program, and plenty of opportunity for self-expression (desirable and undesirable). Differences in pupil abilities, interests, and motivations create many chances for disruption in classrooms. On the other hand, skilled classroom management can make teaching go so smoothly that it seems almost effortless.

As discussed in Chapter 1, recent research on discipline and classroom management is concerned with how the teacher maintains order with a classroom group. Investigators have discovered a number of strategies that teachers can use to prevent and cope with pupil misbehavior in classrooms. The model of discipline that they have been studying is the group dynamics model. The central problem of the teacher is how to work effectively with the class group and deal with authority problems in classrooms. This chapter is concerned with that problem.

TEACHER AUTHORITY AND HOW TO HAVE IT

Teachers and pupils are brought together in classrooms for one purpose—instruction of the rising generation. Everything that teachers do in the classroom is with that aim in mind; they are there to teach. And pupils are there to learn, or are they? Some come to school ready and eager to learn; others are there as unwilling conscripts. The law says that willingly or not, children must go to school. If the teachers are to meet their professional responsibility they must control unwilling pupils and help them to master the curriculum. This is not always easy in an era when open challenging of authority in classrooms has become commonplace.

Yet though disruptive behavior by pupils is hardly uncommon, some teachers seem to experience little or any of it in their classrooms while their colleagues who work with the same kinds of children seem to meet defeat and frustration at every turn. The difference does not appear to lie in the use of teacher authority, if teacher authority means autocratic, dominating behavior and overt use of power. (Indeed it may be that the teacher who is having trouble is an authoritarian who deals with children heavy-handedly.) Teacher authority does seem to be at the heart of successful group management. But there is all the difference in the world between teacher authority as a *quality* which pervades everything the teacher does in the classroom and authoritarian behavior. It is the presence or absence of the former, teacher authority as a quality, which appears to make the difference between a smoothly operating classroom and a classroom that is more often than not wildly out of control. Let us examine this quality in terms of actual teacher behavior. What is done by teachers who have authority in their classrooms?

Explain the Subject Well

When pupils who like their teacher are asked why, they frequently respond, "She explains things." The ability to explain and clarify is central in teacher authority. In his research on teacher attributes associated with liking the teacher and motivation to learn, Jacob Kounin found that liked teachers were described by pupils as explaining things well and disliked teachers as explaining things poorly and, further, that pupils who liked their teachers and were motivated to learn also *felt more like behaving themselves* in class than those who disliked their teachers.[1] Teachers who explain so that pupils can understand are regarded as competent by pupils and are thus invested with authority. Stated as a principle:

> **Sixth Principle:** *Teaching effectiveness, as perceived by pupils, invests the teacher with classroom authority.*

Make the Work Interesting

Kounin also found that liking a teacher and motivation were associated with the teacher's ability to make the subject "interesting."[2] This concurs with the findings of many studies on teacher effectiveness. In David Ryans' famous study on teachers' personality characteristics, for instance, teachers judged by observers as "stimulating" and "creative" tended to have pupils who were judged by the same observers as "alert" rather than "apathetic."[3] But although Ryans categorized the ability to be "creative" as a "personality characteristic," making work interesting might better be viewed as a teaching task. Any teacher can, with effort and good planning, make what is to be learned more interesting and stimulating for pupils. (Unfortunately, it must be observed that some teachers can make the most interesting subject dull. These teachers often lack authority in their classrooms as a result of their poor teaching.)

Be a Good Manager

Children regard the teacher who can get the class working and behaving as a proficient manager. Being a good manager in the eyes of pupils

[1] Jacob S. Kounin, *Discipline and Group Management in Classrooms* (New York: Holt, Rinehart and Winston, 1970), p. 45.

[2] Ibid., p. 42.

[3] David G. Ryans, *Characteristics of Teachers* (Washington, D.C.: American Council on Education, 1960).

also invests the teacher with authority. In his research Kounin found that liking the teacher and motivation to learn are associated with managerial proficiency. That is, liked teachers tend to be seen as good at managing the class (getting pupils settled, working, and behaving) as well as good at teaching (making the subject clear and interesting).[4] Now this finding that there is an association between being a good manager in the eyes of the class and liking the teacher is very significant because children who like their teacher want to behave themslves in class. The converse is undoubtedly also true: youngsters who perceive their teachers as poor managers (unable to get the class settled, working, and behaving), do not feel like behaving themselves, thus compounding the miseries of the teacher who is a poor manager.

How, then, does a good manager act? More to the point, how do teachers behave who get their classes working and behaving? The following are some of the ways they appear to act and perceive their role.

1. Order is viewed as a part of the instructional process. By giving directions and asking questions the good managor can do two things at once, get pupils to do their work and handle individual misbehavior that is not serious (but could be if allowed to get out of hand).
2. Discipline is task-focused instead of person-focused. *Pupil behavior or misbehavior is discussed in terms of the goals and requirements of the lesson.* (If Johnny is misbehaving he is told that if he does not listen he will not understand the work. He is not told that his antics are giving his teacher a migraine headache.)
3. Related to the foregoing, good managers guide pupils rather than criticizing them.
4. The teacher is prepared to teach. Preparedness means that the teacher knows what he or she is doing and is, therefore, an authority. Children and adolescents cannot be fooled. They know if the teacher is prepared. While preparedness can invest the teacher with authority, lack of preparation diminishes authority and invites behavior problems. This is easy to understand from the pupils' standpoint. Why behave if there is nothing worthwhile to do in class?
5. "Withitness," communication by the teacher to the class that he or she knows what is going on and "overlapping," the ability to attend to two classroom issues at once, were discussed earlier (see Chapter 1). They are mentioned again here because they have been found to be closely related to managerial success. Kounin concluded when reporting his research on "withitness" and "overlapping" that teachers wanting to be good managers should work on these two proficiencies.[5]
6. Teachers who want to be good managers should be aware of and use available classroom support. The use of teacher aides, specialists, reme-

---

[4] Kounin, op. cit., pp. 41-42.
[5] Ibid., p. 91.

dial teachers, supervisors, and media can result in more efficient classroom management. This idea is discussed further later in this chapter.

The Momentum of Teaching
and Pupil Behavior

The momentum or flow of classroom activities is of great importance for discipline. When activities move along at an appropriate pace, teachers experience fewer behavior problems than when activities are slowed down and seem to drag.[6] Momentum is of particular importance in self-contained classrooms where teachers and children are in each other's company for hours each day. Unless teaching activities move ahead the way they should, the whole program may be bogged down, leaving children hideously bored.

What is an appropriate pace for teachers? This is difficult to answer because when the pace is right, there is little to remark on except that classroom operation seems effortless. When the pace is wrong, it is obvious to even the most inexperienced observer, and most of all to the class. Activities do not flow but move by fits and starts. There are irritating slowdowns while teachers engage in carping criticism about pupil behavior. And, finally, as if that were not enough, teachers get sidetracked from the lesson they are teaching—and may not get back on the track.

Although seemingly obvious, it is sometimes forgotten that teachers themselves govern the flow of activities in their classrooms. An appropriate flow generates productive energy for teachers and pupils. When activities are held back or interrupted for reasons having nothing to do with the activity itself, pupils' working energy wanes as does their interest. Teachers have it within their power to regulate classroom momentum.

Jacob Kounin has made a major contribution to our understanding of classroom momentum. He contends, and rightly, that teachers who want their classrooms to operate smoothly must watch what he calls "movement management." That is, how they begin, continue, and end activities and how children move physically from one part of the room to another (going to the reading circle from their desks, for instance). Kounin has come up with a list of what are essentially "do nots"— teacher behaviors that can interfere with the smooth operation of classrooms or cause momentum to drag.[7]

[6] Ibid., pp. 92-108.
[7] Ibid.

Thrusts.   Teachers suddenly issue an order or make a statement without looking first to see what children are doing or if they are ready to hear the message.

Dangles.   The teacher starts an activity, then moves to another activity without finishing the first one (leaving it "dangling"). Then she or he returns to the first activity.

Truncations.   A truncation is like a dangle except that the teacher does not resume the unfinished first activity.

Flip-flops.   A teacher actually terminates an activity, telling pupils to put the materials away. After beginning another activity she or he suddenly returns to the terminated activity. Kounin gives this illustration:

> The teacher said, "All right, let's everybody put away your spelling papers and take out your arithmetic books." The children put their spelling papers in their desks, and, after most of the children had their arithmetic books out on their desks, the teacher asked, "Let's see the hands of the ones who got all their spelling words right."[8]

Stimulus-Boundedness.   The teacher is deflected from the goal of the activity by an irrelevant and accidental stimulus. To illustrate, while she is giving a spelling test she may happen to see a piece of paper on the floor and suddenly say, "How did that piece of paper get on the floor? Who is responsible? John, will you put it in the basket please." She may walk around the room looking for other pieces of paper on the floor before resuming the test.

Overdwelling.   The teacher dwells on an issue longer than is necessary to get the message across to pupils. They already understand but the teacher keeps on talking. When the issue is the behavior of children, overdwelling can become nagging or preaching. Overdwelling can slow down the momentum of activity. For instance, during creative writing, one teacher talked at length about the need for children to be "good citizens" and not bother those who were trying to write. (This was exasperating for the 99 percent of the class who were trying to write.)

Fragmentation.   A second type of slowdown is fragmentation, when teachers have individual members of a group do something singly that

8 Ibid., p. 101.

the whole group could do at once. (An example is calling children one by one to come to a recitation group.) Another kind of fragmentation is breaking down a task (such as getting ready for arithmetic) into a number of substeps that take an inordinate amount of time.

Movement management is an important part of classroom management. The objective of movement management is a smoothly operating classroom with a steady flow of activities.

THE PROBLEM OF WAITING

As Philip Jackson points out in his fascinating book on the seldom-thought-of aspects of classroom life, typically much of a pupil's school day is spent in waiting.[9] Pupils wait to ask the teacher a question; they wait to answer questions (sometimes not very hopefully if they have already been called on once before or numerous hands are raised); and they wait for further instructions after finishing a test or a task. As Jackson indicates, some of the waiting seems inevitable. Pupils must wait in line for their turn at the drinking fountain. They must wait for the signal to re-enter the school building after a fire drill. When there are large numbers of people entering or leaving a confined space there must be orderly procedures. This is a fact of life whether we are talking about people boarding or leaving an airplane or children entering or leaving the school en masse.

Waiting to have the teacher to oneself for individual help is also an inevitable fact of classroom life. Indeed, as discussed in Chapter 2, children must learn to share their teacher's time and attention just as they share materials and resources. Knowing how to share is important for basic discipline. Clearly some of the waiting that goes on in classrooms is a necessary result of the circumstances referred to earlier—only one teacher per class, large numbers of children crowded into a limited space, and limited resources (only one pencil sharpener and one drinking fountain, for instance).

Nevertheless, not all of the waiting that pupils do is desirable or necessary. Valuable time for learning can be wasted while pupils wait around. Lively interest can actually turn to apathy from the tedium of waiting which also creates opportunities for disruption. How can a teacher deal with the waiting problem? This poses one of the continuing problems of discipline and teaching: the problem of how to keep pupils constructively occupied at all times and circumvent the physical

---

[9] Philip W. Jackson, *Life in Classrooms* (New York: Holt, Rinehart and Winston, 1968), pp. 14-16.

limitations that teachers share with other mortals. (Teachers like everyone else have one voice, one pair of hands, and can be in only one place at a time.)

Early Solutions

Concern about pupils who sat with nothing to do while waiting to "say their lessons" to the teacher dates back to the early days of our public school system. Looking back briefly on the ways that educators tried to deal with the problem is not only fascinating but can help us evaluate present approaches and proposals for the future.

Monitorial Instruction.   From about 1815-1830, a teaching method was in vogue which had all pupils "saying their lessons" all day long without respite. That is, children were involved in constant recitation, moving to a new lesson as soon as one was finished. Known as monitorial instruction, the plan involved the use of pupil monitors. It attracted wide appeal both because it was so cheap (pupils did the work of teachers) and because no time was wasted by pupils in waiting for the attention of their teacher. Though space does not permit more than a brief discussion of monitorial instruction, if the reader can picture an enormous room containing as many as 1000 children being instructed by pupil monitors from stations at the wall, the mass-mechanical character of the method becomes all too apparent. Fortunately this approach, which was mostly used for educating poor children, fell out of fashion within fifteen years after its inception.

A new educational psychology was being born which emphasized the importance of harmonizing the educational process with the natural development of the child. Learning by rote and catechetical instruction were discredited in favor of language development through discussion and writing about real experiences. The new methods sought to help the child develop concepts and the ability to generalize while monitorial instruction consisted of rote and recitation but little or no reflective thinking. Perpetual recitation could not be the answer to the problem of keeping pupils constructively occupied in classrooms.

Mass Instruction.   Not surprisingly, practice lagged behind theory. Although monitorial instruction died as suddenly as it was born, oral teaching en masse (recitation in unison and "concert drill") remained as a method of instructing everyone at once and keeping them out of trouble. This was especially the case in urban schools in the 1890s when a teacher might have a classroom literally teeming with children. (A class size of seventy-five was not uncommon.) As Cremin observed, "Little wonder that rote efficiency reigned supreme."[10]

The Impact of New Ideas.   The idea that children differ in their abilities and interests was another important principle of the new educational psychology and has remained important to this day. The idea of individual differences clashed head on with the practice of using one educational method for everyone, particularly when that method was superficial and mechanical, such as mass teaching by rote. More importantly, perhaps, the practice of controlling a pupil's every action in school, particularly through mechanical methods, was strikingly out of tune with the goal of education in a democratic society, self-direction. An education commensurate with this goal would have to teach pupils to solve problems and control themselves. It was believed by many progressive educators that the problem of waiting (like other aspects of classroom discipline) would be solved when pupils were deeply immersed in activities of interest to them.

The progressive education era came to a close in the 1950s, leaving the problem of waiting largely unsolved. Again, the reason seemed to be a matter of the physical limitations of human beings. Even if children were eagerly working on activities of deep interest to them in a workshop-style setting (this typically was the classroom group approach in progressive schools), sometimes they needed the guidance of their teacher. And there still was just one teacher to go around so children had to wait. Further, if teachers were to meet individual differences, they had to work with individuals, either in small groups or on a one-to-one basis. The children with whom they were not working either had to wait or do something else. But as long as teachers had a say in what was best for children to do, the waiting problem would exist. Children required the help of the one adult who set the requirements and teachers could not solve the widely differing learning problems of all children at the same time.

Seatwork.   One of the earliest educational methods was the most mechanical. Children memorized lessons from their textbooks and then told the teacher what the book said. This was formalized into a period system—a "study period" and a "recitation period." This plan made it possible for a teacher to do two things at once, hear one or more children recite their lessons at the front of the room and supervise those

---

[10] Lawrence A. Cremin, *The Transformation of the School* (New York: Knopf, 1961), p. 21.

pupils who were working at their seats. From time to time during our educational history, it was thought that this system was dead. During the progressive era it actually did disappear in a few schools in which there was no formal curriculum and children worked on problems and activities of interest to them. But it continued to be the prevailing method of working in the average American elementary school (and is today). Classroom subgroups in reading and arithmetic operate much as they always have; the teacher works with one group at the front of the room while the other groups do what has become known as "seatwork." Certainly this system does operate as regimentation in some schools. On the other hand, it can be a way of helping children learn to work by themselves with a minimum of supervision. Moreover, it is possible to combine the workshop idea in which pupils work independently on self-chosen activities with small group instruction by the teacher. This is being done with apparent success in many schools.

The classroom subgroup system is an improvement over having children sit with nothing to do for hours at a time while waiting for a few minutes of their teacher's attention. (This situation prevailed in many one-room schools before the advent of the graded school.) Nevertheless, subgroups are a far from perfect solution to the problem of waiting. When pupils in the seatwork section of the classroom do not know how to do their work they must wait for the teacher's help. Not everyone finishes a given task at the same time. And those who finish first may not have met the requirements of the assignment. Still they wait because the teacher is busy in another part of the room. Even when the system is operating at its best there is often a great deal of waiting.

Strategies for Teachers

In recent years educators have shown renewed interest in dealing with the problem of waiting and the range of ideas for teachers has widened enormously. Knowing about these ideas should increase a teacher's ability to run a classroom smoothly and can lead to improved learning opportunities for children.

Learning Centers. Of considerable promise as a means for preventing wasted time is the learning center. An increasing number of teachers operate their classroom as learning laboratories which include learning centers in various curriculum areas. When a child has finished work in one center, he or she moves to another center (either a selected or an assigned center). Learning centers make it *possible* for children to use their time optimally, to become independent learners, and to pursue studies of interest to them. This is possible but there is no guarantee that this will happen. Children can waste time and become bored and unruly at learning centers just as they can with any other form of classroom organization. On the other hand, an exciting new world of learning can be opened for pupils when they investigate scientific and mathematical concepts of interest to them. The learning laboratory provides opportunities for developing self-direction as well as learning.

Whether these opportunities come to fruition seems dependent on two conditions: what goes into the labs (what the children are to be working with) and whether pupils actually understand what they are to do and how they are to act. Many labs fail because the only materials that children find are worksheets to be completed. When this happens the learning center is not providing children with anything that they could not just as easily do at their own desks. The resulting disappointment and feeling of being duped can create all of the management problems (and more) that the labs were intended to prevent. Learning centers can "fall flat" but they can also fulfill their potential. The difference seems to lie in the amount of preparation that goes into the center. However, it is just as important that pupils know how to work in an atmosphere of freedom. Youngsters who have not reached the basic disciplinary stage are probably not ready for learning centers. For one thing they may be unable to share materials with others—a prerequisite for using learning centers.

Open Classrooms. The open classroom is an American label for the English approach to informal education. Like the learning center, the open classroom is intended to permit children to move about freely, so that they may work purposefully with various materials and resources without being "tied down" to their seats. The role of the teacher is to work among the children advising and discussing rather than standing before the class. Theoretically, since children are working on activities of their own choosing in which, presumably, they have an interest and can work on at their own pace, time wasted from waiting should be minimal. Also, whereas with traditional methods some pupils finish a task sooner than others and have to wait around, in open classrooms this should not be a problem since everyone is working on a different activity (or at least not doing the same thing at the same time).

As with learning centers, open classrooms provide an opportunity for reducing wasted time and increasing learning. However, there is no guarantee that this will happen. Open classrooms make great demands on the teacher's time and require real knowledge of how to build on children's interests—not to mention prodigious amounts of material and resources. Otherwise they are almost certain to fail. To paraphrase what one observer wrote about progressive education: "Like the proverbial little girl with the curl right in the middle of her forehead, an open classroom done well is very good, done badly it is abominable."[11] This is in no way meant to discourage anyone from using the open classroom form of organization. In the hands of a good teacher an open classroom is a thrill to behold. Children are eagerly working toward clearly understood objectives in an environment that fosters inquiry and problem solving. Unfortunately, however, many open classrooms are just open space structures with traditional curriculums. Discipline in open classrooms is discussed in Chapter 6.

Informing Pupils about the Program.   Often pupils wait after finishing their work simply because they do not know what to do next. Their familiarity with the program of activities does not extend beyond the schedule itself. To illustrate, they know that arithmetic follows reading but they do not know what the work will be so they cannot get started. Hence they mark time until arithmetic. For these children school is like a theatrical production with the curtain descending between acts. No one knows what the next act will be like until the curtain goes up. (The teacher has not shared this information.) And there is no way of speeding up the production even if one is ready and anxious to get started.

This way of running a classroom results in an enormous waste of pupils' time, slows down the momentum of learning, and encourages dawdling. (Why complete a task as soon as possible just to wait?) No one can look back on his or her own school days, however happy they may have been, without recalling moments of impatience when one wanted to get on with the work.

Teachers can take a giant step toward solving the waiting problem by sharing the plan of work for each day or each week with pupils. The program can be put on the board (but not while the class is in session) or dittoed and distributed. When pupils know what is supposed to come next they feel more secure and businesslike in the classroom. The classroom is more likely to operate smoothly instead of by fits and starts. Furthermore, knowing the program can help children learn to budget their time. As noted, pupils who are able to do so can participate in planning. However, whether or not they are involved in making the plan they still need to know what it is.

The plan should be easy for pupils to follow. The best way to ensure clarity is to write the plan as simply as possible.

Continuing Projects.   A far-from-radical innovation (many teachers

---

[11] Ibid., pp. 348-349.

have used it for years) is to have each child involved in a continuing project—one that can be taken up when other work is done. A library book kept in the child's desk is one such project. (Indeed some teachers insist that every child have a library book.) Other examples of continuing projects are murals, research projects, writing projects (stories, plays, and books written by the children themselves), and crafts. Additional activities are children hearing each other read (in groups of no more than three children, preferably two) and reading in the library corner. For library corners to have lasting appeal to pupils, the shelves must always be well stocked with new and attractive books. Some teachers add to the attractiveness of the corner with throw rugs and comfortable chairs.

Involvement versus Waiting: The Recitation Group.   Pupils doing seatwork are not the only ones who often spend much of their time waiting. Those in recitation groups also may be waiting. On the other hand, they may be actively involved during the whole lesson, even when not called on to show what they know or can do. The difference—whether children wait or are involved—depends on the teacher.

Waiting to be called on does not mean that a child is involved in the lesson. We can just recall from our own childhood experience what happens when pupils are called on in a predetermined order: non-reciters often do not listen to the other reciters but look ahead to the page or problem in which they will have to demonstrate their own ability. Or worse, they may be paying no attention to the lesson whatsoever, poking or annoying those around them. Kounin offers some practical suggestions for maintaining the attention (and thus the involvement of the group).[12] First, teachers should avoid procedures where pupils know who is going to be called on next. Kounin gives two illustrations of teaching the same content, one when there is a predetermined order of reciters and one when children are not called on in any particular order.

> Ten children are seated in a semi-circle in a reading group and Miss Smith is seated in front of them holding flash cards. Each card has a single word printed on it. The teacher announces, "Today we'll read a word and then think of a word that rhymes with it. We'll go around in a circle starting with Richard."

> Miss Jones is seated in front of a subgroup of children at the reading circle. She is holding a stack of flash cards saying, "who can read the next one." She pauses, holds up a card and says, "John." John says, "Cook." The

12 Kounin, op. cit., pp. 109-124.

teacher says, "Fine. Now who can name a word that sounds like it?" The teacher pauses again, looks around, and calls on Mary.[13]

In Miss Smith's reading group the children knew who was going to recite next. There was no suspense in her approach and the children could easily turn their attention from the lesson to something else until it was their turn to recite. But in Miss Jones' reading group a child was never sure when he or she would be called on. Therefore the child was more likely to be *thinking* about the answer to a question even when not called on.

Does the way in which teachers call on reciters really matter for classroom discipline? Asking himself this same question, Kounin conducted a study to determine whether different techniques of calling on reciters created varying degrees of pupil alertness and made any difference in their behavior. He found a positive relationship between what the teachers did to keep children "on their toes" and children's behavior. In Kounin's words: "Teachers who maintain a group focus by engaging in behaviors that keep children alerted and on their toes are more successful in inducing work involvement and preventing deviancy than are teachers who do not."[14]

According to Kounin, the following behaviors by teachers can keep pupils "on their toes":

1. Methods used to keep pupils in suspense before calling on a pupil, such as pausing, looking around, or saying, "Let's see . . . , who can. . . ."
2. Selecting reciters randomly rather than in predetermined "round robin" fashion.
3. Alerting children who are not performing that they might be called on in connection with what a reciter is saying or doing (if the reciter does not know the answer or makes a mistake).
4. Introducing new and interesting material into the lesson (an idea or a visual aid).

The following behaviors, however, should be avoided as they reduce the involvement of nonreciters.

1. Preselecting a performer before the question is even asked.
2. Using a predetermined sequence for reciters so that children know when they are or are not going to be called on. (This was previously mentioned but its importance cannot be overdrawn.)
3. Becoming completely absorbed in the performance of a reciter instead of keeping the focus of attention on the group.

A compelling demand on children by their teachers is what Kounin

[13] Ibid., pp. 109-110.
[14] Ibid., p. 123.

calls *accountability*.[15] A child who is reciting is showing what she knows or how well she is able to do something. She knows the teacher is fully aware of what she is doing in connection with the task. In this sense she is being held accountable. But the important question is how many of the children in the group who are not reciting are also being held accountable? The answer is determined by what they are doing while a child recites. All children should be actively involved in doing something related to the lesson. (Thinking of the answer themselves, reading along silently while another youngster is reading aloud, or checking an arithmetic problem in their workbooks are examples of active engagements for nonperformers.)

Kounin suggests several ways that teachers can hold nonreciters accountable, such as asking them to hold up their work, requiring them to recite in unison, checking their work during another child's recitation, and asking for the hands of those who are ready to perform— requiring some of them to do so. One of these suggestions—recitation in unison—is of particular interest in view of our earlier discussion on mass recitation. Suffice it to say that this method should be used sparingly to avoid rote and mechanical teaching. Rote efficiency is not the objective of group management.

Finally, Kounin's concept of pupil accountability is similar to pupil responsibility as discussed in the section on the stages of discipline. But there is a fundamental difference between accountability and responsibility. With accountability the pupil acts in a certain way because the teacher holds him responsible. Responsibility occurs when the children behave in a certain way on their own initiative. When they are responsible, pupils (or adults) direct their own behavior. If they are held accountable, they are directed by others. In view of our goal for discipline, self-direction, the difference is an important one. Responsibility is necessary for self-direction.

What is being said here is that asking a pupil to hold up his workbook to expose what he has or has not done may be holding him *accountable,* but it does not necessarily make him *responsible.* Responsibility is more likely to develop when pupils know the reason why they are performing a task. Otherwise the basis for their actions becomes "because the teacher says so." Pupils who are simply held accountable often do not know what to do when the teacher is not there to hold them accountable. (Bedlam may result when the teacher steps out of the room for a few minutes.)

Finally, holding pupils accountable is not synonymous with good teaching. It can in no way substitute for teaching that makes concepts

[15] Ibid., pp. 111-112.

and procedures clear and interesting. The latter is the best basis for pupil attention that a teacher can have.

Support for Teachers.   "The goal of individualized instruction without adequate support may well be the straw that breaks the classroom teacher's back."[16] So wrote one educator in a discussion on the need for teachers to have assistance if they are to reach and teach all of the pupils in their charge. Earlier it was pointed out that a great deal of pupil waiting occurs because there is only one teacher to go around. Waiting can be considerably reduced and teaching carried on more effectively when teachers have the support of specialists, aides, tutors, and student teachers. The use of self-instructional materials by pupils is another form of support for teachers. Research shows that pupil performance can be improved (*become twice as good or better*) when teachers can delegate some of their instructional responsibilities to professionals and nonprofessionals.[17]

Thus one of the best hopes for dealing with the waiting problem rests in the development of programs which provide teachers with needed support. In many cases, teachers themselves will have to take the initiative through their professional organizations. However, most administrators are anxious for teachers to work as efficiently and effectively as possible and are therefore receptive to the idea of tutoring programs which utilize the services of older students and adults in the community. Teachers must make their classroom needs known rather than suffering in silence. (The latter is in the worst possible interests of children.)

However, volunteers can never compensate for unrealistic pupil-teacher ratios. Children must have the help that they need to develop as far as they can. This requires that they have the time and attention of qualified professionals.

SUMMARY

The central problem of the teacher is how to work effectively with the class group and deal with authority problems in classrooms. Teachers who have authority in their classrooms (as perceived by the pupils) explain the work well, make it interesting, and are good managers (get the class settled and working). Teachers who are good man-

---

[16] Douglas G. Ellson, "Tutoring," Chapter 5 in *The Psychology of Teaching Methods*, Seventy-fifth Yearbook of the National Society for the Study of Education, Part I (Chicago: University of Chicago Press, 1976), p. 141.

[17] Ibid., p. 142.

agers view order as part of the instructional process, guide instead of criticize, and use available classroom support. Activities flow steadily rather than sporadically.

Waiting for the teacher's attention wastes valuable time, turns interest into apathy, and creates opportunities for disruption. Educators have long been concerned about the waiting problem. In past eras continuous recitation and mass instruction by rote were tried and abandoned. Classroom subgroups can be a way of helping children to learn to work by themselves. Useful ideas for increasing learning opportunities and preventing wasted time include learning centers, open classrooms, continuing projects, and pupil knowledge of the daily program.

To maintain the involvement of pupils in recitation groups, teachers should avoid calling on pupils in a predetermined ("round-robin") fashion. Injecting new material into a lesson and using methods to keep pupils in suspense before calling on a pupil can increase involvement. Nonreciters can be held *accountable* by asking them to hold up their work or asking for the hands of those ready to perform. However, holding pupils accountable does not substitute for making concepts clear and interesting (good teaching). Moreover, our goal is to make pupils responsible—behaving a certain way on their own initiative. This is most likely to happen when they understand why they are performing a task. Responsibility is necessary for self-direction.

Problems and Activities

1. In this chapter it was pointed out that pupils like teachers who explain well. In your opinion, what should teachers do when explaining a concept or a procedure to make it clear for pupils?
2. In connection with problem 1, demonstrate by explaining a concept or a procedure either to a group of pupils or fellow students. Was the explanation successful?
3. Do you think that pupils are good judges of their teacher's competency? Why or why not?
4. How does authoritarian behavior differ from having authority in the classroom?
5. As discussed in this chapter, the teacher's authority in the classroom seems associated with certain abilities such as explaining well, making work interesting, and being a good classroom manager. In your opinion, is this list exhaustive? If not, what should be added? Support any additions.
6. Under the topic **Be a Good Manager,** there was a discussion of these do's and don'ts:
    (1) Control is viewed as part of the instructional process not separately.
    (2) Discipline is task-focused instead of person-focused.
    (3) Pupils are guided rather than criticized.
    Do these suggestions seem reasonable to you? You can test this by recalling a situation in which you were teaching (or when you were a pupil).
7. In your opinion can a "thrust" (issuing an order without first looking around to see what is going on) endanger class control? Why?
8. What is your opinion of the method of asking children to recite in unison as a means of getting everyone involved?
9. What is the theory behind open classrooms as a way of dealing with the waiting problem?
10. In connection with problem 9, can this theory be applied in self-contained classrooms as well? Explain.
11. Do you think that children should know the program of work for the day (or week)? Support your answer.
12. What method would you use for selecting pupils to recite in recitation groups?

Lack of Attention
and Teacher
Expectation

5

One of the most frequent practical problems of teachers is the inattentive pupil who distracts others. Since this is an emergent discipline problem with circumstances that vary from situation to situation, there are no pat answers. Nevertheless, there are some practical guides that teachers can use in dealing with pupils' lack of attention and staying power. These ideas are discussed in this chapter.

ATTENTION AND DEVELOPMENT

Fuller and Bown note that researchers consider the first stage of learning to teach a "survival stage."[1] Since pupil attention is irrevocably related to class control it is one of the survival concerns of beginning teachers. Whether or not the teacher can gain and hold the attention of a class is recognized as a major determinant of survival as a teacher.

While it is true that the experienced teacher is generally not as concerned with attention as a survival factor, pupils' lack of attention is a source of anxiety for experienced teachers.[2] Besides the fact that lack

[1] Frances F. Fuller and Oliver H. Bown, "Becoming a Teacher," Chapter 2 in *Teacher Education*, Seventy-fourth Yearbook of the National Society for the Study of Education, Part II (Chicago: University of Chicago Press, 1975), p. 37.

[2] Thomas J. Coates and Carl E. Thoreson, "Teacher Anxiety: A Review with Recommendations," *Review of Educational Research*, Vol. 46 (Spring 1976), p. 167.

of attention makes teachers anxious, there are other reasons why this problem merits close attention. Pupils who can neither listen nor follow directions are having a developmental problem in discipline. Being able to listen and follow directions are pupil responsibilities for basic discipline. Moreover, they are necessary if pupils are to master the curriculum. Other reasons for concern about lack of attention are considered in the following section.

Discipline as Responsible Attention

Perhaps the problem that tries a teacher's patience most is the inability of some children to stay with a task long enough to complete it. On the other hand, there are others who do the job but without the close attention to details that is required for good work. This results in inaccuracies, omissions, and in short, shoddy work. These youngsters lack self-discipline or the ability to persevere with a task or an activity and give it the patient attention needed to do a good job. There are three reasons why we as teachers are concerned about children who do slapdash, incomplete work: (1) the immediate purpose of the learning task has been lost; (2) these youngsters are becoming accustomed to inferior performance; and (3) they often disturb others around them.

The first and third reasons are of immediate concern because we want children to accomplish what they have set out to do, without disturbing the learning atmosphere. However, the long-range problem—the habit of doing a poor job—is perhaps the most serious. This can influence learning and educational opportunities. Furthermore, the independence which we seek to foster in children requires perseverance: being able to work without becoming distracted. Last, but not least, self-discipline in terms of personal responsibility for one's work is required in any job or profession. While we usually associate the idea of self-discipline with pupils in classrooms, lest we forget, self-discipline is enormously important out of school—in any responsible position. When James B, a sixth grader who can do his work well, has trouble staying in his seat and attending to a task, we are concerned about his lack of focus on the task and the effect on other children. He has his mind on the high school football game after school. (His brother is the star quarterback.) The problem is that James' work is slipping on football days and there is every reason to believe that it will continue to do so since the football season is just beginning. James' attention to his work is becoming far too irregular to be effective. Although his careless mistakes and omissions cannot go unchallenged, the situation could not be called catastrophic because lack of concentration in classrooms is not a life or death matter.

Attention to matters having nothing to do with one's job can have catastrophic results out of school. The crash of an airlines jet which brought death to 72 of the 82 persons on board was attributed by the National Transportation Safety Board to "poor cockpit discipline."[3] The safety board said that this lack of discipline had been reflected in crew conversations on topics ranging from used cars to politics, matters having nothing to do with the operation of the plane, and that the crew had failed to keep track of their altitude. Conversation that was not pertinent to the operation of the plane and therefore was distractive and reflected a casual mood, had played a definite role in the disaster.

The point in the foregoing discussion is that discipline as responsible attention is of great importance in every field of life. Helping children learn to stay with a task until it is completed and to pay careful attention to details is part of our job as teachers. In other words, it is not just important from the standpoint of better order in our classrooms or ensuring that youngsters do the work of the school. Discipline as the ability to follow through on responsibility is a goal unto itself.

INTEREST AND ATTENTION

Some writers on educational methods imply (or state outright) that when content and methods of teaching are organized in accord with pupils' interests and abilities, there will be few if any lapses in pupil attention. This is somewhat an oversimplification of the problem. The idea that what we teach and how we teach should be worked out in accordance with children's interests and abilities is one of the time-honored principles of good teaching. We cannot expect children to be interested in work that they cannot do. And taking advantage of children's existing interests when planning lessons is just common sense.

But interest does not automatically generate the application and adherence to procedures necessary for doing a good job on an assignment—not even when the assignment is self-chosen. Youngsters may be interested in an activity and still fail to finish it because they are easily distracted and unable to stay with anything for very long. This is a problem troubling many teachers in open-classroom situations in which children select their own learning activities. Theoretically, interest in a self-chosen task is supposed to generate the power necessary to complete the task. But the problem of reluctant learners and learners

[3] *The New York Times,* July 17, 1975, p. 58.

who choose unwisely is noticeably absent from such theories.[4] And as every teacher knows, some children blow hot and cold on self-selected projects. (Discipline in open classrooms is discussed in Chapter 6.) The point here is that whatever the administrative arrangement (open classrooms, self-contained classrooms, and the like), effective teaching and learning require that children be able to direct their attention to and complete a task. This brings us to the seventh principle:

Seventh Principle: *Discipline is the ability to attend to a task.*

Concentrated learning is integral to self-discipline and good classroom discipline. This is easiest when children find schoolwork exciting and satisfying. According to Robert Havighurst, about half of the children in primary grades find learning to read or perfecting their skill in reading (many youngsters come to school already able to read) "interesting and rewarding."[5] Reading is especially interesting for eight- and nine-year-olds when they can apply their skills, that is, when they can read for pleasure or for information.

Attention and Application of Skills

Pupils will be most likely to give learning tasks absorbed attention when the curriculum provides them with opportunities to put their skills to work. But without such opportunities schoolwork lacks meaning and purpose. When reading consists of hour after hour and day after day of blank-filling in workbooks or dittoed worksheets (as it does for many children), reading will become a deadly bore. As Lavatelli, Moore, and Kaltsounis state, "There is hardly a more depressing sight than a classroom where children spend 50 percent of the school day working mindlessly like ants, routinely filling in blanks on worksheets."[6]

Strangely, it is the poor reader who is most often taught reading as drill and skill and rarely, if ever, has an opportunity to apply those skills.[7] If we want these youngsters to become readers, they must be given opportunities to read for enjoyment. Skills taught by the school

---

[4] Ann C. Berlak et al., "Teaching and Learning in English Primary Schools," *School Review*, Vol. 83 (February 1975), p. 220.

[5] Robert J. Havighurst, *Developmental Tasks and Education*, 3rd ed. (New York: McKay, 1972), p. 26.

[6] Celia S. Lavatelli, Walter J. Moore, and Theodore Kaltsounis, *Elementary School Curriculum* (New York: Holt, Rinehart and Winston, 1972), p. 76.

[7] Daniel Tanner and Laurel N. Tanner, *Curriculum Development: Theory into Practice* (New York: Macmillan, 1975), p. 603.

must serve purposes that are recognized by learners. This recognition comes with chances for learners to apply their skills. The point cannot be overdrawn that children will be least likely to attend to a task when it seems to them to lack purpose.

This is not to say that children do not find the task of developing a new skill in writing, spelling, or arithmetic interesting. Given a dynamic, encouraging teacher, most children will be interested in mastering skills. But their energies should not be devoted to needless repetition. A pupil who clearly understands an arithmetical operation should not be asked to do more examples of the same kind but should go on to master another operation.

There are many exciting ways that children can put their skills to use. Solving real problems in the classroom, neighborhood, and community requires the use of academic as well as social skills. Attending to a task becomes less difficult when that task involves real people and their problems. Writing stories or papers based on personal experiences, running a post office (youngsters in one school ran a bona fide post office), or producing a play are just a few examples of putting skills to work. Moreover, skills improve with use.

DEALING WITH TASK INATTENTIVENESS

The following are ideas that teachers can use in situations in which pupils either do not stay with a task long enough for completion or rush through it, giving it a lick and a promise.

1. Directions given to pupils should be concise and to the point. Confusion and distraction can be caused by too much teacher talk. Excessive talk competes for the learner's attention with the task at hand.
2. Find out if the pupil understands just what he or she is supposed to be doing. A frequent cause of task inattentiveness is failure to understand the task. The best way to determine whether this is the problem is to ask the learner what he or she is doing and why.
3. In connection with point 2, teachers should make certain that they understand what they are explaining to pupils. As Jane Martin points out, "it *is* possible for someone to have explained a thing yet not to have understood it"[8] (italics supplied). However, inattention may stem from pupils' difficulties in understanding the work. If the teacher does not understand it either, it is highly unlikely that the teacher's explanatory efforts can lead to clarification for pupils.
4. Older pupils can make an outline of the procedures involved in an activity and check them off as each step is followed. This requires that the activity be given close attention.

[8] Jane Martin, *Explaining, Understanding, and Teaching* (New York: McGraw-Hill, 1970), p. 17.

5. Pupils who have difficulty completing their work should be assigned limited tasks at first, extended as the child's self-discipline and self-confidence increase.

6. The number of distractions that come between the pupil and the work should be reduced. Desks should be free of clutter. Noise and visual stimulations should be minimized.

7. Help should be available for pupils who lack tolerance for frustration and will abandon a learning task at the slightest difficulty. Some youngsters are easily confused and discouraged. Others seems to be looking for an excuse to do something else that appears to hold more pleasure for them at the moment. If the teacher cannot give children who have a low tolerance for frustration the time and special attention needed, other methods must be used or discipline problems may occur. An immediately usable idea which is often effective is to pair a pupil who stays with a task until it is completed because of the pleasure it affords him with a youngster who lacks perseverance. The achieving peer can function as a role model. This idea is most easily implemented in heterogeneously grouped classes.

8. Expect that pupils will complete the task successfully. Ultimately it may be the teacher's expectation, either positive or negative, that is the most powerful single factor in task attentiveness. (The "expectancy phenomenon," mentioned briefly earlier, is considered in the following section.)

9. Follow through on requirements until they have been reasonably met. In the case of James B discussed earlier, the teacher found that frequently checking James' work was the best approach. She was undeviating in the requirements of the assignment, but not punitive. This youngster was an able pupil who needed firmness and direction. When he realized what he could expect from his teacher there was no more problem. This case was a complete "success."

10. Be quick to notice when children are frustrated and irritable because of boredom. Lack of variation in methods of teaching is one common cause of boredom. One of the most overused and abused methods is discourse (talk) by the teacher. A good disciplinarian knows that teaching is more than conveying information and that children cannot be expected to sit still and listen indefinitely or by the time they are to start on a task they will be hopelessly bored with it. Listening for hours invites mischief. In the same vein, too many oral reports are as bad as too few and too much making and modeling is as bad as too little. As George Sheviakov and Fritz Redl predicted some years ago in their classic book on discipline, "Boredom will always remain the greatest enemy of school discipline."[9]

11. Some children live in constant fear of assault—from their peers, from

[9] George V. Sheviakov and Fritz Redl, *Discipline for Today's Children and Youth* (Washington, D.C.: Association for Supervision and Curriculum Development, 1956), p. 54.

their parents, or from neighborhood gangs. Their fears often result in lack of attention in the classroom. It is not always easy to detect this fear and it is frequently overlooked as a cause for inattentiveness as one teacher of urban disadvantaged pupils writes:

As a product of a middle-class suburban family, I have never really experienced this kind of fear. I find it difficult to imagine what it is like to bear the scars of a parent's wrath or to witness a stabbing in some back alley. It is little wonder that these children cannot keep their minds on school work and often become belligerent themselves.

The problem of meeting pupils' safety needs is discussed in Chapter 10.

EXPECTANCY AND ATTENTION

Does the teacher's opinion and expectations of Johnny and Susie affect their performance? The recent fascination of researchers with what has been variously called the "Pygmalion effect," "self-fulfilling prophecy," and "expectancy phenomenon" has generated findings with implications for the problem of inattention. In this section we will be looking at the efforts of researchers to detect and state the effects of teacher expectations on pupils.

Recent interest in the self-fulfilling prophecy dates from the landmark study by Rosenthal and Jacobson which proposed that pupils live up, or down, to their teachers' expectations of them.[10] These two researchers found that teachers express their opinions consciously and unconsciously in word, facial expression, and gesture and that teachers who believe that their pupils are bright teach harder. *Pygmalion in the Classroom* was sharply criticized on methodological grounds. Robert Thorndike found "basic defects in the data that make its conclusions (although they may possibly be true) in no sense adequately supported by the data."[11]

However, it was the question raised in Thorndike's parenthetical statement that continued to interest researchers. Were the findings of the study true? A growing number of researchers have tried to find out, focusing their efforts on various aspects of the problem.

[10] Robert Rosenthal and Lenore Jacobson, *Pygmalion in the Classroom* (New York: Holt, Rinehart and Winston, 1968).

[11] Robert L. Thorndike, Review of *Pygmalion in the Classroom* by Robert Rosenthal and Lenore Jacobson, *American Educational Research Journal*, Vol. 5 (November 1968), p. 708.

Opportunities for Pupils To Respond

In 1966, two years before the Rosenthal and Jacobson study was published, Jackson and Lahaderne described the striking differences between pupil-teacher contacts in the same classroom:

> For at least a few students, individual contact with the teacher is as rare as if they were seated in a class of a hundred or more pupils, even though there are actually only 30 or so classmates present. This observation calls into question the conventional view of looking upon each classroom as a unit whose participants have shared a common educational experience.[12]

Inequalities of teacher-pupil contacts may also be viewed as inequalities of educational opportunity, particularly, if as Good found, teachers tend to provide more opportunities for participation for pupils they assess as high achievers.[13] The subjects in Good's study were pupils in four first-grade classrooms in two predominantly white working-class neighborhoods and their teachers. The teachers were asked to rank their pupils in order of achievement and these rankings were used to select pupils for observation who were classified as "high," "low," and "middle." Twelve pupils were selected for observation in each classroom. Each time the teacher gave one of the pupils an opportunity to respond, an observer entered a tally beside that child's name.

Good found that "opportunities to respond were closely related to pupil achievement as rated by the teacher," and that "Teachers consistently gave higher achievers significantly more chances to speak in the classroom than low achievers."[14] Low achievers tend to have short attention spans. As Good points out, being ignored by the teacher will not help the low achiever overcome this deficiency. Good's point is an important one for classroom discipline as well as achievement. Since, as Good says, giving pupils limited opportunities to respond is "likely to sustain inadequacies," it is also likely to arrest development in discipline. Like academic progress, upward movement through the stages of discipline is impeded for low achievers by depriving them of opportunities to respond.

A particularly important finding of the study was that first-grade reading activities in which teachers worked with small groups afforded pupils with a more nearly equal opportunity for participation than

---

[12] Philip W. Jackson and Henrietta M. Lahaderne, "Inequalities of Teacher-Pupil Contacts," Expanded version of a paper delivered at the American Psychological Association Convention, New York City, September 3, 1966.

[13] Thomas L. Good, "Which Pupils Do Teachers Call On?," *The Elementary School Journal*, Vol. 70 (January 1970), pp. 190-198.

[14] Ibid., pp. 195, 197.

whole-class activities.[15] Since the amount of time teachers spend working with pupils in small groups tends to decline as pupils move through
the grades, the opportunities of low achievers to respond in class may
also decline. Whether this is indeed the case is an important problem
for research.

Time for Response.   Another dimension of opportunity for response
is how long teachers wait for an answer to their question before they go
on to another pupil. One researcher found that teachers wait longer for
pupils whom they consider to be bright. When they increase their waiting time for "slower" pupils, they get greater responsiveness.[16] Since
attention is an increment of responsiveness they also get increased
attention. Hence giving pupils more time to answer is another approach
for dealing with lack of attention.

Prompting.   Studies indicate that teachers prompt the pupils whom
they believe to be bright toward the right answer, also encouraging
greater responsiveness from these pupils. "I guess we don't expect an
answer [of the poor students]," said one teacher. "So we go on to someone else."[17]
    Calling on pupils often, giving them time to answer, and prompting
them communicates to pupils that the teacher expects them to do well.
Conversely, ignoring them as they compete for opportunities to answer
questions, waiting only a second (as many teachers do) before going on
to the next pupil, and giving no hints as to what the answer might be,
communicates unfavorable expectations. Perhaps when the feedback
that they receive communicates that they are not expected to do well,
pupils are convinced that they cannot compete successfully. This is part
of the Pygmalion theory. Another part is that "teachers literally teach
more to those of whom they expect more."[18] The implications of this
theory for the problem of inattentiveness seem twofold: (1) teachers
should be aware of what their actions communicate to pupils and seek
increased responsiveness from pupils with learning and behavioral deficits, and (2) teachers should take care not to water down the content of
what is taught to these pupils. Central to the teacher's efforts should be
attempts to clarify concepts and procedures that pupils find difficult.
Abandoning the content for something less substantive communicates

---

[15] Ibid., p. 194.
[16] Robert Rosenthal, "The Pygmalion Effect Lives," *Psychology Today*, Vol. 7
(September 1973), p. 61.
[17] Ibid.
[18] Ibid.

to the pupils that they are being abandoned. Such pupils may then think, "Why pay attention? My teacher never gives me the hard questions because I can't do the work."

Attractive versus Unattractive Pupils

Recent interest has also been directed to the question of whether teacher expectancy for pupils' academic achievement is biased by pupils' facial attractiveness. Clifford and Walster have presented evidence which suggests that teachers are biased by pupils' attractiveness.[19] According to Clifford and Walster, teachers perceived attractive children as having a higher IQ, greater educational potential, and more interested parents than unattractive pupils. In her research, Karen Dion found that adults show differential treatment toward attractive and unattractive children in situations in which their behavior is identical.[20] She found that when a transgression was committed by an attractive child, it was perceived as less undesirable than the same act committed by an unattractive youngster. In her conclusions, Dion expressed concern "that adults' assumptions about a child's character, particularly, the type of behavior expected from him, may ultimately be communicated to the child, potentially influencing his self-evaluation."[21]

However, two studies conducted by LaVoie and Adams, found that teachers' predictions about pupils' academic potential and their assessments of pupils' parents, peer relations, attitudes, and work habits were biased by pupil conduct, not attractiveness.[22]

While the findings of LaVoie and Adams that pupils' conduct is a more powerful factor than attractiveness in influencing teacher expectancy conflict with the findings of Clifford and Walster and Dion, teachers might best consider both factors (conduct and attractiveness) as potentially affecting their pupil expectancy. The point is that we need to be aware of the factors that *could* negatively influence our evaluations of pupils and impede our efforts to deal with lack of attention.

[19] Margaret M. Clifford and Elaine Walster, "The Effect of Physical Attractiveness on Teacher Expectations," *Sociology of Education*, Vol. 46 (Spring 1973), pp. 248-258.

[20] Karen K. Dion, "Physical Attractiveness and Evaluation of Children's Transgressions," *Journal of Personality and Social Psychology*, Vol. 24 (November 1972), pp. 207-213.

[21] Ibid., p. 213.

[22] Joseph C. LaVoie and Gerald R. Adams, "The Chosen Ones: A Study of the Effects of Children's Conduct, Sex, and Facial Attractiveness on Teacher Expectations," Mimeographed research report, University of Nebraska at Omaha, 1972; and Gerald R. Adams and Joseph C. LaVoie, "The Effect of Students' Sex, Conduct, and Facial Attractiveness on Teacher Expectancy," *Education*, Vol. 95 (Fall 1974), pp. 77-83.

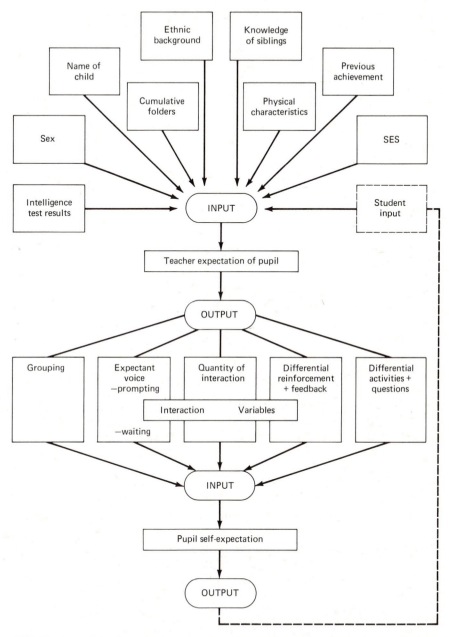

FIGURE 5-1   *The Braun-Neilsen-Dykstra Model of the Behavioral Cycle between Teacher Input and Learner Output (Source: Carl Braun, "Teacher Expectation: Sociopsychological Dynamics," Review of Educational Research, Vol. 46, Spring 1976, p. 206.)*

Carl Braun takes the position "that there is a close relationship between the teacher's expectations for the learner, the teacher's treatment (output) of the learner, and ultimately the child's self-expectation."[23] He puts forward a graphic illustration of the cycle between teacher input and learner output which is reproduced in Figure 5-1, the Braun-Neilsen-Dykstra Model. Although space does not permit a discussion here of all of the factors, they are important and substantiated by research. Race and socioeconomic status (SES) are especially potent sources of input.[24] However, the point of emphasis is that teacher expectation has an important and formative influence on a pupil's self-expectation and output. The teacher's expectation is communicated to a pupil by, among other things, grouping, voice, quality and quantity of interaction, questions, and activities. A teacher can create a climate of warmth around a pupil with an expectant voice, opportunities to respond to and ask questions, and activities that show confidence in the pupil's ability. All of these communicate that the teacher has positive expectations. When this is the message received by the pupil, inattention is less likely to be a problem than when the message is negative.

SUMMARY

Gaining and holding the attention of learners is essential for class control—and for survival as a teacher. Children who can neither listen nor follow directions are exhibiting a developmental problem in discipline. Moreover, the ability to follow through on responsibility is also an important part of discipline. For these reasons and the more obvious negative effects on learning and class control, teachers are concerned about inattention.

Teachers can deal with this crucial problem by giving directions concisely, finding out if pupils understand the task, *and* making certain that they themselves understand what they are explaining to pupils. Older pupils can make an outline of the activity. Boredom is a frequent cause of inattention and a deadly enemy of discipline. Boredom is less likely when teachers vary their methods. Attention is more likely when the curriculum provides learners with opportunities to apply their skills.

Teachers should expect learners to finish a task successfully. The "expectancy phenomenon" appears to be an important factor in attentiveness and involvement in work. Learners may live up or down to their teachers' expectations of them.

[23] Carl Braun, "Teacher Expectation: Sociopsychological Dynamics," *Review of Educational Research*, Vol. 46 (Spring 1976), p. 205.

[24] Ibid., p. 193.

Problems and Activities

1. Do you believe that not being able to do their work well will produce task inattentiveness in children? Why? If your response is affirmative, how can teachers deal with this factor in classroom discipline?
2. In your opinion, is the ability to stay with a task until completion an important educational goal? Why?
3. When will a child attempt to attain the goals of a task in the face of obstacles or difficulties? What are the implications of your answer for teaching and curriculum planning?
4. Do you believe that by providing children with opportunities to use skills, teachers can decrease the number of discipline problems stemming from task inattentiveness? Give reasons for your answer.
5. In view of your response to question 4, what suggestions would you make to the teacher in the situation described below?

   Helen D, the fourth-grade teacher in Room 305, is having trouble getting Charles to pay attention in reading. Since Charles is a very poor reader, Helen has decided to put him on a diet of nothing but phonics. Day after day, Charles sits day dreaming or looking out of the window. He only returns to reality when Helen calls on someone at his table. Games with phonics are not the answer either. Charles pays attention at first but when he isn't called on he drifts back to his daydreaming. Charles only withdraws during reading. In arithmetic, music, and art, his lethargy disappears and he seems to be another child. Helen believes that for a slow child like Charles reading should consist only of repetitive practice of word recognition skills. Meanwhile, although Charles is quiet, Helen has the feeling during reading that Charles is beginning to harbor hostile feelings toward her.

6. What are the problems inherent in attempting to regulate behavior by telling pupils what not to do? How can these problems be avoided?
7. Robert Rosenthal proposes a four factor theory of the influences producing the Pygmalion effect. Teachers who have been led to expect good things from their pupils appear to

   (1) create a warmer social-emotional mood around their "special" students **(climate)**
   (2) give more feedback to these students about their performance **(feedback)**
   (3) teach more material and more difficult material to their special students **(input)**
   (4) give their special students more opportunities to respond and

question **(output)** [Robert Rosenthal, "The Pygmalion Effect Lives," Psychology Today, Vol. 7 (September 1973), p. 60]

Do you believe that these factors hold implications for dealing with lack of attention? Explain.

8. Based on his research, Robert Rosenthal has put forward the idea of "expectant voices," that is, that the tone of voice conveys the teacher's expectations and can influence pupil performance. [Robert Rosenthal, "The Pygmalion Effect Lives," Psychology Today, Vol. 7 (September 1973), pp. 56-57.] Do you believe that teachers may unconsciously use a different tone of voice when posing questions to bright and slow pupils? If your answer was affirmative, do you think that this affects pupil output? Support your answer. If your answer was affirmative, in your opinion how can this problem be dealt with?

Discipline in Special Settings

6

Whatever the physical design of a classroom—be it a large, open space or a confined space with four walls—the teacher's responsibility is the same: to involve pupils in learning activities that are more engrossing and attractive to them than undesirable alternatives (disturbing others, fighting, wandering about aimlessly, daydreaming, and the like). Similarly, it makes no difference for the teacher's responsibility whether pupils are working independently, in small groups, or as a class; pupils still must be absorbed in the task at hand. The reasons for occupying pupils in approved ways are both instructional and managerial. We want our pupils to meet the requirements of the curriculum and we want to maintain order in our classrooms.

Nevertheless, different architectural designs make different demands on teachers' classroom management. Also, when pupils are divided into small groups or work alone, different strategies are required than when teachers work with the classroom group. Most teachers seem to have no trouble understanding the whole-class mode of instruction in the self-contained classroom. The reason is obvious. Most teachers attended self-contained classrooms in which whole-class teaching, with the teacher at the front of the room doing most of the talking and asking questions, was (and is) the predominant mode of instruction. Very often when these teachers find themselves in rooms without walls they feel queasy and uneasy. This is understandable. All too frequently, teachers are given little or no preparation for the new situation. Teachers need to know just how the demands on them differ in various kinds of settings and what they must do to make the setting work for them instead of against them. This chapter concerns ways of working with pupils in special settings.

OPEN CLASSROOMS

The architectural design of a classroom is just that and nothing more. The physical plan of a classroom tells us nothing about how instruction is carried on. More important than the structural design are the activities that take place inside the structure.

An open classroom is a large area without walls in which several classes and teachers meet. Whether open education goes on in an open classroom is another matter entirely. As noted in Chapter 4, many open classrooms are simply open spaces housing traditional programs.

Open Education

What, then, is open education? While educators tend not to agree on a precise definition of open education they do seem to agree that a major objective of open education is to help children learn to meet new situations in creative, responsible ways (that is, to use thinking skills in solving problems). It is of interest and importance that this is also a goal of the personal-social growth model of discipline.

Educators also seem to agree on the following: (1) open education encourages small groups of peers to work together on problems of mutual interest; (2) open education allows children to move freely around the room as they work; (3) open education provides a rich environment for learning (an abundance of materials and books); and (4) open education takes place in a flexible setting; the classroom is usually divided into functional areas rather than a single fixed unit. (Space use is determined by the pattern of instruction; teachers usually work with small groups and individuals in the functional areas rather than with the class as a whole.)

An Educational Concept.   From the foregoing it is clear that open education is an educational concept, not an architectural concept. Open education is as possible in a conventional (self-contained) classroom as it is in an open space classroom.

Role of the Teacher: Conflicting Viewpoints.   There are certain aspects of open education about which educators openly disagree. Some educators think that the curriculum should consist wholly of activities which evolve from pupil interests. According to Herbert Kohl, the role of the open classroom teacher is to help pupils "pursue what interests them" and, further, that "the things that work best in class . . . are the unplanned ones, the ones that arise spontaneously."[1] Following this line of argument, Kohl tells teachers that they must let students say " 'No,' to what you want them to learn no matter how much stake you have in it," so that students can maintain their "freedom."[2] Finally, Kohl suggests that children handle their own behavior problems (such as the problem of taking things from each other's coat pockets) by discussion and holding mock trials, although "this may take time—time that will be taken from reading and science and social studies and other supposedly basic work."[3]

Kohl wants children to learn to take responsibility for their own learning and behavior and rightly so. But experienced teachers know that teachers need to share in curriculum planning, both to be accountable with information about what is transpiring (to the administration, community, and parents), and to give guidance as it is needed. Experience has taught us that the program of activities must be planned, either by the teacher alone or cooperatively with pupils, whatever the form of classroom organization. But this is especially the case with open classrooms. As pointed out in Chapter 4, if it is to operate successfully, an open classroom requires a great deal of planning.

Suggestions like Kohl's are not very helpful when the public begins to ask questions about the educational program. The public is (and should be) concerned about what goes on in the schools. Open education that follows a model like Kohl's can lead to charges that the schools are neglecting discipline and the "basic skills." The feeling that children are not receiving a good education can result in loss of support for the schools and "back-to-basics" movements. Both of these can undo the great educational gains made by programs which bring a wider range of experience into the curriculum than the three R's and are based on the principle that learning is best when the learners can use their skills in real situations.

The view of open education held by most open educators is very different from that of Herbert Kohl. They do not believe that the teacher is best who moves into the background while children follow their interests. On the contrary, they believe that teachers are responsible for establishing standards of work and behavior and that teachers

---

[1] Herbert R. Kohl, *The Open Classroom* (New York: Random House, 1969), p. 20.
[2] Ibid., p. 73.
[3] Ibid., p. 30.

must extend as well as help to develop pupil interests. Open educators are concerned with the development of academic skills. But they believe that skills develop best when children use them (along with their imagination and creativity) to solve problems.[4]

Finally, open educators are concerned with children's feelings relating to locus of control. An objective to which most open educators would probably subscribe is to develop in children feelings of internal (versus external) control. This again calls to mind the personal-social growth model of education.

In sum, the definition of open education held by most educators does not call for an abdication by teachers of responsibility for planning the program of activities and setting standards for work and classroom behavior. Open education does not view child freedom in the negative "freedom-from" sense, but in the positive "freedom-for" sense: freedom for pursuing clearly understood goals.

We will return shortly to the problem of how teachers can implement open education approaches. We turn now to the management problems that teachers must deal with in rooms without walls.

Management Problems in
Open Space Classrooms

According to advocates of open plan schools the purpose behind the room without walls is flexibility. It is intended to permit teachers to use space freely in conducting a variety of educational activities. For many teachers the open setting has worked out well. Either the design of space fit their concept of teaching from the start or they changed their concept of teaching to fit the open plan. Other teachers, however, have had difficulties in managing large groups of pupils in unconfined spaces. They have been unable to take advantage of the instructional opportunities offered by open classrooms due to their problems in managing pupils. What one observer ventured to predict has come to pass. Some teachers in open classrooms are devoting "even greater energy to keeping order, gaining attention, and keeping pupils actively engaged in classroom activities than to encouraging pupils to follow their own interests, to inquire freely, and to work at their own tempos."[5]

---

[4] For a discussion on the meaning of open education, see Herbert J. Walberg and Susan Christie Thomas, "Open Education: An Operational Definition and Validation in Great Britain and United States," *American Educational Research Journal*, Vol. 9 (Spring 1972), pp. 197-208; and Susan S. Stodolsky, "Identifying and Evaluating Open Education," *Phi Delta Kappan*, Vol. 57 (October 1975), pp. 113-117.

[5] Robert Dreeben, "The School as a Workplace," in Robert M. W. Travers (ed.), *Second Handbook of Research on Teaching* (Chicago: Rand McNally, 1973), pp. 463-464.

Granted this, the instructional advantages cán outweigh the troublesome aspects of learning to work in an open setting. And as pointed out earlier, teachers are responsible for keeping pupils engaged in classroom activities no matter what the architectural design of the classroom or the approach to education being followed. Nevertheless, when classes meet in relatively unconfined spaces teachers can and do encounter unfamiliar problems in classroom management. These problems, which seem to fall into three general categories, merit close attention.

1. *Distractions.* There are more distractions in open space than in conventional classrooms. There are large numbers of pupils working on a variety of activities. (Even if teachers use the whole-class method of teaching, there may be three or four classes being conducted simultaneously in the same unbounded space.) There are two kinds of distractions in open classrooms: *visual* and *auditory.* Since the space is larger than a conventional classroom and there are more pupils to observe, there are more visual distractions for pupils. Also, open space environments are noisier than self-contained classrooms because there are more activities going on at the same time and because some activities are inherently noisy. (The sound track of a movie, for instance, makes that teaching aid noisy.) One teacher described the problem:

   If a teacher shows a movie to his class, he will find some 200 ears inclined toward it, and more than likely will soon have 100 children crowded into his corner because the other teachers could not compete with the sound track. The same holds true for games, and each teacher must constantly be aware of the noise levels in his corner, for when multiplied by four, even a hum becomes a roar.

2. *Avoidance of work.* Since children in open classrooms usually have more freedom to move about the room it is easier for them to avoid work.

3. *Problems in enforcing rules of conduct.* The distractions referred to above make it more difficult for teachers to enforce classroom rules. It is harder to enforce rules in a large society than in a small society. An open space classroom containing 120 pupils is a larger society than a bounded classroom with 30 pupils.

Dealing with Distractions.   Many of the distractions in open classrooms are caused by *conflicting activities*; for example, a noisy game going on in one part of the room distracts pupils who are trying to write poems and stories in another part of the room. Conflicting activities require separation. Pupils who are reading and writing need to work in a place that is free of distractions. And children who are playing must be able to play without undue constraints. One possible solution is for the teachers who share the room to plan *compatible activities*

Mount Saint Mary's College
Emmitsburg, MD 21727

at the same time. Examples of compatible activities are independent study, reading for pleasure or for information, creative writing, a social studies assignment in map making, practicing spelling and handwriting, and the use of self-instructional materials. A way of handling small group projects (with groups of from two to six pupils) is to schedule them for the same time of day for all classes. Even when team teaching is not going on in an open space classroom, teachers should plan cooperatively so that the activities that go on are as compatible as possible.

Another solution for the problem of conflicting activities is to have pupils who are reading and writing work in the library. This is not always possible, however, since not all schools have libraries and those that have them usually accommodate classes on a scheduled basis.

A third solution is to create an enclosed space where pupils can work in privacy. Alcoves can be made with bookcases, or partitions can be put up. (Teachers have shown great ingenuity in making alcoves for quiet work.) While this does not entirely solve the problem of auditory distractions it does deal with the problem of visual distractions.

The problem is that the classroom must be flexible enough to allow both freedom of movement and concentrated attention. This problem can be solved by careful planning if teachers are willing to change by adjusting their ways of working to new demands. Many teachers who have learned new ways of working (for instance, team teaching in which the number of children they are responsible for at a given time varies with the nature of the work) would not go back to a self-contained classroom if given the choice. It is foolish to insist (as some do) that the only solution to the problems experienced by teachers is to turn open classrooms back into self-contained classrooms.

On the other hand, when an open plan classroom does not provide enclosed spaces where pupils can work in privacy (or teachers can work with one child or a small group), this problem can be solved in the course of other modifications to the school building. It is important to point out in this respect that teaching methods and patterns of organization are in a continuous state of evolution and school buildings must serve changing demands.

Pupils and Open Space Architecture.   Although moving to an open setting from a self-contained classroom is not easy for teachers, what is sometimes forgotten is that pupils are equally unprepared. As Robert Sommer points out in his fascinating book on the use of space, teachers will find it worth their while to spend time discussing with pupils ways that the classroom environment can be made more tolerable (ways to reduce the noise level, for example).[6] This is good advice for all teachers, not just teachers in open space classrooms.

But teachers also need to spell out for pupils how the environment in an open setting can, through its flexibility, aid rather than hinder learning. More specifically pupils must see the arrangement of desks and tables as functional, and therefore changeable, parts of their classroom environment. Tables and chairs are moved and pupils move around the room as activities demand. In other words, pupils should be helped to understand that open plan architecture is designed to accommodate the different activities in which they will be involved. Explaining the purpose of the classroom design helps pupils to know how they will be expected to work and act in an open classroom. This will facilitate a smooth transition. Pupils are more apt to get settled into their work without undue confusion than if they are kept in the dark about the problems and purposes of an open space setting (and what they must do to make it work).

Sometimes pupils seem to be avoiding work but the real problem is their failure to understand what is expected of them. The key to the problem is to explain goals and procedures clearly. The alternative is not a cheerful one: pupils moving aimlessly about a broad expanse, wasting their energy in random behavior, and distracting others (if only on account of their visibility to large numbers of pupils).

Open Education and Basic Discipline

An important aim of open education is self-directed inquiry. An ideal teaching situation would occur when all or most children are at the developmental level required for this kind of instruction. But this is the ideal, not the real. Clearly not all children are at this developmental level (and those who are still need guidance from the teacher). Although open learning emphasizes independence, some children are unable to handle independence responsibly. Independence is the ability to make their own "structure" in an unstructured learning situation, that is, to identify a problem that interests them and develop a plan for solving the problem. Children who have not reached the basic disciplinary stage cannot be expected to do this. Generally they do not perform well in an unstructured learning situation. They may even respond with hostility and confusion. These children may seem to be avoiding work in their open space classroom but the problem is that

[6] Robert Sommer, *Personal Space: The Behavioral Basis of Design* (Englewood Cliffs, N.J.: Prentice-Hall, 1969).

the method of teaching being used is unsuited to their level of development. Teachers must match their teaching methods to the developmental level of their pupils. This is as true in an open space setting as it is in a self-contained classroom.

The point cannot be overdrawn that whatever the teacher's educational philosophy, some children need close direction. We hope that we can help children develop a self-disciplined style of learning but not all children are at this stage when we are brought together with them in a classroom without walls or any classroom. Assignments for these children must be more structured than for those who have learned self-direction. (See Chapter 5 for a discussion on lack of attention.)

Finally, it should be emphasized that the long-range goals for learning and behavior are the same for children who are not able to handle independence responsibly as for those who are. The basic goal is to get children to the stage at which they can think for themselves and manage their own behavior. Children can begin to make decisions about their learning under teacher direction, by degrees. Even in the most structured learning activities, as work is checked the teacher can ask the youngster to suggest what he or she feels comes next in the learning process. (This helps to develop responsibility and engagement in work.)

In an open space classroom, as in any classroom, the teacher should be prepared to offer direction and help. As children are able to do so, they should be allowed to establish some goals and means themselves.

Contracts

Gaining and holding the attention of large numbers of pupils in a broad expanse is not a simple matter. Some pupils find the school program uninteresting. Although the same problem exists in self-contained classrooms it is harder to deal with in a large room with many distractions. Some teachers have used contingency contracting, or "contracting" with pupils as a means of getting them to do work that they find hard or uninteresting. The teacher arranges a contract for each pupil. The contract states that upon satisfactory completion of a small task in a least preferred subject the pupil will complete another small task in the next preferred subject and so on through all areas of the curriculum, after which the cycle begins again. Small contracts are considered best for maintaining quality of work.[7]

The contract is seen as a means of individualizing instruction as well

[7] Robert G. Packard, "Do We Have To Do What We Want Today? Structure in an Open Classroom," *Teachers College Record,* Vol. 74 (May 1973), pp. 556-557.

as attracting and keeping pupils' attention on their work. Another idea behind contracts is that through successful accomplishment of work in an unpreferred subject, the subject will gain interest for the learner. In theory, then, all areas of the curriculum would eventually be of interest to the learner.[8]

Contingency contracting methods are based on the theory of operant conditioning, applying the work of B. F. Skinner. According to Skinner, many of the effects that are considered matters of motivation are, in operation, "simply the arrangment of contingencies of reinforcement."[9] Hence the model of discipline and learning on which contracts are based is the behavior modification model.

As Good, Biddle, and Brophy point out, studies show that contingency contracting can work in classrooms, however long-term studies are needed "to insure that the gains from these procedures hold up over time and that the procedures do not involve undesirable side effects."[10]

Some teachers report that the idea of a contractual arrangement with their teacher is initially of interest to pupils but interest soon falls off. Since the attraction for pupils lies in the agreement rather than the work itself, this is understandable. When the novelty of contracts wears off pupils and teachers are left exactly where they were before—with the problem of motivation.

What seems to happen is that pupils do the work mechanically. They view it as something to be gotten over with as soon as possible and do not become involved. The process for them is akin to working on an assembly line in a factory; they do the work (the small task) but remain isolated from the work. Contracts are a factory method imposed on pupils.

Can teachers combine contracts with intrinsic motivation? This seems theoretically untenable since contingency management is based on the principle of operant conditioning with the use of extrinsic rewards. Problems with motivation when using contracts seem to stem from the fact that "the medium is the message."

As Good, Biddle, and Brophy state, many writers have objected to contingency contracting on philosophical grounds, believing that it is degrading to pupils, too manipulative and that pupils will become overly dependent on extrinsic rewards, eroding the goal of lifelong learning.[11]

[8] Ibid.

[9] See B. F. Skinner, *The Technology of Teaching* (New York: Appleton, 1968), p. 11.

[10] Thomas L. Good, Bruce J. Biddle, and Jere E. Brophy, *Teachers Make A Difference* (New York: Holt, Rinehart and Winston, 1975), p. 72.

[11] Ibid., p. 71.

Contracts are manipulative. The learner is doing something unappealing for the privilege of doing something less unappealing and so on until the chain is completed. This approach is out of tune with the aims of open education which stress the development of self-direction. It is also in conflict with the viewpoint that teachers are most likely to succeed in holding pupils' attention when pupils feel that they are learning how to do the things that they need to do in the world.

Psychological orientations (in this case, behaviorism) are based on a human viewpoint. As Bruce Joyce reminds us, "There is a powerful message in each of the alternative stances for the nature of man and his education."[12] While his point was made in connection with approaches to teacher education, it holds equally well for educational methods in lower schools. Contingency management is based on the view that learners are automatic and externally controlled.

Working at One's Own Pace

One of the basic principles of child development is that individuals learn at different rates. This is of tremendous importance in planning instruction. As discussed earlier, pupils do not finish their work at the same time. Open education is one approach for dealing with this problem. Learning in the open classroom is supposed to proceed at the child's own rate which is good. Education has come a long way since all pupils were regarded as identical peas in a pod. But there is confusion in schools about precisely *what* is meant by pupils proceeding at their own pace. This confusion has made it easy for some pupils to avoid work. The following case is illustrative.

> Recently Mrs. G was called in by her son's teacher, Barbara F, because John, a seventh grader at Turnbull Middle School, was not doing his work. As an illustration, Barbara pointed out that John had been procrastinating for three weeks about a topic for independent study, spending the time daydreaming or just "fooling around." "Don't you tell him, I mean, tell him that he *has* to get it done in a certain amount of time?" asked Mrs. G. "Oh, no," explained Barbara. "We believe that children should learn at their own pace." "My son has no pace," responded Mrs. G. "He won't work unless you give him a 'push.'"

Although Barbara was a dedicated teacher and anxious to teach in accord with developmental theory, she misunderstood the concept of

---

[12] Bruce Joyce, "Conceptions of Man and Their Implications for Teacher Education," Chapter 5 in *Teacher Education*, Seventy-fourth Yearbook of the National Society for the Study of Education, Part II (Chicago, Ill.: The University of Chicago Press, 1975), p. 144.

differences in individual rates of learning (or if she understood the idea, she did not understand how to apply it in the classroom). Individual rates of learning should not be confused with willingness or unwillingness to do the work. It is important for children to have the time that they need to complete an assignment. But Mrs. G was quite right. A teacher (or parent) could wait indefinitely for a child to do something if the child was led to feel that he or she had an infinite amount of time to do it. Barbara had told her class that they could turn in their independent study projects when they were able to do so, but she failed to point out that "able" does not mean the same as "want" or "feel like."

The confusion could have been avoided in the first place by giving children a reasonable amount of time to finish their projects and indicating clearly when the projects would be due. Or the teacher and class could have made the decision cooperatively as they planned the activity together.

Actually, Barbara failed to make clear *just what her expectations were for the assignment*. In attempting to follow the precepts of letting pupils "pursue their own interests" and "work at their own pace" she gave pupils very little guidance. This turned out to be a mistake. John (and most of the others) had no idea of how to proceed with an independent study project. Problems that interested the pupils should have been discussed as possible topics for independent study. Children engaging in independent study need to be given careful guidance and taught the necessary skills as they work.

Confusion about "pace of learning," when this results in letting children go their own way without proper guidance or direction and without a clear understanding of standards and requirements, can lead to discipline problems. Often what looks like "avoidance of work" by pupils is due to their not knowing what is expected of them. This can be a real problem in open space classrooms where pupils may be expected to work independently much of the time.

Rules of Conduct in Open Settings

Problems of enforcing rules in an open classroom can be traced directly to conditions already discussed; incompatible activities, distractions, lack of clarity about the work itself, and an erroneous interpretation of the individual differences principle. Turning pupils loose without adequate supervision even with the best of pedagogical intentions can cause chaos in a self-contained classroom. In an open space situation it can cause pandemonium. Many of the problems that teachers have in keeping order will be eliminated or at least decreased as they deal with these factors. But it must be remembered that in order to live together in one room teachers need to sit down with each other and work out their expectations for pupil behavior. Without a policy for classroom discipline, inconsistency will reign supreme. Inconsistency on the part of one teacher in a self-contained classroom can cause problems for that teacher. But when the classroom is being shared by three or four teachers, inconsistency compounded can lead to chaos instead of education. Actually, it is in the inconsistency of the teachers managing the open classroom, rather than in the physical design, that we can locate much of the trouble that teachers experience in discipline.

Conflicting Models of Open Education

Two models of open education are described below. The models differ markedly and have important implications for discipline and learning.

Model A

In Model A there is neither large nor small group instruction. Each pupil pursues his or her own work and there is little pupil interaction (except unsought interaction when pupils get bored and restless as they frequently do in this classroom). The room is divided into "interest centers" with activities in the centers consisting largely of programmed materials and worksheets. The reading program consists entirely of what the children call "programming," filling in blanks on page after page of a programmed reading workbook. Sometimes in the language center the children take an assignment card and work on the instructions it gives. It might have instructions to write a story or answer some questions cut from a textbook and pasted on the card. In this classroom there is very little contact with the teacher. The teaching style is that of individual task supervision at a low cognitive level. Teachers talk with children on a "one-to-one basis" but most of the teacher talk in these conversations is task supervision such as, "Have you finished this worksheet yet?" There is no attempt to use thinking skills for problem solving because the emphasis is almost exclusively on "skill development."

Model B

In Model B there are times when the teacher finds it appropriate to teach the whole class (or they watch or listen to something as a group). Generally however, the principal form of organization is small groups with some independent activity. We frequently see pupils in pairs or threesomes reading to one another. Sometimes there is peer tutoring. The reading program is individualized with children selecting their own reading materials. Skills are taught (usually in groups) as the teacher notes those skills in which children need practice. When working with individuals and groups the teacher tries to pose provocative questions and to stimulate effective thought and action on the part of learners. In Model B, pupils may be seen working on group projects. It is felt that social responsibility (concern for others) cannot develop unless pupils help other pupils answer their questions. Individual creativity is also emphasized in this classroom. Even less skilled children do some creative writing every day and several have made and bound their own books.

While both models appear to be based on the individual differences principle (which lies at the heart of open education), Model A differs in a very significant way from Model B. The method of working in Model A gives the appearance of allowing the pupils to work independently at their own pace. Actually, most of the work is more narrow and less interesting than the work in many "traditional" classrooms. In Model B, on the other hand, children are using reading material that is attractive (to them) in form and content. Their experience with books is positive, pleasurable, and even, at times, exciting.

In Model A, the teacher has all but withdrawn from the children. This teacher believes erroneously that open education means only independent work and children learn more when teachers remain silent. The teacher in Model B believes that whether a teacher talks or remains silent depends on the situation. In some situations expository teaching (talk) to the whole class seems like the best way; in other situations (particularly when dealing with small groups), the teacher does not talk as much as group members. In working with individuals the teacher asks questions that go beyond the recall of facts or factual teacher statements. "What do you think?" or "What would you do to find out?" are often heard in Model B because the teacher believes that the best way to help children learn to ask questions of a high cognitive level is to ask them.

In Model B the teacher has decided to cultivate certain social skills and attitudes because this teacher has a clear idea of the kind of people who should emerge from the schools. These people should be able to make sound decisions alone or with others. They should have empathy for others and feel a personal need to help others when they need help. The teacher in Model B believes that personal and social growth is an interactive process and neither can happen without the other.

In Model A the children have as long as they need to complete a task but since the program of activities is so mechanical, the process breaks down when children get bored with repeating the same patterns. Many children have fallen behind on their programmed reading. Absenteeism is quite high in Model A. In Model B, the teacher is concerned about maintaining a steady flow of activities as a way of holding pupil interest. Children are given a reasonable amount of time to finish their work but not so much time that momentum sags. Children are seldom bored in Model B. The classroom is run like a workshop with children eagerly engaged in activities of interest to them. In Model A the classroom is like a factory. Learning resembles working on an assembly line or doing piecework. Some of the children want to please their teacher and be "good workers" but even those who try their best are hideously bored in this open classroom.

Model A and Model B are located in schools only a few blocks apart from each other in a small city. Model A has all of the problems of traditional education that open education was intended to solve (and more). Model B represents an advance over traditional education. The importance of the learner is recognized. Children are learning to work together on common problems and skills are being used as well as developed. In Model A children are kept occupied with busy work and have no opportunity to immerse themselves in creative work of their own.

Although there are a few children with emotional and learning problems in Model B, generally speaking discipline is not a problem. Most of the children are too involved in the program of activities to turn to unapproved ways of behaving.

THE SMALL GROUP SETTING

In this section we will be discussing the small group as a learning situation. By this we do not mean teacher-led recitation groups but groups of children working together cooperatively and somewhat autonomously on an activity. (The teacher-led recitation group was discussed in Chapter 4.)

Why Do Small Group Work?

Although sadly neglected in many classrooms, learning how to work cooperatively on a common problem is an important part of development. In fact, one cannot get beyond the basic disciplinary stage without being able to work cooperatively for a socially constructive purpose (see Chapter 2). Although basic discipline, being able to listen and follow directions, is essential for school learning it is only a turning point in a person's development. We want pupils to be able to manage their own lives rather than being managed by others. In order to know how to make wise decisions and solve the practical problems of life children must be able to identify a problem, gather the relevant facts and develop a plan of action. Moreover they must put the plan into action and determine whether or not the problem has been solved.

The small group setting is important for yet another reason: being able to contribute to a group project or discussion helps a child become confident as well as competent. Both are important for development.

The rules and components of small group discussion (one person talking, taking turns talking, listening, thinking, and learning from one another) are nothing more or less than rules for classroom behavior. Therefore, if the group is really following the group discussion process we do not have to be concerned about pupil behavior; discipline is built into the process. Moreover, the behavior learned should "rub off" or transfer to other classroom activities (large group discussion, for instance), thus having a generally uplifting effect on classroom discipline.

If the group is working well on its own and is, thus, controlling itself instead of being controlled by the teacher, children are learning self-direction, the ultimate goal of education and discipline.

Organizing for Small Group Work

Some teachers who try small group work in their classrooms do not get "results" (except the kind of results that lead them never to try again). Seemingly, at the heart of teachers' problems with small group work lies the mistaken idea that the whole class must be involved in small group work at the same time. Teachers have always leaned toward the whole-class method of teaching. A logical extension of this method is to divide the whole class into small groups. But some children may be unprepared for this kind of learning experience. Or worse, nearly everyone may be unprepared. Children may not even know what the word discussion means, much less what it means to act as a leader (chairman) or a group member. In this case the activity has little chance for success.

Educators no longer subscribe to the notion that everyone has to be involved in the same activity at the same time. (Actually, this idea has long been out of favor.) Probably the best way to start with small group work is to begin with one group. Teachers can work with the small group, training them in problem solving and group discussion skills while the rest of the class is doing independent work. When this small group finishes its work it can be split and new members added to work on new problems or projects. This way there will be some trained members in each group.

The ultimate number of groups will depend on the readiness of pupils to be small group members and the nature of the work to be done. A word must be said about ways of determining whether a child is ready for small group activity. Some educators feel that children are not ready to work in a small group unless they can listen and follow directions, that they are at the basic disciplinary stage. This would seem particularly important for the initial group trained by the teacher. Other educators feel that children learn through exposure to learning models (people who learn well). Following this principle, a teacher could conceivably assign unsocialized children (those not yet at the basic disciplinary stage) to a trained group. But if the teacher decides to do so, a good policy is to outnumber the unsocialized by the socialized. In other words if the group contains six members, only one or two at the most should be below the basic stage.

The Importance of Roles.   A good way of teaching group discussion skills is through roles. "What does a leader do? Does he just start the discussion?" are the kinds of questions that teachers should ask in the training process. Responsibilities of the group should be established in the first session. These responsibilities or jobs might include: having a problem to solve, gathering information (facts), asking questions, making a plan to solve the problem, trying the plan, and seeing if the plan worked.

Giving each group member a responsibility can provide structure for the discussion. One way of doing this is to identify group tasks such as being the leader, giving information, questioning, adding different ideas, and judging. The tasks can be written on cards and distributed to the children. Each group member can practice one role during a session or can practice different roles. Eventually the children should realize that a good group member practices more than one role.

The Problem.   As noted in Chapter 2, while some group activities fail due to pupils' lack of ability to engage productively in group discussion, others fail because the pupils' work does not hold their interest. Is the problem real? Is it of interest to pupils? These are questions that teachers must ask themselves if they want group activities to succeed. There is no point in spending a great deal of energy teaching children how to work together on a common problem if the problem is in no way connected with their lives or interests. Problem solving should be meaningful work, or be similar to play if the problem challenges and deeply engages the learner.

Real problems for pupils to work on are considered in Chapter 8. It may be, however, that the teacher will want to assign a discussion topic having to do with a school activity. Pupils and teachers can select the topic cooperatively, for example, a money-raising project. (The "problem" which group members must solve is how to go about raising funds.) Other examples might be planning a field trip or a mural.

INDEPENDENT STUDY

It is hoped that this chapter has dispelled some of the myths about independent study, particularly the myth that independent study proceeds best when the teacher steps into the background and throws the child completely on his or her own resources. Nor should independent study by pupils be seen as a way of "freeing teachers for other things." When done properly, independent study takes time and requires careful planning just the same as any other classroom activity. In fact, if it is to be productive instead of shallow, independent study often requires that children be taught the concepts and procedures of research as they work. Teachers should first learn the concepts and procedures involved in experimental, historical, and descriptive research themselves. Otherwise, the experience may be less than worthwhile. Behavior problems can also ensue since pupils do not know what to do or how to do it.

Independent study is one strategy for individualizing learning. It can give pupils a chance to develop their own interests as well as new ones. Here again a teacher can run into problems, however, since not all pupil interests are of equal value. (This problem was dealt with in Chapter 3 and will not be discussed here.)

Although independent study is usually associated with pupils following a personal or general interest, what is often forgotten is that one child pursuing one problem (or part of a problem) is simply a way of organizing for teaching and learning. As such, independent study is a way of helping pupils to meet the requirements of the curriculum. This is sometimes forgotten in discussions about independent study which present it as a way of freeing pupils from the restrictions of the curriculum. Independent study can work well within the framework of the ongoing curriculum. For instance, children studying ecology can work independently on such problems as pollution, conservation of natural resources, noise, zoning, community beautification, and so on.

When all is said and done, however, the important thing to remember is that the principles for good teaching are the same as they are for any classroom method. Pupils must be helped to grow, starting from where they are. The direction should be from a carefully structured plan (structured by the teacher or cooperatively with pupils) to self-planning and self-direction. Pupils should never be given more than they can handle, but on the other hand the problem should be sufficiently challenging to hold their interest until the work has been completed and given them a sense of satisfaction and accomplishment.

The principles of good teaching and effective discipline apply, no matter what the design of the classroom or form of organization (one-to-one, small group, or whole class).

This point can be stated as a principle and seems a fitting note on which to end the chapter.

Eighth Principle: *No matter what the classroom design or how pupils are organized for instruction, the principles for effective teaching and discipline apply.*

SUMMARY

While it is true that open settings offer instructional advantages, they present special problems in classroom management. Explaining the purpose of the classroom design (how it can aid learning) helps pupils to know how they will be expected to work and act. It is also helpful to discuss with pupils ways that the classroom environment can be made more tolerable (whether or not it is an open setting). Teachers sharing an open classroom can eliminate many problems by working as a team. Auditory and visual distractions caused by *conflicting activities* can be minimized by planning *compatible activities* at the same time.

Open education encourages small groups of youngsters to work together on problems of mutual interest and helps pupils learn to use thinking skills in solving problems. (These are also goals of the personal-social growth model of education.) Space use is determined by the pattern of instruction. Clearly, open education is as possible in a conventional classroom as it is in an open space classroom.

Children who have not attained basic discipline do not perform well in an unstructured learning situation and may respond with hostility and confusion. In an open classroom as in a conventional classroom, teaching methods must be matched with development in order to help pupils progress to the next stage.

A way to begin small group work is to start with one group. The group can be trained in problem solving and group discussion skills while the rest of the class is doing independent work. When its work is finished, the group can be split and new members added to work on a new problem (with trained members in each group). While some educators feel that pupils are not ready to work in a small group unless they are at the basic disciplinary stage, others feel that children learn by working with learning models (pupils who work well). Giving each group member a responsibility provides structure for the discussion.

When properly guided and supervised, independent study can afford children and youth a maximum opportunity for intellectual development. Whether the teacher is using independent study, large group, or small group instruction, the principles for effective teaching and discipline apply.

Problems and Activities

1. Are there differences in the demands on teachers for classroom management between open space and conventional classroom settings? If so, what are they?
2. Draw up a list of things that teachers can do to make an open space setting work for them instead of against them.
3. Is open education an educational concept or an architectural concept? Why?
4. In view of your response to problem 3, is it possible to have open education in a self-contained classroom? Explain.
5. As discussed in this chapter, Herbert Kohl believes that children in open classrooms should settle their discipline problems by "discussion or a mock trial," although this will take time from reading and "other supposedly basic work." [Herbert R. Kohl, The Open Classroom (New York: Random House, 1969), p. 30.] What is your opinion of a mock trial held by pupils as a way of dealing with discipline problems? (It may be helpful to review the discussion in Chapter 2 on Piagetian theory concerning children's moral development in framing your answer.)
6. Draw up a list of incompatible classroom activities and a list of compatible classroom activities. How, in your opinion, can teachers in an open space classroom best solve the problem of incompatible activities?
7. Do the responsibilities of a teacher for children's learning differ in accord with the architectural design of the classroom? Why?
8. How would you prepare pupils to work in a new classroom environment?
9. What is your opinion of contracts as a way of getting pupils to work in a situation with many distractions?
10. Which of the two models of open education described in this chapter, Model A or Model B, seems tied most closely to the personal-social growth model of discipline? (See Chapter 1.) Why?
11. In connection with problem 10, which of the two models of open education do you prefer and why?
12. What can teachers do to help ensure the success of small group work?
13. In this chapter it was pointed out that small groups that function well can have a generally beneficial effect on order in the classroom. How is this so?
14. Do you think that self-directed group work is an important method of instruction? Why?
15. Do you feel that children should be at the basic disciplinary stage before they participate in a small group project? Support your answer.

The Ecology
of Classroom
Discipline

7

Many factors or ingredients enter into effective discipline. While it is not within the teacher's power to supply all of these ingredients (such as home training), others are well within the teacher's control. For example, teachers control the factor of teaching: they can make the work clear and interesting to pupils and, as we have seen, this is of critical importance for discipline. A teacher is also free to try out new ideas for curriculum improvement in his or her classroom. One illustration previously discussed was the use of literature to start pupils learning. Another, discussed in the next chapter, is building a curriculum of social responsibility. How the teacher runs (manages) the classroom is a major factor in discipline that is under the teacher's control. (In fact, teachers *must* operate their own classrooms. No one else can do it for them.) The point is that there are a number of factors in classroom discipline that are under the teacher's control. These factors relate to each other as well as to discipline.

In addition to the factors in classroom discipline that an individual teacher can actually control, are the factors that a teacher can influence. Generally, the factors controlled by teachers are instruction, curriculum improvement, classroom management (including grouping for instruction), classroom climate, and evaluation of learning. The factors that teachers can influence but cannot control include parent-teacher relationships, parental attitudes, parental guidance of pupils, out-of-school elements, administrative functions, and pupil welfare. Figure 7–1 pre-

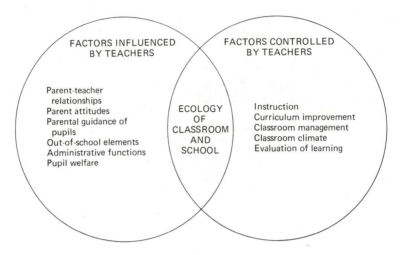

Figure 7-1   *Factors Controlled and Influenced by Teachers*

sents a composite view of the factors controlled and influenced by teachers. These factors are not discrete but are interactive in the setting of the classroom and school.

An ecological approach to discipline can prove useful, as expressed by this principle:

Ninth Principle: *By identifying and dealing effectively with the factors under their control and influence, teachers can, in most cases, tip the ecological balance in favor of discipline.*

This chapter focuses on the factors in classroom discipline which are accessible to teacher manipulation. By identifying and working systematically with these factors teachers can do much to tip the ecological balance of discipline in their favor. Some of the factors (teaching, curriculum, and classroom management) have already been discussed in detail and will not be considered again here. Pupil welfare is discussed in Chapter 10.

ECOLOGICAL FACTORS INFLUENCED BY TEACHERS

Out-of-School Factors

Teachers should be aware of the out-of-school factors in classroom discipline and try to extend favorable factors and counter those which are unfavorable. Television viewing, movies, the deliberate education pupils receive at home, and the incidental learning they acquire from the streets (in an urban environment) all shape classroom behavior. "Every family has a curriculum, which it teaches quite deliberately and systematically over time."[1] So points out Lawrence Cremin in a wonderful little book on the ecology of education.

Social scientists are fond of remarking that the home seems to have a greater influence on pupil behavior than the school. While the home doubtlessly exerts a profound influence on children, the school remains the most powerful instrument of a democratic society for providing opportunity for all. Teachers should not think in terms of what schools cannot do but rather in terms of what schools can do, separately or in combination with other influences on children. Much can be accomplished by working with parents. The home and school together can be overwhelmingly powerful.

Administrative Factors

Teachers do not control all of the school factors in classroom discipline. Certain factors are controlled by the administration (principals, assistant superintendents, superintendents, and school board members). How the school is organized (including grouping practices), class size, support for teachers (specialists, aides, materials, and media) are administrative factors in classroom discipline. For instance, whether a school has ability grouping or heterogenous grouping has an influence on classroom discipline (see pp. 133–134). Although the administration controls matters such as the nature and size of classroom groups and teacher support, teachers are having more to say about these and other influences on their work. This is partly due to the growing power of teachers unions and professional organizations. But it is also a result of the growing awareness of administrators and teachers themselves that teachers must participate in the decisions that affect their classroom effectiveness. Thus in some schools the efforts of teacher committees to make changes in grouping policies and practices have been extraordinarily successful. In others teachers seem to have had little influence. However, in all fairness, the problem is sometimes a lack of teacher interest rather than a lack of teacher influence.

Parent-Teacher Relationships

The relationship between parents and teachers can deeply affect pupils' classroom behavior—for good or for evil. When pupils can see the

---

[1] Lawrence A. Cremin, *Public Education* (New York: Basic Books, 1976), p. 22.

cooperative interest of parent and teacher in their school progress, they realize that their home lives and school lives are not independent of each other. Knowing that their parents and teachers are in communication and care together about their progress can have a beneficial effect on pupils' classroom behavior and motivation to learn. Moreover, a parent's positive attitude toward the teacher is quickly sensed by the child and increases the teacher's chances of working effectively with the child.

But when parent and teacher are enemies or work at cross-purposes the effect on the child's behavior can be devastating. Pupils' sense of security is threatened whenever there are sharp differences of opinion among or between what psychologists call the "significant others" in their lives—that is, between their parents or between parents and teacher. Because of this insecurity (which may amount to the feeling that the bottom has fallen out of the world), a youngster may be unable to concentrate on schoolwork, or may react in a different way by attempting to play one adult against another. However, the point is that children are usually well aware of their parents' feelings. If children are led to believe that the teacher is in the wrong or incompetent, they will not be motivated to act properly or do their work.

Parents and teachers have in common a desire that the children do well. If teachers can just keep that common ground in mind as they work with parents, it will be easier to develop cooperation and mutual respect. As the professional whose responsibility it is to do everything possible to help the child learn, the teacher must take the lead in developing cooperative relationships with parents. Teachers who want to tip the scales in favor of good discipline should encourage parents to feel like partners in the educational process. It does not make good sense to ignore or leave out one of the most potent ingredients in effective discipline, positive parent relationships.

Building the Relationship.   In developing a productive cooperative relationship with parents, it is important to open home-school communication as early as possible in the school year. Introducing oneself to parents and guardians is usually appreciated and may be done with a simple phone call or a home visit. Another way (the best way in my opinion) is to invite parents as a group to the school just to get acquainted with one another and the teacher. If a parent cannot attend he or she should be made to feel welcome to come and meet the teacher at another time. At the very least, parent and teacher should get acquainted by telephone.

Although the group meeting with parents can be a purely social affair, some teachers may see it as an opportunity to acquaint parents with the educational goals for the year. In this case, care must be taken to provide time to talk informally so that the social purpose is also met.

Being human, most people react more positively to those individuals that they know and like socially than to complete strangers. This is the reason why teachers and parents should get to know each other before they have to communicate on a professional basis about the progress or lack of progress of pupils. When they know and like each other, conflicts are less likely to develop between parents and teachers. Moreover, teachers are likely to gain the support and cooperation they must have.

Parent Roles in Education.   The nature of parent-teacher relationships can vary from parents and teachers being in communication about children's school progress to actual parent participation in the educational program. If the focus is on communication, it must be made clear to parents that they are welcome in the school. Many parents feel uncertain about whether their presence would be welcomed by teachers and administrators or whether they would be looked upon as intruders. What we are seeking is parental interest in their children's school performance. Parents' interest in their children's schoolwork has the effect of shaping the children's attitudes positively toward schoolwork. This fact has led to a dramatic shift in educational opinion about the role of parents in the educational process. Teachers used to look upon parents as persons who interfere with the educational process. Now all significant adults in the children's world are seen as partners in their education and many schools have programs involving parents as participants in the educational program. But if parents are to maintain a high level of interest in their children's schoolwork, they must feel free to visit the school to discuss their children's progress. This is so whether or not the parents participate in some phase of the educational program.

Parents as Teachers.   In cases in which a pupil needs help to overcome a learning problem, work can be sent home by the teacher by prior arrangement. But for home teaching to succeed, two-way communication is necessary. Some parents may be unable to visit the school as often as they would like to confer with the teacher about their youngster's progress and what they should do next. An idea found successful by some teachers for dealing with the problem is two-way communication on tape. Tape cassettes can be recorded and exchanged by parents and teachers. The teacher records what learning activities the child is involved in and suggests to parents what they can do at home to help the pupil. The cassette is sent home with the child. After listening to the tapes and following the teacher's suggestions, the parent records the results for the teacher (along with any questions he or she may have) and returns the cassette with the child. Taped interaction between home and school is one answer to the need for two-way communication between parents and teachers.

Parents who wish to help their youngsters increase their skills and knowledge should be encouraged to do so. This is so whether the children perform well on learning tasks or have learning problems. The objective is to provide every pupil with optimum opportunity to progress as far as he or she is able. A mother hearing her child practice reading every evening can help that child progress. This may make the difference between high or average achievement for some children and average or poor achievement for others. The idea should be for the home and school to complement and extend the efforts of each other.

Parental Participation in the Classroom.   There are two basic principles behind parent participation in the program of the school. First, participation can lead to parental interest in their children's school progress which can have a positive effect on learning. Second, parents will lend their support to the school to the extent that they can identify with the school. The support of parents is good for classroom discipline as well as learning.

For these reasons teachers are evolving new patterns for parent participation in the classroom. Parents have always served as volunteers to assist in certain school activities such as class parties and field trips. Increasingly, however, they are serving as volunteers in capacities more closely related to the instructional process. Parents donate countless hours to working with individual children in an attempt to help them overcome their learning disabilities. In some schools, mothers assist in the library (by reading to small groups) and help with creative dramatics. Mothers teach their craft specialties to pupils (embroidery, knitting, crotcheting, flower arrangement).

Parents should volunteer in their child's classroom. This helps to build cooperation between home and school and makes the child aware of that cooperation.

Reluctant Parents.   Some parents are loathe to have anything at all to do with the schools. It is almost impossible to get them to come in for conferences. The reason may be that their recollections of their own teachers are negative. Or it may be that they were made to feel intimidated by a teacher at a previous conference. One of the best ways to open home-school communication with these parents is to plan a field trip and ask them to come along. This involves them as participants in a less threatening situation than a classroom. As many parents as possible who want to go along "for the ride" should be included. These parents should then be invited to visit the classroom some morning or afternoon to observe. Afterward a discussion session can be conducted in which parents may ask questions (if they wish) concerning the educational program.

These parents may or may not continue to serve as volunteers. But of most importance is that the teacher has helped them to understand what is going on in the classroom. In helping to change indifference or hostility into feelings that are constructive and supporting, the teacher has effectively facilitated classroom operations.

Parent-Teacher Conferences

The parent-teacher conference has become a major way of reporting pupil progress to parents. The growing use of this method has improved the amount and quality of information available to parents. While this is important enough there are two additional advantages of conferences: (1) conferences do not stop with reporting, they are an opportunity for constructive planning and (2) conferences provide a real flesh-and-blood connection between home and school: parent and teacher are in face-to-face communication and pupils are aware of this.

That their mothers or fathers know or have spoken with their teachers cannot but affect the children. Since this relationship between the significant others in the children's lives is centered on them it demands something of them. But what these demands are and whether they result in a clear course of action is what counts. The conference can be constructive and helpful if it goes beyond reporting pupil behavior and includes task setting. On the other hand, it can be destructive and disheartening for the child if all that comes out is the feeling that "my mother and teacher have it in for me."

In his study on parent-teacher conferences in three New Jersey school districts, school psychologist Hugh Carberry found that most parents were willing to talk freely about their experiences with conferences. As Carberry points out, the positive and negative comments of parents provide teachers with clues on how to handle parent-teacher conferences.[2] The following are some examples of positive comments:

> Kristin's teacher always gives me a feeling that there's hope and there are strategies that we can try to motivate her.

> John's teacher last year was really great. I felt that he really understood and liked my child.

[2] Hugh H. Carberry, "Parent-Teacher Conferences," *Today's Education*, Vol. 64 (January-February 1975), p. 67.

Jack's teacher is open and doesn't come across as a know-it-all. She's a good human being.

I know Helen isn't doing well because the teacher and I have already talked. I'm looking forward to our next meeting because the teacher has asked Helen to sit in with us and maybe we can hash a few things out in a three-way conference.[3]

The following are some negative comments:

I always feel as though the teacher is questioning whether I am a good mother.

Last year the teacher seemed to think she was doing me a favor by having John in her classroom.

Last year the teacher talked to me as if I didn't know anything about education, and he really didn't want to hear my observations of Jenny at all.

Whenever I go to these conferences, the teacher and I usually just compare notes on how difficult Paul is, and we both end up feeling hopeless.

The conferences are a waste of time. I never get any information. The teacher never wants me to help.[4]

In reading over these comments, one is struck by how the positive comments seem to cluster around what is perceived by parents as the teacher's positive and constructive approach and the negative comments on what is seen as a negative approach. Parents who like the teacher perceive him or her as liking their child, honest about the child's progress and willing enough to help the child to map out a plan. The teacher plans with parents, treating them as partners, not subordinates, and does not maintain a "professional distance."

On the other hand, teachers who prompt negative reactions from parents are perceived as unwilling to listen, unwilling to share information about the child, being overly conscious of their professional status (to the point of making parents feel inferior), thinking negatively instead of planning what to do and, worst of all, not liking the child.

In sum, teachers who want the support of parents would do well to be constructive in their meetings with parents. Of course this takes work. Teachers must determine the direction of tasks for pupils before each conference. But the results in terms of parent support and pupils knowing exactly what they must do, not to mention the wholesome effect on classroom discipline, are more than worth it.

[3] Ibid.
[4] Ibid.

Unavailable Parents.   No matter how a teacher may try to establish cooperative relationships, some parents are very difficult to communicate with effectively. Included in this group are the parents who do not come to conferences. Unfortunately, these are usually the parents with whom teachers need to confer the most. Sometimes the parent is the sole support of the family. To make a classroom visit at the scheduled time would mean missing a day's wages. In such cases the teacher should plan the conference for a time when the parent can be there. Usually if the teacher shows understanding for the parent's predicament, the parent will make every effort to see the teacher.

Other parents have small children at home and cannot afford the price of a baby sitter. Schools can provide baby sitting services for these parents during conference time. The time and trouble it takes to reach unavailable parents is well worth it.

Parents with Low Expectations.   Some parents are difficult to work with because they do not believe that their children's academic weaknesses can be overcome. They may say, "Well, I was never good in arithmetic either," or "No one in my family could ever write a straight sentence." Even worse they may advise, "Don't expect anything from Susie because she's stupid."

Pupils' concepts of their ability are the products of the expectations of the pupil held by significant others, particularly parents. Therefore it is of critical importance that teachers help parents to realize that their children's academic performance can be improved. One way is by pointing out how the children have improved or done well. This can develop parental confidence in their children's ability. Another way is by giving the parents actual responsibility for enhancing the children's concept of their ability. Parents should know that their evaluations and expectations can shape their children's self-concept of ability and affect their academic performance. This was demonstrated some years ago in a now classic experiment involving underachieving junior high school pupils in Michigan. Their achievement was significantly increased between the seventh and ninth grades by raising the academic expectations and evaluations of their ability held by their parents. This was accomplished through parent education focused on how parents could help their children acquire an enhanced self-concept of academic ability.[5]

[5] Wilbur B. Brookover, et al., *Improving Academic Achievement Through Students' Self-Concept Enhancement—Self-Concept of Ability and School Achievement,* Project No. 1636, U.S. Department of Health, Education, and Welfare, Office of Education, October 1965.

In sum, teachers who want to improve achievement would do well to enhance parental evaluations of their children's potential.

Hostile and Aggressive Parents.   Sooner or later every teacher will probably be faced by a parent with a grievance, imagined or otherwise. A parent may open the conference by saying, "I certainly think it's unfair of you to give Lisa a B+ on her spelling test when you gave Robert Jones an A− and he missed the same number of words," or "I hear that you're having more trouble with discipline than Bobby's teacher had last year." If the parent's complaint is based on fact (as it was in the case of the spelling test), the teacher should admit that a mistake was made and thank the parent for bringing it to her or his attention. If the comments are unfounded, the teacher should calmly and diplomatically explain the real situation. Teachers should not be aggressive or abrupt in explaining that there is no truth to a parent's comment. Being on the defensive can only lead to added resentment. In the case in which Bobby's mother tried to put the teacher on the defensive about discipline problems, the teacher handled the comment by saying that Bobby's teacher last year was excellent but that the children this year were a well-motivated group, presenting no unusual problems with discipline.

Occasionally an irate parent will come in, insisting that he or she be seen immediately. As Walter St. John suggests in his guidelines for dealing with angry adults, the best policy is to meet with aggrieved persons promptly, if possible in a private setting where they can talk without being interrupted.[6] The teacher should listen carefully, giving the angry person a chance to tell the whole story. It is important that the teacher not interrupt *even if he or she disagrees.* "When the initial verbal onslaught ends and nonverbal clues suggest that the grievant is more relaxed, ask questions in an interested but nondefensive manner in order to clarify confusing points," advises St. John.[7]

Very often, an angry person begins to develop better feelings simply from talking. This is why it is very important to let aggrieved parents talk fully. As a well-known college president once quipped when asked the secret of his success in handling irate students: "I've learned to be a charismatic listener." When a teacher listens carefully to an upset parent, the parent may be willing to listen to the teacher later.

When the problem has been resolved, the conference should be ended on a positive note by thanking the parent for coming and bringing

[6] Walter D. St. John, "Dealing with Angry Adults," *Today's Education,* Vol. 64 (November-December 1975), p. 82.

[7] Ibid.

the matter to attention. How the conference ends is of critical importance for a future cooperative relationship with that parent.

When parents know and like the teacher they are much less likely to become angry. Their feelings of support are too powerful. Hence if a situation develops in which the teacher appears to have made a mistake, they are more likely to approach it rationally than emotionally. This is why it is so important to get to know parents early and put down foundations of trust.

Pupils as Conference Participants.   Usually the child is not present at parent-teacher conferences. However, some schools have changed their policy to include the children as participants. This is in accord with changing attitudes toward the role of children in their education. Current thinking holds that it is important for children to participate in setting goals for learning and evaluation of their work. After all, it is their work. Therefore they should have a place at the conference table.

There is yet another reason for including the pupils. When the child hears firsthand about how he or she is doing in school, there is less likelihood of what was said being misconstrued by parent to child. On the other hand, when the pupil is not present, the substance of what the teacher communicated to the parent can be mutilated misleadingly by the parent. What the youngster gets secondhand may be very different from what was actually said. The following case is not unusual.

> When told that her son was doing good work in school, Mrs. T became anxious. "Is he at the top of his class?" she asked. "No," replied the teacher, "but I'd say he's in the top third. He's a very hard worker and seems to be working up to his ability. I think that we can all be pleased." After the conference Mrs. T told her son (who was anxiously waiting outside the classroom door), "Your teacher told me that you could do better if you tried harder. You could even be at the top of your class. Your trouble is that you are bright but lazy."

Parent-teacher-pupil conferences can do much to alleviate the pressure put on their children by over-anxious parents.

Certain parents who are having discipline problems with their youngsters see the two-way conference as a means of gaining more control over them. When a child is curious about what happened at the conference they may say, "You'd better watch out. Miss Jones really has it in for you." This can have a devastating effect on the relationship between teacher and child. In the pupil's thinking the teacher has betrayed her or him, though on the contrary, the teacher may have been positive and supportive.

There are, then, two substantial reasons for having pupils present at conferences: the pupils can be involved in setting goals (educational and behavioral) and can personally hear the evaluations of their work and achievements.

A study involving children, parents, and teachers, representing grades one through six, found that after the children had participated in two conferences, the majority of parents, teachers, and children were "strongly in favor" of keeping the child permanently as a conference participant.[8] Although interesting, this is an isolated study. The problem of pupils as participants needs to be widely researched before it can be concluded that parents and teachers generally favor including pupils on the conference team.

There are problems in including pupils that proponents tend to gloss over. First the idea seems to work best when children are doing well in school. Children want to hear the favorable report of their teacher and communication is comfortable and easy between teacher and parent. But if a child is not doing well and has limited ability it may be difficult for parent and teacher to talk with the child there. Also some parents may find it difficult to ask questions about the pupil's work with the pupil present.

Nevertheless, the advantages of the child seeing the cooperative interest of the parent and teacher in his or her school progress and hearing the teacher's encouraging remarks (in addition to the other advantages described) may outweigh the disadvantages. It is also possible that the disadvantages can be eliminated with planning. There is only one way to find out. Schools can test the three-way conference experimentally, evaluating it carefully before adoption.

Finally, if the pupils are not included in the conference, the teacher should review with them what will be discussed with their parents before the meeting. Pupil-teacher conferences should precede parent-teacher conferences.

Television and Pupil Behavior

Many teachers are concerned about the long hours spent by children viewing television. They feel certain, from listening to children's talk, that children are exposed to a considerable amount of televised violence. They hope that children watch and forget but are troubled by the thought that children might learn and remember. The content learned could lead to aggressive behavior.

The deepest suspicions of these teachers have been confirmed by

---

[8] Joseph A. Saeli, "Parent/Teacher/Child Task-Setting Conferences," *Phi Delta Kappan*, Vol. 56 (December 1974), pp. 287-288.

research. Hundreds of studies have confirmed that television is one of children's most frequent waking activities. As a monumental study conducted by Congressional request points out, "there appears to be no question that violent television fare is available in overwhelming abundance and that children do watch these programs both frequently and regularly."[9] Conducted by more than fifty researchers, the inquiry concluded:

> At least under some circumstances, exposure to televised aggression can lead children to accept what they have seen as a partial guide for their own actions. As a result, the present entertainment offerings of the television medium may be contributing, in some measure, to the aggressive behavior of many normal children.[10]

The summary of the report stressed that exposure to violence on television very likely only affected children predisposed by many factors to aggressive behavior. However, Dr. Robert Liebert, a researcher who reviewed all of the research done in the inquiry, said in a *New York Times* interview that the studies "quite clearly" demonstrated "that watching violence in a television context can instigate aggressive behavior in children."[11]

Liebert pointed out that none of the studies suggested that televised violence was the only cause of violence but it was one cause that can be altered more easily than a family's emotional climate or economic status: "We don't want to take the baby sitter away," he said, "We just want to keep her from committing murder in the living room."[12]

As for the report's assertion that only a small number of children were affected by exposure to television violence, Dr. Liebert argued that research showed that of only a small number of cigarette smokers, "some" cigarette smokers with a predisposition to malignancy develop lung cancer. "A modest relationship is clearly enough to take action," he said.[13]

But there are other aspects of the problem that merit attention. First, we must think of the victims as well as the aggressor. There are many innocent victims of violence and whether their aggressors amount to a

---

[9] Robert M. Liebert, "Television and Social Learning: Some Relationships between Viewing Violence and Behaving Aggressively (Overview)," in *Television and Social Behavior*, a report to the Surgeon General's Scientific Advisory Committee; Vol. 2 (Washington, D.C.: U.S. Government Printing Office, 1972), p. 9.

[10] Ibid., p. 30.

[11] *The New York Times*, February 19, 1972, pp. 1, 63.

[12] Ibid., p. 63.

[13] Ibid.

tiny or a large proportion of all children and youth exposed to televised violence is hardly the point. (Indeed, one aggressor can have many victims.) Society must be protected. Second, granted that violence in television programming does not have an adverse effect on the majority of our nation's children and youth, those adversely affected tend to be concentrated in urban areas where most of the violence in our society occurs. In urban schools there are large groups of children predisposed by various factors to aggressive behavior. By contrast in suburban schools there may be very few. This does not mean that exposure to televised violence leaves the middle-class child unaffected. Nor does it mean that the problem of the influence of televised violence on unsettled children is not a problem of the society as a whole. Violence cannot be confined to one school or one city block.

Instead of dismissing the effects of televised violence as insignificant because only some children are affected, the television industry should meet its responsibility to all children and all society. At this writing this has not happened. And because the report did not make a strong indictment of televised violence, it did not prompt remedial action by the government. Due to the power of commercial interests, television violence may be with us for some time to come.

Television is a powerful medium for learning. As such it is an enormously important factor in the ecology of education. Teachers need to develop ways of countering the negative influences of television on children and extending the positive influences. We will turn to this problem shortly.

Effects of Television Aggression on Children's Willingness To Aggress. Violent program content appears to increase the willingness of children to aggress. A study involving kindergarteners through twelfth graders obtained information on children's choices after they watched television programs differing in the amount of violent content.[14] (The programs were taken from the air without editing.) Each child in the experiment was presented with a series of lifelike situations such as, "You're standing in line for a drink of water. A kid comes along and just pushes you out of line. What do you do?" The child was asked to choose between two responses, an aggressive response ("Push them") and a nonaggressive response ("Go away"). The study found a significant relationship between the amount of violence in the television program a child viewed and his willingness to select physically aggressive

<hr>

[14] Aimee Liefer and Donald F. Roberts, "Children's Responses to Television Violence," *Television and Social Behavior*, Vol. 2 (Washington, D.C.: U.S. Government Printing Office, 1972), pp. 43-180.

responses after television viewing. A second finding of interest was that children more often chose physical aggression at an older than at a younger age.

In another study two groups of elementary-school-age youngsters were exposed to excerpts from television shows, one group to excerpts depicting aggression (a brutal fist fight, a shooting, and the like) and the other group to an exciting but nonaggressive sporting event.[15] Afterward, the children in both groups were given opportunities to either hurt or help another child by pushing either a red or a green button. The children were told that pushing the green button would help another child but that pushing the red button would hurt him or her. They were also told that the longer they pushed the button, the more the other child would be helped or hurt. Younger children (ages five to six) showed a greater willingness to hurt after observing the aggressive program. More importantly, the average depression of the *hurt* button was more than 75 percent longer in the aggressive program group than in the nonaggressive program group.

These studies have implications for classroom behavior. It may be that the aggression shown by some children in their interaction with peers (pushing, shoving, fighting) is at least partially an outcome of repeated exposure to aggression on television.

The Influence on Children of Televised Violence.　　When the home is weak in efforts to control the development of aggressive attitudes, the relationship between exposure to televised violence and children's attitudes becomes more powerful. Nor are middle-class children immune to the effects of exposure to aggressive television. In their research into the relationship between television violence and aggressive attitudes, Dominick and Greenberg found that "for relatively average children from average home environments, continued exposure to violence is positively related to acceptance of aggression as a mode of behavior" and that, further, such aggressive fare makes a "consistent, independent contribution to the child's notions about violence. The greater the level of exposure to televised violence, the more the child was willing to use violence, to suggest it as a solution to conflict, and to perceive it as effective."[16]

[15] Robert M. Liebert and Robert A. Baron, "Short-Term Effects of Televised Aggression on Children's Aggressive Behavior," *Television and Social Behavior*, Vol. 2 (Washington, D.C.: U.S. Government Printing Office, 1972), pp. 181-201.

[16] J. R. Dominick and B. S. Greenberg, "Attitudes Toward Violence: The Interaction of Television Exposure, Family Attitudes, and Social Class," *Television and Social Behavior*, Vol. 3 (Washington, D.C.: U.S. Government Printing Office, 1972), pp. 329-333.

What Teachers Can Do

Encouraging Parental Supervision. Teachers cannot control the viewing habits of children. But teachers can make parents aware of the problem and suggest that parents supervise television viewing. The viewing of many preschool youngsters is unsupervised, especially in disadvantaged homes. Teachers can suggest that parents direct their children to television programs more likely to lead to positive effects on cognitive and social development, such as *Sesame Street.*

Encouraging Reading and Use of Libraries. Teachers can also encourage children to read books. As Cremin points out, if one takes an ecological approach to education, educational institutions such as schools and public libraries should be viewed as relating to and complementing each other.[17] Children should be taught to use and enjoy the services of the public library. This is one educational institution that will be available to them for the rest of their lives. Schools and public libraries can extend the influence of each other. And both can counter and neutralize the harmful effects of aggression on television. Working in concert, the school and library are more powerful than either one or the other in isolation.

Counter-aggression Messages. The following statement, taken from the national study on the relationship between televised violence and the attitudes and behavior of children, is of profound significance for the task of the teacher:

> If indeed, as evidence shows, the more disadvantaged are more aggressive in attitude and experience; if this aggressiveness is strongly reinforced through a steady exposure to television fare of their own choosing; and if few counter-aggression messages are received from family, peers, or other socializing agencies, then the consequences are of paramount social importance.[18]

As the socializing agency with which all children come in contact, schools must provide counter-aggression messages. Although this must be done in all schools, it is of critical importance in schools serving disadvantaged children. Schools can do this by teaching that there are nonviolent ways available to people for settling their conflicts and by demonstrating what they are. They can do this by dealing with children

---

[17] Cremin, op. cit.

[18] Bradley S. Greenberg and Thomas F. Gordon, "Social Class and Racial Differences in Children's Perceptions of Television Violence," *Television and Social Behavior,* Vol. 5 (Washington, D.C.: U.S. Government Printing Office, 1972), p. 205.

in nonviolent ways. (Hitting children teaches violence as a solution to conflict.) And they can do this by teaching social responsibility and immersing children in opportunities to engage in socially useful activities.

Teachers can also provide counter-aggression messages by helping children become aware of the "curriculum" they are being taught on television (violence as well as other content) and to learn how to deal critically with this curriculum and its values.

Co-curricular Clubs.   Finally, schools can do much to counter the effects of violent television content by interesting children in other kinds of leisure-time activities. Co-curricular clubs can be organized to foster interests in stamp collecting, coin collecting, science, photography, dance, and creative writing. Clubs are hardly a new idea. Educators have long known that clubs hold a strong appeal for children and youth and that informal pupil activities can have at least as powerful an influence on the lives of children as the formal curriculum. But the club idea needs to be implemented today as never before as a means of helping youngsters to become doers instead of viewers.

ECOLOGICAL FACTORS CONTROLLED
BY TEACHERS

Grouping and Pupil Behavior

How children are assigned to classrooms is an important factor in the ecology of classroom discipline. In some schools children are randomly assigned. Since they are a heterogeneous group the teachers expect some children in the class to have more self-control than others and different levels of performance. Their expectation, positive but certainly undramatic, is that each child will advance as far as possible that year in intellectual and social competence. They expect that their efforts will promote the child's learning and anticipate few serious discipline problems.

In other schools pupils are assigned according to ability or achievement. Since they are (supposedly, at least) a homogeneous group, the teachers have expectations about their behavior based on the level of the group. High-achieving pupils are expected to behave better in class and learn more than low-achieving pupils. Almost inevitably teachers get what they expect. Those pupils who are expected to behave and perform well do so and those who are expected to misbehave and do poorly do so. As noted earlier, a teacher's attitude seems to be a self-fulfilling prophecy.

Assigning pupils to rooms by ability is a fairly common practice. Many children are misassigned to low groups and are capable of doing good work but are penalized by the teacher's low expectations. Being assigned to an ability group affects pupil performance. Pupils assigned to low groups are bound to suffer from deep feelings of inferiority. The teacher has a Herculean task to erase these feelings. There is only one way that it can be done, by expecting that pupils can and will achieve and good teaching. Anything less reduces educational opportunity for children.

If schools were to use the findings of research to decide whether to group pupils by ability, this way of assigning pupils to classrooms would be abandoned. For research fails to show that academic achievement is improved by grouping pupils of like ability together. Despite the research findings and the fundamental problems associated with ability grouping (low achievers are deprived of high-achieving role models, for example), many schools continue to group pupils by ability. The reasons cannot be discussed here. As noted, a school's grouping procedures are usually decided by the administration, although in some schools teachers participate in this decision.

Grouping within Classrooms.   An ecological factor controlled by teachers is how they organize pupils for instruction. Many teachers group pupils by ability for reading and mathematics and some also group for social studies and science. In many respects the arguments against ability grouping within the classroom closely parallel those at the school level. Ability grouping may deprive the less-motivated pupil of association with well-motivated peers. Although some would argue that they attend the same classroom this is not the same as working together.

Moreover, being in the bottom group can be personally humiliating to pupils. The problem is compounded if, as often happens, they are in several or every bottom group in the room. This may lead to loss of self-respect. Without self-respect a youngster is less educable and less likely to progress upward through the stages of discipline.

Finally, ability groups can be rigid stratifications. Once classified as slow, pupils often remain in a low group even when achievement plainly merits transfer to a higher group. However, this argument advanced in opposition to grouping need not apply to grouping within classrooms. Teachers can regroup pupils as often as necessary. Classroom subgroups have the advantage of flexibility. Subgroups can be formed when needed and dissolved when their purpose has been fulfilled. That is, pupils who have similar needs can be put together until their needs have been met. When the skill has been mastered, the group has served its purpose and should no longer exist. Groups are to serve purposes; they are not sacred entities to be served. As Good and Brophy state:

> Too often groups are convenient devices that keep teachers from thinking and prevent them from effectively dealing with problems. Teachers place children into high, middle, or low groups and then do not think about them again but they have to think about them. Grouping can be a powerful tool if teachers use it as an effective way of organizing students for learning specific skills and if the teachers disband groups once their usefulness ceases and form new groups as new needs become apparent.[19]

Teachers who maintain ability groups should frequently review assignments to high, middle, or low groups. The teacher's guideline for grouping can be summed up in one word: *flexibility*.

A word must be said about the importance of providing opportunities for pupils of various abilities to work together in a variety of situations. Low achievers need to work with models of academic success. A frequently advanced idea is the use of peer tutoring. Children teaching other children can be of great value to both tutors and tutees. But this is not the same as being engaged together in a common quest for knowledge or the solution of a problem. Low achievers need to be in learning situations with high achievers for the modeling effect to work. One way to meet this objective is to assign pupils to small heterogeneous groups for science or social studies, allowing each member of the group to make an individual contribution toward the solution of a problem or project. Each group member can be assigned a specific task by the teacher, in accord with the pupil's ability or interests.

Evaluation and Pupil Behavior

Simply by virtue of its communication to pupils of their success or failure, evaluation is a factor in the ecology of discipline. Repeatedly being labeled a failure can cause pupils to stop trying and impel them toward problem behavior. On the other hand, pupils who receive positive feedback about their relation to the school are likely to be encouraged and partake eagerly of whatever fare happens to be on the curricular menu. These pupils seldom pose discipline problems.

There is more than an element of incongruity in expecting failure to inspire pupils to do better. Yet one hears from many quarters that what is needed is "toughness" in evaluation of pupils' learning and discipline problems will disappear. If the problems disappear as a result of failing

[19] Thomas L. Good and Jere E. Brophy, *Looking in Classrooms* (New York: Harper & Row, 1973), p. 260.

more pupils, it will be because the pupils themselves disappear, from dropping out. Children who fail in school constitute the majority of dropouts. When pupils drop out the school may be relieved of their presence but the story does not end there. The cost of their failure is paid by society. In human and monetary terms that cost is staggering.

Evaluation can be a positive element in the ecology of discipline if it points out clearly to pupils what their next steps are in learning. But for this to really make a difference, pupils must know where they are headed. Youngsters should be given a bird's-eye view of what they will be expected to learn at the end of the year or some other period in their school lives. This helps to make sense of schooling. But it also provides a gauge for determining progress or lack of it, and helps to keep pupils working constructively toward an objective.

When pupils are having trouble meeting the goals of the school certain persistent questions arise, such as whether the pupils are meeting their responsibilities. Do they do the work? Do they ask questions when they do not understand? If they are not meeting their responsibilities, they should be asked what they can do to make things turn out differently. This is a good point to begin planning changes for the future.

On the other hand, they may have met their responsibilities but made little progress. Here it should be noted that in addition to the assessment of knowledge and understanding, a second function of evaluation is to diagnose learning problems. Diagnosis should be followed by a plan for the next teaching steps. A third function of the evaluation of learning is the evaluation of instruction. When pupils have problems it may be due, at least in part, to the method used by the teacher. These functions of evaluation were put forward by Ralph Tyler.[20]

Evaluation is many-sided. But one of the most important aspects of evaluation is how it relates to another factor in classroom discipline, the classroom climate. Evaluation must take place in an atmosphere of encouragement. Teachers must provide opportunities for pupils to achieve and show confidence that pupils can become competent. This is what is meant by a climate of encouragement.

In sum, evaluation can be a positive factor in classroom discipline if it is constructive and looks forward, not backward. One should not focus on what the pupils failed to do but on what they can do next.

[20] See Ralph W. Tyler, "The Objectives and Plans for a National Assessment of Educational Progress," *Journal of Educational Measurement*, Vol. 3 (Spring 1966), p. 1.

SUMMARY

Effectiveness in class control is something to be achieved systematically. By identifying and working with those factors under their control and influence, teachers can do much to tip the balance of discipline in their favor. In doing so, they are taking an ecological approach to discipline.

Parent factors (parent-teacher relationships, parent attitudes, parental guidance of pupils) are potent aspects of the ecology of classroom discipline. Together the home and the school can be overwhelmingly powerful. But teachers must take the lead in getting to know parents and planning with them as partners in the child's education. Parents like and support teachers who are constructive in their meetings with parents. Pupil performance can be improved by raising parental evaluations of their children's ability. When teachers listen carefully to an aggrieved parent, the parent may be willing to listen to the teacher later. If parents know the teacher and foundations of trust have been put down, they are less likely to become upset.

Including pupils in parent-teacher conferences can exert a positive effect on class control. Pupils see firsthand the cooperative interest of their parents and teacher in their school progress and can participate in setting their own educational and behavioral goals. If the pupil is not included, a pupil-teacher conference should precede the parent-teacher conference.

Studies show that televised violence may be contributing to the aggressive behavior of normal children as well as those predisposed to aggressive behavior. Teachers can counter the negative and extend the positive influences of television by suggesting that parents supervise viewing and by building activities around programs that address important areas of learning and can help the child develop an awareness of how people "say" things by television and film. Pupils should learn to deal with the "curriculum" that they are being taught on television. Teachers can seek to extend reading interests and the influence of puplic libraries. Co-curricular clubs can be an extraordinarily effective device for developing new leisure-time interests.

Grouping within the classroom and pupil evaluation are factors in the ecology of discipline that teachers control. They can work as positive forces if grouping is flexible, giving low achievers opportunities to work with models of academic success, and evaluation is constructive, taking place in a climate of encouragement.

Problems and Activities

1. In your own words, explain what is meant by an ecological approach to discipline. What does it mean to you as a teacher?
2. In what ways do parents influence classroom discipline?
3. In connection with problem 2, describe briefly what teachers can do to influence each parent factor (see Figure 7-1) favorably for discipline.
4. Do you think that pupils should be present at parent-teacher conferences? Support your answer.
5. In this chapter it was pointed out that concepts held by parents of pupils' ability influence pupils' self-concepts of ability. In your opinion, is this finding important for classroom discipline? Why?
6. In view of your response to problem 5, should teachers try to enhance parents' low opinions of pupils' potential? If so, how can this be done?
7. When a parent comes in with an unfounded accusation against the teacher, should the teacher give the parent a chance to tell the whole story when obviously it is without foundation in fact? Explain.
8. In schools in which pupils do not participate in parent-teacher conferences, do you think that teachers should hold conferences with pupils beforehand, informing them about the nature of the report to their parents? Why or why not?
9. Can schools counter and neutralize the negative effects of violent television content? If so, how?
10. What is the best attitude a teacher can have when teaching low-ability groups?
11. Why do you suppose many schools continue to group pupils homogeneously when this practice is unsupported by research findings and there are so many arguments against it? Consult the literature on grouping to see if your speculations are correct.
12. Do you feel that pupils should be grouped for reading and arithmetic? If so, would you periodically review assignments to groups? Why? In your opinion, how often should this be done?
13. What can a teacher do to ensure that evaluation of pupils is constructive rather than destructive?

Socializing
the Unsocialized

8

Perhaps the saddest shortcoming of unsocialized children is that they lack empathy. They seem insensitive to the needs and rights of others and unconcerned about their feelings. The behavior of unsocialized children is mindless and uncontrolled. They disrupt the learning efforts of their classmates (and their own learning as well). They have not developed reciprocity. It will be remembered from the discussion in Chapter 2 that reciprocity (understanding the viewpoint of others and balancing that viewpoint with one's own) is necessary for socialization. Effective class control depends on socialization. This chapter is concerned with ideas for socializing unsocialized pupils.

SOCIALIZATION, THE NECESSARY OBJECTIVE

Increasing numbers of children are growing up without adequate socialization. In many cases the problem is a home and community that has failed as a socializing agent. The school is left with the job of helping unsocialized children learn what are considered correct and incorrect responses in a social situation. (The school is a social situation.) While some would argue that socializing children is not the job of the school, that argument becomes purely academic when one is undergoing the experience of working (or attempting to work) with unsocialized children in classrooms. Overcoming defects in the socialization of children may be a matter of survival. For the authority of the teacher is virtually meaningless when children are neither aware of nor concerned about the consequences of their actions. Thus although the curriculum guide may say nothing about socialization, and teachers sometimes wonder if it is their responsibility, many teachers are in situations in which they cannot get by without pursuing this objective. Unless teachers and children can get along together in classrooms nothing else in the curriculum guide is possible. Also, even if teachers are not in eminent danger of losing their jobs due to "failure to maintain discipline," unsocialized children can make classroom life less than pleasant.

Moreover, self-direction in children is our overriding educational goal. Socialization is inherent in self-direction. Random, unthinking, unsocialized behavior is the very antithesis of self-direction. Developing self-direction in children means helping them to become responsible individuals who know how to act and how not to act and who care about the consequences of their actions for themselves and others. Thus we as teachers are legitimately concerned with socialization in our classrooms.

REDIRECTING NEGATIVE BEHAVIOR

What we hope for goes deeper than acceptable manners and ways of behaving. We want the unsocialized child to be a responsible person who contributes to the well-being of others rather than exploiting them. We seek a caring and doing individual. Our goal, therefore, is not to eliminate the emotional energy of the unsocialized child, but rather to utilize it toward growth. The problem is to channel destructive energies into socially acceptable and useful activities. This is a matter of redirection.

Actually, redirection is what we do all the time in teaching. As John Dewey wrote in *Democracy and Education*: "All direction is but redirection; it shifts the activities already going on into another channel."[1] Thus the problem of redirection is in our domain as educators. It is not something that we could leave to psychologists and guidance counselors (even if they were available in large numbers) because it is basically an instructional procedure. Moreover as educators we are supposed to nurture social responsibility in children and youth. This must be done if the rising generation is to do their part in making a better future.

---

[1] John Dewey, *Democracy and Education* (New York: Macmillan, 1916), p. 26.

Principle of Redirection

Tenth Principle: *Socialization requires the redirection of destructive behavior into socially useful behavior.*

Although the short-range goal of any method in dealing with behavior problems is to end the misbehavior, it is not to end activity. The desired objective is that the pupil change what he or she is doing to something else; in this case we hope to substitute socially useful for destructive behavior. The long-range objective is to develop social responsibility.

We want children or youth to obtain pleasure from their actions. But we want the satisfaction to come from the good of the result for others as well as themselves. Implementation of the principle requires that misbehavior be ended without dampening activity. Perhaps they will be more active in school than they have ever been before. But their behavior will be socially useful rather than destructive.

This implies that we as teachers must have a conception of the kind of individual who is to eventually emerge from the school. A teacher cannot recognize opportunities for planning activities for social growth without a clear picture of this person. In developing this conception, it is helpful to know that a democracy demands a very special kind of citizen—one with the power of self-direction and the disposition and ability to assume social responsibility. If we want children to contribute to the improvement of society as adults, rather than to its detriment, we must give them opportunities to learn by experience. Examples of such opportunities are suggested later.

Theory behind Redirection

Those who have tried it know that exhortations to "behave yourself or else" are utterly ineffective with unsocialized children. Such verbalization leads to confusion rather than clarification for the children are given no direction about what they should be doing. Put another way, there is no redirection of activity. Threats do not inform children as to what they should be doing. As a rule, they merely make the offensive behavior seem more appealing. Studies show that the undesirable behavior should be pointed out so the children know exactly what they *should stop doing,* and the desired behavior stated clearly so that they know exactly what they should be doing.[2] These studies are discussed

---

[2] Justin M. Aronfreed, "Aversive Control of Socialization," in W. J. Arnold (ed.), *Nebraska Symposium on Motivation 1968* (Lincoln, Nebr.: University of Nebraska Press, 1968); and Jacob S. Kounin and Paul V. Gump, "The Ripple Effect in Discipline," *The Elementary School Journal,* Vol. 59 (December 1956), pp. 158-162.

in Chapter 9. The point here is that children's energies have already been set in motion; they are already doing something. Unless they know what to do instead, their energies cannot be rechanneled. Verbal explosions to "stop that or you'll be sorry" thus may result in worse rather than better behavior.

Method of Redirection

Social responsibility begins when the teacher points out the value of a child's accomplishment for others when appropriate. The good behavior should be reinforced by pointing out the positive effects for others in the classroom as well as for the child. This should never take the form of moralizing but simply mentioning in passing (in a whisper if others are working) how the child has contributed to making the classroom more pleasant and conducive to learning for others. The point is that socialization requires giving or, to put it more strongly, giving up something: the right to do what one feels like doing at a given moment. Through recognition of the good to others as well as oneself, the habit of giving can be reinforced. For example, Jerry's noisy inattention and turning around bothers his neighbors and interferes with their work. He appears to be neither aware of nor concerned about the consequences of his actions for others. When Jerry does exhibit prosocial behavior, however briefly, his teacher pauses alongside Jerry's desk. "That's the way," she says softly. "And thank you for your attention. You're a good neighbor."

Next, the pupil should be given social responsibility. This is necessary for socialization and the development of self-direction and for providing experience in contributing to the well-being of others. A special time can be set aside for socially useful activities or they can be integrated into the ongoing curriculum. The advantage of a special time is that the activities are easily identifiable as socially valuable. This is of utmost importance. Integration into the curriculum depends on three conditions: the nature of the social responsibility, the nature of the curriculum, and whether learners can still make the connection between the activity itself and its social value if it is part of some larger curriculum objective.

But granted this, any curriculum worth having does not leave the development of social responsibility to chance. What we teach and how we teach should provide children and youth with carefully planned opportunities to formulate and meet social goals and should imbue them with the spirit of service to others. Both types of socially useful activities, those which arise from special opportunities or events and those emerging from the curriculum, are discussed in the following section.

When their energies have been channeled in socially useful directions, children should be able to make the connection between what they are doing and the needs and feelings of others. This immediately rules out any busywork as a socially valuable activity.

DISCIPLINE-DEVELOPING ACTIVITIES

Activities that Lead from Special Opportunities

The following examples are socially useful activities that teachers can try with their pupils. Some of them are very short and others extend over a period of time. They include individual and group activities.

Make humorous posters for a children's health center. Introduce the activity to individual youngsters with the question, "What kind of picture would you like to see if you were in the hospital?" The posters can be made available to young hospital patients. (Pupils should not be asked to make posters for a children's hospital if they are not needed.)

Make reading kits. Older children can make a series of shoe-box reading kits filled with personalized reading games for the use of primary-grade children. Materials used are 3 × 5 cards, pictures from magazines, and glue.

Improve the environment. Pupils take Polaroid pictures of aspects of their environment which need to be changed. They then develop a plan for making the needed improvements and put the plan in motion. (This idea can be carried out in conjunction with science and social studies.)

"Adopt" senior citizens. Junior high schoolers participate with residents of nursing homes in a number of activities including reading to them, going for walks, playing games, or listening. Individuals and groups can perform special services for senior citizens on request. One group engaged in this activity registered senior citizens to vote. Senior citizens can also be hosted with parties, fashion shows, and choral concerts.

Serve as volunteers in the special education classroom. In schools in which there are classrooms for severely retarded children, fourth, fifth, and sixth graders can give the retarded youngsters encouragement and help.

Make and bind books. Primary-grade children enjoy making their own books and these generally turn out to be the most frequently checked-out books in the school library.

Establish a buddy system. Primary students can orient kindergartners to the school building, facilities, rules, and regulations. (A buddy system is a good procedure for making new pupils of all ages feel at home in school.)

Make a nature trail for studying outdoor life. This was done by a group of fifth and sixth graders who cleared a mile-long trail and planted trees that were donated.

Wage a campaign against school vandalism. Selected upper elementary-school pupils can sponsor a Vandalism Prevention Week. Schools with beautification and anti-vandalism projects often experience a sharp decline in vandalism. When this happens it is particularly rewarding for the sponsors of such campaigns. These children have feedback that what they have done has made a difference. The objective of the social approach to discipline is to develop the feeling of being a contributing member of society.

Serve as advisers on textbook selection. Pupils of all levels and abilities can provide valuable counsel on texts and reading books.

Compose questions. Unsocialized children seldom give correct responses to questions because they answer impulsively rather than reflectively. Ask them to make up one question on a given topic which will be posed to their classmates.

Make articles for use by handicapped individuals. One ninth-grade metal-shop class designed and made adjustable wheelchair trays for handicapped persons to use at the local community recreational center.

Finding Opportunities for Socially Useful Activities

The foregoing ideas are only representative. Others can be fashioned by teachers to meet the special needs of individual children and youth, the school, and the community. Two criteria which should be used in selecting or designing activities are the social significance of the activity and its power to develop empathy in the unsocialized child.

There is a constant stream of opportunities for socially valuable activities. We can take our cues from special community needs. For example, in one middle-class community where the divorce rate was high, there were many lonely and troubled children. Attacking the problem cooperatively, elementary and senior high schools seized upon it as a wonderful opportunity for social growth. High school students were matched with a young child who needed someone with whom to relate. Each "big brother" or "big sister" saw his or her young charge at least once a week. Together they chose some out-of-school activity (bowling, shopping, trying a new hairdo, or simply taking a walk around the block). In the process of building a relationship, the younger children seemed to gain a measure of self-confidence which carried over into other school activities. For the high-schooler, the commitment to the relationship (with its inevitable ups and downs) was a personally fulfilling learning experience. The pleasure came from meeting the needs of others as well as the feeling of being a contributing member of the community.

A news item that captures the attention of children may lead to a socially valuable activity. To illustrate, fifth graders in a ghetto-slum school followed news accounts about a three-month-old girl who was admitted to the hospital after her father had beaten her and tried to sell her for money to buy narcotics. The father was in jail and the child was not released to the mother because there was no assurance of the mother's ability to care for her baby. Knowing that the battered baby was literally worse off than any orphan, the fifth grade raised $21 to give to the baby. Their teacher realized that this experience in making a contribution to the well-being of the baby would be most valuable if the children could deliver the money to the proper authorities personally and see the baby. This was arranged and a more empathetic experience can hardly be imagined. After the visit to the hospital, one child commented that what the baby really needed was not money but a mother and father to care for her. "If she's adopted, I hope she won't find out that her real daddy tried to sell her," he said. Previously this boy had seemed oblivious to the needs and feelings of others. The teacher felt this to be the most important educational experience that these children had ever had. But the credit belongs to her for recognizing and embracing an opportunity for social growth instead of letting it slide by.

The point of emphasis in the foregoing is that we are literally surrounded by opportunities to cultivate social responsibility in children, and thus help them progress through the stages of discipline. Real life is pregnant with possibilities for creating socially useful activities. All we have to do is recognize them. We do not need a divining rod to do so. What is needed is a clear idea of the social attitudes we hope to inculcate in children.

Activities that Lead
from the Curriculum

Certainly the curriculum itself should seek to develop social responsibility in pupils. Pupil responsibilities for the constructive and generative stages of discipline require that they be given opportunities to identify real problems, propose and test solutions. While such opportunities are now commonplace in social studies, environmental studies, and the like, they are less common but just as possible in other curriculum areas. The following ideas for socially valuable activities illustrate this point.

Teach lessons on counting change and computing interest rates. Selected pupils can plan and teach practical mathematics to others in the class. They can provide counsel on how consumers can avoid being cheated when making purchases.

Teach minicourses. High school students can teach minicourses in art, music, public speaking, and dance at elementary schools. They can also provide tutorial services for elementary pupils.

Make canes for blind people. A high school English class sanded and painted more than 70 canes. The students were reading about Helen Keller in the play, *The Miracle Worker.* They visited a center for blind people and found that it was possible to help the blind by becoming actively involved in a project. The cane idea was suggested and the students quickly adopted it, giving up their lunch periods to complete the job. This activity was socially valuable because the canes provided the blind people with a measure of safety and security without which their freedom of mobility would have been curtailed.

Produce plays. Junior high school drama students can develop productions with which they tour elementary schools. One group developed two productions, the first geared to kindergarten through grade four and the second for fifth and sixth grades. All dialogue was improvised and and props, costumes, and scenery were made by the pupils in the drama class. The production for older children dramatized a historical event (Salem witchcraft trials), integrating the audience into the dramatization. An informal discussion followed the dramatization, making it important that the "theater troop" be informed of the historical facts. This idea should also be useful for any teacher within his or her classroom.

Make equipment for kindergarten rooms. In one school system, high school vocational education students remodeled 40 old high school workbenches for the use of kindergartners, thus providing an excellent learning activity for children, and one to which they reacted with obvious delight.

Plan and prepare a nutritionally sound lunch and invite another class as guests. Pupils of all levels need to develop useful concepts about diet and health. At the luncheon, selected children can explain why certain foods were included on the menu.

Paint permanent murals. Under the guidance of an art teacher or the local museum of art, elementary school youngsters can paint permanent murals on the walls of the school cafeteria, thus improving the physical environment of the school. In one school, every child, kindergarten through grade three, participated in this activity which depicted their city. The mural was viewed by parents at a potluck dinner held in the cafeteria. In another school, every youngster assisted in the painting of a large outdoor mural in the school yard.

Social Responsibility and the Social Studies

As the foregoing ideas demonstrate, socially useful activities can and should grow out of virtually every area in the school curriculum. Nevertheless, it is the social studies which offer the most possibilities for activities involving service to the community. First of all, study of the community leads to ideas for improving the community. Second, an important aim of the social studies is to develop a sense of social responsibility in children and youth.[3] While some pupils develop a feeling of social obligation because they come from homes in which there is a spirit of public service, others will never have this feeling unless it is cultivated by the school. Although giving children a sense of responsibility to their community is a general aim of education, it is a specific aim of the social studies. On the whole, social responsibility is poorly taught. Teachers are still more inclined to have children study *about* community problems than give them firsthand experience in identifying and ameliorating community problems. Both reading and actual experience are needed if children are to develop a spirit of community service.

Finally, many unsocialized pupils have a feeling of alienation from the community.[4] Whether they overcome this feeling and develop instead a sense of community loyalty may depend largely on experiences provided by the school. These experiences are within the province of the social studies. If the children or youth do not get them in social studies they may never have them.

Certainly citizenship is a responsibility which we as teachers must prepare children to assume as adults. However, it would be a mistake to think of the children as citizens only in terms of their future. They have present capacities as contributing members of society. If we as teachers provide an environment to help the children utilize their capacities in the present, we are providing the best possible insurance that they will meet their social responsibilities in the future. How can an elementary school youngster contribute to the well-being of the

---

[3] John Jarolimek, "Some Reflections on a Decade of Reform in Social Studies Education," *Journal of Geography*, Vol. 69 (October 1970), pp. 388-389; and Daniel Tanner and Laurel N. Tanner, *Curriculum Development: Theory into Practice* (New York: Macmillan, 1975), p. 489.

[4] Robert J. Havighurst, *Developmental Tasks and Education* (New York: McKay, 1972), pp. 75-82.

community? Ideas come from study of the community. For example, in one social studies class, a survey of community recreation facilities revealed that there was no safe place for children to use their sleds, causing many sledding accidents each winter. The class planned and made a snow slide on the side of a hill and developed rules and regulations for its safe use.

A group of junior high schoolers studied their small town and found an appalling situation with regard to the sewage system: it did not include the underprivileged neighborhoods. The children launched a vigorous campaign and persuaded the town government to extend the sewage system.

Sixth graders in a decaying urban neighborhood conducted a survey of the physical needs of the area. Topping the list was a park where older people could come and sit on oppressive summer days and mothers could bring their babies and young children; the nearest park was miles away from this apartment-house neighborhood. With the blessing and guidance of community leaders, the children cleared a vacant lot of rubble and planned and built a "vest-pocket" park. This activity was rich in possibilities for intellectual and social growth and afforded the pupils great personal satisfaction. Such activities teach social responsibility in a way that is not possible by simply reading and discussing community problems.

Socialization and Fate Control

One of the problems that compound the difficulty of working with unsocialized children is that they seldom feel responsible for their actions. They tend to feel that their misdeeds "happen" to them. They lack the sense of control over events which is so necessary for self-direction. In teaching social responsibility through socially useful activities we have a rich opportunity to convey to children that their actions do make a difference, and that behavior should be targeted to a desired outcome. A sense of fate control is part of socialization and essential for self-direction.

The last stage of a social studies activity is evaluation: pupils decide whether they have solved the problem of concern to them. For example, in the case of the sewage system, was the campaign to extend it successful? However, an affirmative answer is not enough. Our pupils should also be able to make the connection between what they have done and its benefits for others.

We want children to learn that through thoughtful action, people in a democracy can improve their society. This is probably the most important goal of the social studies. The process of teaching children to guide action with thought is also the process of socialization. Thus it is clear that the social studies have a crucial role in the socialization of children. One of the best ways that this can be done is through socially useful activities.

An Anthropologically Sound Concept

One of the reasons why we have so many discipline problems and why juvenile crime statistics are shooting up at an alarming rate is that we have failed to induct children into a satisfying role in society. Unlike societies in which children are systematically inducted into full participation into the social group, our complex society performs this function in a haphazard and almost indifferent fashion terming the in-between state, adolescence. It is small wonder that we find so many confused and alienated children in our classrooms; the wonder is that there are not more. It is a biological and psychological fact that humans must find some satisfying outlet for activity. In simpler societies in which what is learned transfers directly to living, the children can direct their energies toward accepted educational ends. For the road to achievement is open to them and there are clear signposts along the way.

In our society there is very little harnessing of child and adolescent energy either by the school or other institutions in society. Children cannot be expected to live without an outlet for their energy and this outlet may take the form of antisocial behavior. This is a great tragedy, because most children are ready, willing, and eager to become deeply involved as citizens. Learning to become socially responsible is one of the developmental tasks of childhood and adolescence.[5] Giving children a chance to become socially responsible can combat behavior problems.

The point is that giving children opportunities to engage in socially useful activities is an anthropologically sound idea. Activities such as the ones discussed in this chapter build self-respect, self-confidence, and a commitment to community welfare. They serve to induct pupils into their role as citizens and as a bulwark against discipline problems. While this is very important in elementary school, it becomes crucial in junior high school. This is the age when children become uncertain about their role in society and need opportunities to build self-esteem and social loyalty. Also, as any junior high school teacher knows, it is a period of ebullient energy which can be a positive force if properly channeled, but a source of unhappiness if dissipated or directed toward antisocial ends.

[5] Ibid.

CRITERIA FOR DISCIPLINE-DEVELOPING ACTIVITIES

Should activities be carefully structured or should pupils devise their own ways of getting the job done? What about the unsocialized children who are incapable of exercising self-discipline—can I risk involving them in a group activity? How many children should work together on an activity? Typically, these are the questions teachers ask as they approach the specifics of socially useful activities. They are considered here along with suggestions for maximizing the chances for successful outcomes.

Activities Should Be Structured

Well-structured activities are what we are seeking. However, an activity *becomes* structured through cause-and-effect planning and a review of the consequences. (The snow-slide activity on page 148 is an illustration.) *The structure is in the activity* (diagnosis of the problem, planning a solution, putting it into action, and reviewing the consequences). This is so regardless of who plans it.

There is no denying that unsocialized children and all children need guidance if they are to learn how to structure an activity. But the more children are involved in planning an activity, the more they are likely to feel that their actions really matter, that they have a social value. In addition, cooperative planning does not mean that activities are unstructured. Cooperatively planned activities can be as patterned as teacher-planned activities. (On the other hand, activities planned by teachers can also be formless.)

Planning with others requires communication. Listening to the suggestions of others is just as much a part of communication as making suggestions. Some children cannot listen long enough even to follow the most simple directions. They must be able to do so before they can participate in planning. Independence in managing themselves is learned by degrees. As shown in Chapter 2, being able to listen and follow directions comes first. Next comes participation in developing procedures for reaching a goal.

Unfortunately many teachers simply leave children at the listen-and-follow-directions stage instead of gradually freeing their capacities to become responsible persons. Children should move from social responsibility that is given by the teacher (along with clearly understood procedures) to acquiring a sensitivity to the needs of others and the ability to propose and try out ideas for meeting these needs.

The Minimum Number of Students
Needed Should Work on an Activity

Activities may be tailored for groups or individuals. A group can be formed either by interested volunteers or teacher assignment. In general the number of pupils working on a given activity should be no more than needed to accomplish the task. This is because more children than are required to do the work can cause discipline problems. The purpose of socially valuable activities is to combat, not cause, misbehavior. However, this does not obviate whole-class activities, all-school activities, system-wide activities, or even national activities. A national land utilization survey was conducted in England through the assistance of school children in every region.

Some class activities require subgroup organization. An example is the junior high drama class referred to earlier which toured elementary schools. Members of the class worked on props, scenery, costumes, ideas for improvisations, and acting. Thus the class organized itself quite naturally into subgroups.

On the other hand, at times teachers, for reasons of their own, want the whole class to share in a socially valuable experience. Trips, for instance, are a way of providing concrete experiences for children who need to relate to people and situations that would otherwise remain remote from their lives. To illustrate, it was not enough for the class of fifth graders in a previous example to read about the abused baby. The trip produced the empathy desired because the class moved into the real world of the baby.

Activities Should Hold
Personal Interest

Some children, for whom a group situation is ordinarily inadvisable because they cannot work in close proximity to others (the temptation to poke, punch, quarrel, and interrupt is overwhelming), will become productively engaged with others if they feel personally related to the activity. In other words, interest in the task outweighs the need to disrupt. Of course this is what we hope for in all areas of teaching. Teachers can best facilitate the development of sympathetic identification with a school or community problem by relating it to children's own experience. In the example in which the youngsters constructed a snow slide, the problem was related to their own experience in finding a place to play. Needless to say, personal identification with an activity is facilitated by a teacher who proceeds as though children can make a contribution of value to the school or community.

When a task of social significance holds high interest for unsocialized children, this is a sign that they may be ready to develop the social skills necessary for living and working with others.

Activities Should Involve Genuine Problems

In giving children social responsibility we hope to convey to them that their school and community are improvable and that they have the power to make conditions more pleasant for others, starting perhaps in their own classroom. Redirection of negative behavior serves not only to end the misbehavior but to develop a spirit of service and the habit of thinking about the feelings of others as well as themselves. Therefore it is absolutely essential that activities be based on real school and community needs. This procedure cannot succeed if it is based on busy work or contrived problems. Fortunately opportunities abound for activities that are genuinely socially useful.

Children Should See the Result of an Activity

One cannot overstate the importance of pupils actually seeing how their work has brought pleasure to others. A group of unsocialized teenagers who were involved in making braille bingo cards (a very tedious process) grumbled about how they would never do it again. But when they saw the cards being used at a community recreation center, they grinned and patted each other on the back for making the game possible. The point at which making the braille cards became a socializing experience was when the teenagers saw the cards being put to use by blind people. Similarly, the point at which the activity of collecting money for the abused infant (in an earlier example) had the most power to socialize was when the children actually saw the baby.

In conclusion, this approach to socializing unsocialized children is essentially hopeful, both from the standpoint of classroom behavior and society. Seeing children who were engaged in destructive behavior developing personal-social competence and sensitivity to the needs and feelings of others can afford us great personal and professional satisfaction.

SUMMARY

Unsocialized children function on impulse, doing what they want when they want, regardless of its effect on others. If teaching is to be possible, teachers must pursue the goal of socialization. However, socialization is also important because pupils cannot be self-directing if their behavior is random and unthinking. Schools have not only the right but the obligation to help pupils become socialized.

What we seek goes beyond mechanical obedience to rules and good manners. We want pupils to become sensitive to the needs and problems of others, to plan and act on solutions—to become socially responsible. Social responsibility is part of socialization. The approach to socialization put forward in this chapter is to redirect destructive energies into socially constructive activities. Socially useful activities can lead from the curriculum or special opportunities. An example of an activity leading from the curriculum, in this case a social studies unit on ecology, is a neighborhood beautification project. An example of a socially useful activity leading from special opportunities is to provide special services for senior citizens who are residents of nursing homes. The heart of the impact of these activities lies in their reality; they are ways of helping pupils meet real social problems.

Socially useful activities are an effort to provide situations conducive to developing empathy. Pupils should be able to make the connection between what they are doing and the feelings and needs of others. Socially useful activities can convey to pupils that their actions make a difference. This is important for developing internal locus of control and a satisfying role in society.

Activities may involve individuals, small groups, or the whole class, depending on the nature of the activities. Pupils should see for themselves how their work has brought pleasure to others. Socialization is developmental and to be continuously attained.

Problems and Activities

1. What is your assessment of the idea of redirecting negative behavior into socially useful behavior?
2. Develop a socially useful activity for fourth graders, using the guidelines suggested in this chapter. If possible put the plan into action. Evaluate the activity by determining whether the children are able to make the connection between what they are doing and the needs and feelings of others.
3. Developing social responsibility is an important aim of the social studies. Plan a social studies activity which will help children develop a sense of community responsibility. (Use any grade level that interests you.) If possible, put the plan into action.
4. How can socially useful activities help children to develop a sense of fate control? Give illustrations.
5. In giving junior high school pupils opportunities to engage in socially useful activities are we acting on knowledge from anthropology? Justify your answer.
6. In connection with problem 6, do you think that socially useful activities at this age can decrease discipline problems? Why?
7. Why is it absolutely essential that socially useful activities involve real problems?
8. In this chapter it was pointed out that pupils should actually see the result of their work and how it has brought pleasure to others. Why is this important for socialization? For fate control?
9. Why is empathy important in socialization? In your opinion will the method discussed in this chapter help to develop empathy in unsocialized children? Why?

Dealing with Discipline Problems

9

Although attention to ecological factors can move the balance in favor of discipline and this, in itself, is of enormous importance, it cannot totally eliminate discipline problems. Some pupils have not reached the basic disciplinary stage. It is one task to guide pupils toward developing the responsibilities in this stage, such as the ability to listen and follow directions. It is quite another, however, to deal with the minute-by-minute disruptions that these pupils can cause in classrooms. Moreover, even pupils who have reached the basic disciplinary stage can become unruly and out of control. Therefore, the teacher's concern for classroom discipline is twofold: (1) the teacher must be able to control disruptive pupils and involve them in learning (in some ways a simultaneous process); (2) the teacher must help pupils move upward through the stages of discipline. Hence the teacher has both immediate and developmental concerns. These short-range and long-range concerns are overlapping rather than mutually exclusive, as will be seen. This chapter will attempt to provide insights into what should happen when pupils behave in unacceptable ways.

Before beginning consider that *all* teachers experience behavior problems. How they handle them makes the difference. (Some teachers handle their problems so well that they do not appear to have problems.)

ACCEPTABLE VERSUS UNACCEPTABLE BEHAVIOR

Obviously, the behavior of pupils who disrupt the class is unacceptable. We are concerned because they are interfering with the learning efforts of other pupils. Moreover, our nerves are on edge because, as even the most inexperienced teacher knows, disruptive acts are often contagious. (We can remember our own school days when some mischief-maker dropped a book thereby creating a deafening epidemic of book-dropping.)

In this chapter our main concern is with behavior that disrupts and disturbs the class. However, this should *not* lead the reader to think that all other behavior is acceptable in classrooms. The behavior of a youngster who is daydreaming and unable to begin a paper may not interfere with the efforts of others, yet clearly is unacceptable. As pointed out previously, what is acceptable in class may be determined by the learning goal (what a pupil has to do in order to accomplish the purpose of a given activity at a given time). While the youngsters who cannot seem to start their work may not be bothering anyone, they are impeding their own academic progress. Furthermore, these youngsters may become so frustrated and restless that the next time we look, they may be taking a poke at another child. Not being involved in the work can produce discipline problems. This is so with even the most well-mannered pupils.

DEALING WITH DISRUPTIVE BEHAVIOR

Disruptive behavior can take many shapes and forms, some silly and harmless and others dangerous. Clowning, giggling, and talking out loud while others are working quietly are in the harmless category. Experts are divided in their opinions on how to deal with this kind of behavior. Since it seems to be an attempt by the pupil to gain attention, some authorities suggest that it be ignored. Others are concerned about a potential strategic danger of ignoring misbehavior: the misbehavior could spread to other children.

On the other hand, horseplay with sharp instruments such as knives or scissors must be stopped immediately to avoid disaster. No one has suggested that this kind of behavior be ignored.

Objectives

There are four main objectives in dealing with misbehavior:

1. To end the misbehavior

2. To redirect the pupil into constructive activity
3. To promote long-range developmental goals
4. To continue an uninterrupted flow of classroom activities

In light of the interrelated conception of discipline and learning, it is not enough to end pupils' misbehavior. The pupils must also become engaged in their work. Some teachers make the mistake of having pupils who have misbehaved sit for hours without doing any work instead of helping them to become "rehabilitated learners." The objective must be, as Blom points out, to return the children to the school program as soon as possible.[1] This is true whether the children have been excluded from the classroom because they disrupted it for others or were involved in misbehavior that was settled by the teacher in the classroom.

It is especially important for pupils to begin working again if they have become angry and generated surplus energy that could be directed against others as hostility or resentment. Furthermore, in using their energies constructively, the pupils may begin to feel that they are making progress in meeting the goals of the school. But for this to happen teachers must be willing to let pupils start over again with a clean slate.

Another reason for starting the children working as quickly as possible after misbehaving is that there is less likelihood of a relapse into misbehavior.

Jacob Kounin and Paul Gump developed a strategy for ending pupil misbehavior and returning the pupil to work simultaneously.[2] The teacher defines with clarity the misbehavior and gives the child the appropriate standard of behavior: "Edward, stop bothering Susan and work on your story or read your library book." This strategy can return wayward students to order without reducing educational efficiency. It does not slow down the academic program. On the contrary, it can encourage the rest of the class to continue their work. When teachers clarify what kind of behavior they object to and what kind of behavior they expect, pupils who are watching and listening respond with increased conformance and decreased nonconformance. Thus besides redirecting the problem pupil the strategy can redirect watching pupils who may also be misbehaving. The influence on children who watch the teacher correct a classmate is called a ripple effect. Interestingly, the subjects of Kounin's studies on the ripple effect ranged from kindergarten pupils to graduate students in a college of education. Kounin

---

[1] Gaston E. Blom, "Psychoeducational Aspects of Classroom Management," *Exceptional Children*, Vol. 32 (February 1966), p. 381.

[2] Jacob S. Kounin and Paul V. Gump, "The Ripple Effect in Discipline," *The Elementary School Journal*, Vol. 59 (December 1958), pp. 158-162.

found that college students as well as kindergartners who were not themselves targets of a desist technique were affected by it.[3]

Disciplinary Action and Long-Range Goals.   Whatever means the teacher selects to deal with misbehavior should be consonant with the developmental goals of discipline. It is an unfortunate situation when the disciplinary technique undermines educational and disciplinary goals. As an illustration, giving a pupil an overload of homework as punishment is hardly likely to generate positive attitudes toward education, yet one of the aims of the school is to encourage individuals to seek further education throughout their lives.

Likewise, some teachers unthinkingly use measures that are destructive of developmental goals in discipline. For example, ignoring the clowning and silly child who is unable to even start a paper will not help him reach that first stage of discipline. Disciplinary techniques that the teacher uses to get even with the child are also in conflict with developmental goals. Retribution is at a low level of moral development and is, therefore, a poor technique for a pupil to model. Furthermore it is personally and socially destructive rather than constructive. On the other hand, helping children to find a way to make up for their destructive acts is consonant with the goals of discipline.

The principle that ways of dealing with behavior problems should be in accord with developmental goals is of great importance. Therefore, it will be given a name, the *principle of consonance.*

Eleventh Principle (the principle of consonance): Ways of dealing with misbehavior should be consonant with developmental goals.

Preserving the Learning Atmosphere.   The first three objectives in dealing with discipline problems concern the disruptive pupil. The fourth concerns the class. An effective disciplinary technique should not shatter the learning atmosphere but should permit learning to continue without interruption. However, as one writer observed, it sometimes happens that the control technique used by the teacher disrupts the classroom to a greater extent than the deviancy.[4] This can happen when teachers make mountains out of molehills and overdwell on an incident. Teachers should select their desist techniques in light of the need to preserve the learning atmosphere and keep the program moving.

---

[3] Jacob S. Kounin, *Discipline and Group Management in Classrooms* (New York: Holt, Rinehart and Winston, 1970).

[4] William J. Gnagey, *The Psychology of Discipline in the Classroom* (New York: Macmillan, 1968), p. 33.

This is particularly important in classes of emotionally disturbed children or with a high rate of disruptive behavior. In his study of classroom management problems with emotionally disturbed pupils, Blom found that unless quickly controlled by the teacher, one child's acting-out behavior can ripple through the classroom, causing disorganization.[5] What Blom is describing is an undesirable ripple effect (in contrast to the desirable ripple effect, when a teacher's comments to one pupil result in increased conformance by watching pupils). Remarks made by one pupil to another in a stage whisper and interspersed with sexual curse words are the kind of behavior that Blom found could bring disorganization unless controlled with all deliberate speed.[6] Three other researchers found that teachers who are successful in controlling misbehavior lower the rate of contagion to other pupils.[7]

While control techniques are considered next it would be well to mention some that teachers could use to control the pupil mentioned previously in the stage whisper incident described by Blom. The teacher could try to control the pupil with a stern look. This helps some youngsters, especially if the teacher's "I mean it" behavior includes walking over to the pupil. It did not control the behavior of the emotionally disturbed pupil in this situation. The boy kept on talking and finally had to be taken away from his seat by the teacher who called on the intercommunication speaker for the "standby officer" who took the youngster out of class. Generally, exclusion from class is a last resort and is done in accord with a systematic procedure which includes a warning to the pupil. This procedure is discussed later.

To return to the considerations in controlling disruptive behavior, one final point must be mentioned. In deciding how to deal with a problem, a teacher should consider the effect of what she or he does on the pupils' relationship with their classmates and with the teacher. Peer relationships are enormously important in pupils' lives and a control technique that could lower pupils' status in the eyes of their classmates could, as Gnagey so wisely points out, "trigger more problems than it solves." And as Gnagey goes on to say, "if a control technique is selected that is too harsh or unfair, a deviant may become so angry or afraid that a constructive relationship with the teacher may be virtually impossible from that time on."[8] Gnagey also says, "it would hardly do to gain the control and lose the student."[9]

[5] Blom, op. cit., p. 377.

[6] Ibid.

[7] Jacob S. Kounin, Wallace V. Friesen, and A. Evangeline Norton, "Managing Emotionally Disturbed Children in Regular Classrooms," *Journal of Educational Psychology*, Vol. 57 (February 1966), pp. 1-13.

[8] Gnagey, op. cit., p. 33.

[9] Ibid., p. 32.

Strategies

Before launching into a discussion of what should happen when children misbehave, it may be valuable to take stock of how teachers attempt to handle class problems. In their national study of programs for disturbed children from elementary through senior high school, Morse, Cutler, and Fink found that teachers used three kinds of approaches for maintaining reasonable class limits.[10] First, teachers counseled pupils (individually or as a classroom group) after a problem. Second, pupils were excluded and allowed to return when they said that they were ready to act responsibly. Third, teachers tried to have a good program and reasonable routines. Interestingly, the third approach was considered the best. It is extremely important to know that experienced teachers of disturbed children consider improving the educational program to be the best approach for controlling pupils. This makes perfect sense since classroom discipline must be connected with its purpose, the improvement of learning. Discipline for its own sake never works. It should be no surprise that the choice of teaching materials, the organization of instruction, and the adjustment to individual differences in the classroom should prove to be such important factors in maintaining effective discipline.

While this study concerns the methods used in classrooms containing disturbed children, it has relevance for teachers in regular classrooms. Many disturbed and difficult children are in regular classrooms.

Returning briefly to the second approach, not all experts agree that pupils who have been excluded from the classroom should make the decision about when they should be allowed to return. Hewett, for example, believes that exclusion from class should involve a definite period of time decided on by the teacher rather than the pupils.[11] Exclusion under conditions determined by the pupil could be perceived by the pupil as a reward instead of a punishment.

There are numerous other ways that teachers fall back on to maintain class limits. As revealed by the Morse, Cutler, and Fink study, some of the methods are: reprimands, "counting to five" by the teacher as a warning, making pupils make restitution for damages they cause, withholding recess, late dismissal, isolation, or sending the pupil to the office for discipline. A few of the teachers in the study (6 out of 74) admitted to physical punishment, "unangry" smacking or paddling.[12]

---

[10] William C. Morse, Richard L. Cutler, and Albert H. Fink, *Public School Classes for the Emotionally Handicapped: A Research Analysis* (Washington, D.C.: National Education Association Council for Exceptional Children, 1964).

[11] Frank M. Hewett, *The Emotionally Disturbed Child in the Classroom* (Boston: Allyn and Bacon, 1968).

[12] Morse, Cutler, and Fink, op. cit.

Not all the techniques used by these teachers to control their classes were reported in the study which was conducted by mail surveys. Even if teachers reported all the techniques of which they were aware there were undoubtedly some that they used of which they were unaware. A fascinating study by the late anthropologist Jules Henry found that some teachers who thought of themselves as strict disciplinarians had an incorrect picture of themselves. One teacher was unaware of the reassuring physical touches she gave to pupils when they began to get out of bounds or needed encouragement. She was controlling the class in a way that was unknown to her.[13]

The methods teachers unconsciously use in classrooms are not always supportive and encouraging. Many teachers employ punishment without realizing it. If punishment is used, it should be used consciously. Be that as it may, Henry's point is an important one because it indicates that teachers are not always aware of how they manage their pupils. Without belaboring the point, it seems clear that even very experienced teachers need to become more aware of what they are actually doing in classrooms.

Ignoring Misbehavior. Perhaps the best strategy to begin discussing is the one that requires the teacher to take no action, ignoring the misbehavior. This is not necessarily the easiest strategy. Some teachers are torn between the temptation to say or do something and the knowledge that an incident probably would be better ignored. The inability to ignore is the great weakness of many otherwise good teachers. Ignoring might be the best technique when:

1. The breach of conduct is momentary.
2. The misbehavior is not serious or dangerous.
3. Drawing attention to the incident could interrupt the class or ruin the learning atmosphere.
4. The pupil is usually well-behaved.

The test of a wise decision is whether the class goes on without interruption.

Behavior Modification. Ignoring disruptive behavior has been systematized into an approach for reducing classroom problems. In this strategy, teacher attention in the form of praise for appropriate behavior is used concurrently with ignoring negative behavior. The model of discipline is behavior modification (see Chapter 1). It is being consid-

[13] Jules Henry, "The Problem of Spontaneity, Initiative, and Creativity in Suburban Classrooms," *American Journal of Orthopsychiatry,* Vol. 29 (April 1963), pp. 266-279.

ered here as a control technique and also in terms of its implications for developmental goals.

Behavior modification cannot end a misbehavior "right now" which is one reason why some teachers draw back from this technique. The misbehavior is supposed to end through a process of extinction. Since behavior modification ignores negative behavior it is not a method that can be used when a misbehavior is dangerous, such as when one pupil throws another forcefully to the ground or an aggressive child goes on a rampage of destruction. In these cases quick and decisive action is needed. The pupils must be restrained from indulging in any dangerous acts—held if necessary. (Although as Redl and Wineman pointed out in their classic book on techniques for treatment of aggressive children, this must be done "antiseptically," or on a "behavioral level," so that it is not confused by the children with revenge or rejection.)[14]

Proponents of behavior modification are careful to distinguish between the dangerous misbehaviors for which this method is unsuitable and pupils' classroom behavior which is incompatible with learning. Typically the latter includes: creating noise without permission (vocalization or otherwise), playing, grabbing the property of another pupil, movement from their chair when the pupils have not been given permission to do so, and failing to do work when assigned. Looking at the list of behaviors, one can immediately see a striking parallel with the problems of pupils below the basic disciplinary stage. This is not surprising since most of the children for whom behavior modification is proposed have not achieved basic discipline.

Some studies show that positive results have been obtained when teachers praise appropriate behavior and ignore disruptive behavior. However, O'Leary and his associates took a careful look at these studies, finding that the strategy was not always effective; teachers did not actually ignore all disruptive behavior, and praising appropriate behavior and ignoring disruptive behavior actually created classroom pandemonium.[15]

In their research in classrooms for behavioral problem children, Jones and Miller found that ignoring interrupting behavior in small group discussions was less effective in suppressing this behavior than putting a hand on a pupil's shoulder and making comments such as, "Wait your

---

[14] Fritz Redl and David Wineman, Controls from Within (New York: The Free Press, 1952), pp. 202-203.

[15] K. Daniel O'Leary, Kenneth F. Kaufman, Ruth E. Kass, and Ronald S. Drabman, "The Effects of Loud and Soft Reprimands on the Behavior of Disruptive Students," Exceptional Children, Vol. 37 (October 1970), p. 145.

turn, please." The latter approach led to more orderly discussions than the use of extinction procedures (planned ignoring).[16]

In the use of extinction procedures in classrooms it is important that pupils' misbehavior not be reinforced by their classmates. This requires that the teacher obtain the cooperation of the children's classmates in ignoring the misbehavior. As MacMillan, Forness, and Trumbull point out, this can lead to scapegoating.[17] Certainly teachers should plan very carefully before they attempt to enlist the cooperation of the class in ignoring a classmate's misbehavior. It must be made clear to the class that their classmate has a problem in self-control and needs help. Since they like and want to help him or her they can best do so by ignoring his or her misbehavior.

Some teachers may obtain positive results from the use of reinforcement procedures. Indeed it may be argued that good teachers tend to reinforce desirable behavior (including academic achievement) through social praise and rewards, although these teachers may not ignore disruptive behavior. We may also argue, as we have discussed, that under certain conditions misconduct might be better ignored. Yet this is not the same as the systematic use of conditioning-extinction procedures in shaping children's behavior.

As Howard Garner points out, "behavior modification has been criticized for building dependence on external reinforcers and decreasing internal control or self-discipline."[18] A question that must be asked as teachers make judgments about a control tactic is, *to what extent does it give the pupils insight into their own responsibility for what happens to them?* The aim of the personal-social growth model is to develop internal locus of control. As Lawrence and Winschel point out, "the development of internality appears fundamental to education in a free society. It suggests responsibility and self-reliance—the individual as an effective agent of his own destiny."[19]

The idea that children and youth must be helped to see the relationship between their behavior and its outcome and assume responsibility

---

[16] F. Jones and W. H. Miller, "The Effective Use of Negative Attention for Reducing Group Disruption in Special Elementary Classrooms." Unpublished manuscript, University of California at Los Angeles, Department of Psychiatry, 1971.

[17] Donald L. MacMillan, Steven R. Forness, and Barbara M. Trumbull, "The Role of Punishment in the Classroom," *Exceptional Children*, Vol. 40 (October 1973), p. 88.

[18] Howard S. Garner, "A Truce in the War for the Child," *Exceptional Children*, Vol. 42 (March 1976), p. 318.

[19] Elizabeth A. Lawrence and James F. Winschel, "Locus of Control: Implications for Special Education," *Exceptional Children*, Vol. 41 (April 1975), p. 483.

for both is not new. It has its roots in progressive educational theory and the conception of democracy. In fact the idea that people can control, direct, and improve their own lives and the society in which they live is the democratic ideal. The point is that in our treatment of disruptive pupils (and others as well), we must try to help them to develop a sense of control over the events in their lives. The life space interview is such an approach (see pp. 167–169).

Returning to the discussion on behavior modification, self-direction does not develop out of thin air. A ladder must be built to internal control. Basic discipline must be established first and when properly used, behavior modification can be a valuable building block for basic discipline. Thus behavior modification is not inconsonant with the main goal of education, self-direction.

Training.   When pupils work in disorderly ways, teachers frequently turn to the training model. One pupil may be asked to do something over "the right way" or this demand may be made of the entire class. If Johnny runs in the hall, he may be told "Go back and walk." Similarly, if the class thunders up the stairs ahead of the teacher instead of walking quietly, the teacher may call, "Come back and do it quietly." If the teacher thinks that the misbehavior might be an incipient sign that the class is getting out of control, she may ask them to practice walking up the stairs more than once.

There is more involved here than training. Punishment is also involved. In making pupils practice, the teacher is also punishing them for their misbehavior and, as teachers know, this can suppress the misbehavior, at least for awhile. Although a time-worn and almost disreputable technique, "asking the pupil to do it the right way" can be effective because an alternative to the undesirable behavior is provided and reinforced. Two final points should be mentioned. A rationale should be provided for pupils; even if the reasons for doing something one way instead of another are clear to the teacher they may not be to pupils. And constant criticism or punishment diminishes its effectiveness; pupils become adept at "tuning out" a berating teacher and repeated punishments tend to become "old hat" and cease arousing much anxiety.

Verbal Control: Teaching without Screaming.   Verbal control is usually the first resort of a teacher. This is quite understandable in view of the fact that teaching involves direction and redirection. Therefore verbal control is clearly tied in with teaching. Although verbalization is the strategy that teachers use most to control disruptive pupils, it is not always effective. In this section we will attempt to see how it can be made more effective.

In looking into alternatives to ignoring disruptive behavior when praising and ignoring are not effective, O'Leary and his colleagues found that most teacher reprimands were loud in nature and could be heard by other children in the class. When the teachers were asked to use soft reprimands, audible only to the pupil in question, the frequency of disruptive behavior declined in most of the children. Reversal of the procedure again resulted in an increase of disruptive behavior and return to soft reprimands caused such behavior to decline.[20]

The advantages of soft over loud reprimands are summed up by the researchers as follows:

Soft reprimands offer several interesting advantages over loud ones. First of all, a soft reprimand does not single out the child so that his disruptive behavior is made noticeable to others. Second, a soft reprimand is presumably different from the reprimands that disruptive children ordinarily receive at home or in school, and consequently, it should minimize the possibility of triggering conditioned emotional reactions to reprimands. Third, teachers consider soft reprimands a viable alternative to the usual methods of dealing with disruptive behavior.[21]

There are four additional advantages to soft reprimands. First, such reprimands provide a model of speaking softly. This is important in view of the complaint voiced frequently by teachers that some children do not talk, they shout. Pupils whose communication from adults consists largely of shouted commands and reprimands are apt to respond in kind. As the researchers point out, for the most part disruptive children receive loud reprimands at home and in school.

Second, soft reprimands can have a calming effect whereas loud reprimands can make children jumpy and nervous and unable to concentrate.

Third, in order to be heard, a soft reprimand has to be made while the teacher is physically close to the child and giving him or her individual attention. This can be far more effective than a shout from a distant teacher who is obviously busy with something or someone else.

Fourth, and perhaps most important, soft reprimands require less teacher energy than loud reprimands. The energy saved from screaming can be used more pleasantly in teaching.

[20] O'Leary, Kaufman, Kass, and Drabman, op. cit.
[21] Ibid., p. 146.

A final word: reprimands are not being recommended as a substitute for praise.

Control through Proximity.   Sometimes moving toward disruptive pupils is enough to end their misbehavior. If pupils know how to do their work but cannot seem to resist bothering others, just standing beside them silently and thoughtfully may help them to concentrate. However, there is more than one way to reduce the physical distance between teacher and pupil. Proximity can be achieved when the teacher remains in place and asks to see the pupil's paper or calls the pupil to the blackboard.

Another strategy is to change seat locations, separating pupils whose close proximity to each other is distractive. The attention seeker can be seated directly in front of the teacher so that wherever the teacher looks in the classroom his or her gaze also includes this pupil.

The Psychodynamic Approach.   An approach which has not gained wide acceptance by teachers is the psychodynamic approach which is focused on the need to understand the psychic origin of disturbed behavior and to accept the pupil without censure. The aim is to build up a warm and trusting relationship between teacher and pupil so that formal learning can take place. As mentioned, the psychodynamic model of discipline is influenced by Freudian psychoanalytic theory, and as Hewett and Blake state, "the teacher may assume in part the role of a therapist who attempts to understand the psychodynamics of the child's problems."[22]

Beside the point made earlier that understanding is not enough, total acceptance of disturbed behavior in an atmosphere of warmth and friendliness is pretty hard for teachers to maintain. Teachers have to keep the program of activities moving. Anything that threatens to slow the program down or bring it to an unfortunate end must be dealt with, as must anything that could endanger pupils. This is part of the teacher's job. The permissive orientation of the psychodynamic approach makes it impractical for teachers.

Since the psychodynamic approach is based on the premise that the best way to deal with disruptive children is to accept all of their behavior, it does not help them to learn to discriminate between appropriate and inappropriate behavior. The approach ignores the intimate relationship between basic discipline and cognitive development. It turns

---

[22] Frank M. Hewett and Phillip R. Blake, "Teaching the Emotionally Disturbed," in Robert M. W. Travers (ed.), *Second Handbook of Research on Teaching* (Chicago: Rand McNally, 1973), p. 660.

its back on the social function of the school which is to help pupils learn to live together. For these reasons the psychodynamic approach is inconsonant with developmental goals. There is one final reason: an approach can be neither practical nor wise, if limits are child-determined rather than teacher-determined.

Life Space Interviewing.   Teachers cannot be psychiatrists. But they do have a role in helping pupils whose behavior has exceeded tolerable limits to see their behavior as it really is and to plan constructively for change. Many children lack a sense of reality about their behavior. For example, Kevin may feel that he is being picked on by other children when in reality it is he who is the aggressor. After just so much of Kevin's bullying, some pupils begin to retaliate and he gets into trouble. Lecturing or verbal nagging is likely to detach Kevin further from reality by increasing his hostility against an interfering adult (the teacher). Indeed, even the most reality-related pupil often will become defensive in the face of "a good talking-to" by an adult nor is kind criticism or the promise of rewards or punishments the right approach to use with Kevin. He needs to see his own role in what happens to him so that it isn't always the fault of "those other guys." Furthermore, Kevin needs to develop a sense of inner control—to feel like an agent in his own destiny. The life space interview is a technique with real potential for helping children like Kevin.

In describing life space interviewing, it is, perhaps, best to begin by saying what the technique is not. It is not an attempt to delve into the past events in a pupil's life as a psychiatrist might do. It is, as described by Hewett and Blake, "a form of reality-oriented, therapeutic 'first aid,' in which the teacher discusses a given problem in the immediate context within which it has occurred."[23]

The origin of the life space interview is most interesting. In his work with badly disturbed children in a residential treatment center in Detroit in the late 1940s, Fritz Redl and his associates used what they called a "counter-distortional interview."[24] As the name suggests, the purpose was to correct the distorted perceptions of youngsters about their own behavior. Like Kevin, the children at Pioneer House were deficient in the ability to see how their behavior contributed to a situation. The interviewer's style was to initiate discussion with the youngster about what had happened, and after checking and probing, confronting him with what he had really done, making him aware of his real problems. Unless children understood and admitted that they were

[23] Ibid., p. 674.
[24] Redl and Wineman, op. cit., pp. 262-267.

in fact involved in the misdeed, there was no way to start working with them on the problem.

The foregoing concept was developed into a theory and made operational for teachers. As Redl pointed out, "the life space interview is closely built around the child's direct life experience in connection with the issues which become the interview focus. Most of the time it is held by a person who is perceived by the child to be part of his 'natural habitat or life space,' with some pretty clear role and power-influence in his daily living."[25] We can easily see how the teacher fits this description.

William C. Morse worked out a specific set of procedures for teachers.[26] The steps in life space interviewing are:

1. In a nonthreatening way, ask the pupil to tell what happened. The purpose of this first step is two-fold: to find out the pupil's own perceptions of the event and to be an empathic listener so that trust is established. (If more than one pupil is involved, attention must be given to balanced listening.)
2. Try to determine if the problem is really the central issue. Are there other related problems? As we have seen, learning problems often lie at the heart of behavior problems. Some pupils are so confused and frustrated about their work that they strike out in anger through fighting and hitting.
3. Ask the pupil "Well, what do you think should be done about this?" Often, the pupil will make a self-commitment for change. Some pupils will suggest that they make restitution for destruction that they have caused. As Morse points out, reasonable discussion, in which the factors bearing on the problem are brought into the open, often leads to resolution of the problem at this stage. If not, the teacher must go on to step four.
4. Discuss the realities of what will happen should the behavior continue. Here it is imperative that the teacher know the policies and resources of his or her school. One does not, for example, say to the pupil that he will be suspended if no one is ever suspended from that school.
5. Elicit from the pupil how the pupil thinks he or she might be helped and what the teacher might be able to do to help the pupil control the behavior impulse in question.
6. Develop a follow-through plan with the pupil. What will we have to do if this happens again? The point made in step 4 must be repeated here: any plan must be conceived within the limitations of school resources.

The life space interview can be a technique of great value. The most

[25] Fritz Redl, "The Life Space Interview," *American Journal of Orthopsychiatry,* Vol. 29 (January 1959), p. 5.
[26] William C. Morse, "Working Paper: Training Teachers in Life Space Interviewing," *American Journal of Orthopsychiatry,* Vol. 33 (July 1963), pp. 727-730.

obvious surface evidence often shows up in improved self-control. However, we are concerned with more than overt behavior. We seek genuine change in the pupils and are concerned with helping them to move upward through the stages of discipline. The life space interview is a technique that is designed both to end unacceptable surface behavior and to develop internal locus of control. Therefore it is in accord with developmental goals and meets our principle of consonance.

The life space interview follows the personal-social growth model of discipline.

Group Forces. In and of itself, the class group can be a powerful force against individual misconduct. Often, burned by the scornful look of classmates, pupils will stop clowning and pay attention, anxious to get back in the good graces of their friends. However, an alliance between the teacher and the class group can be that much more powerful. When the teacher makes the point clear that she has the class behind her, misbehaving individuals often come quickly to order. The following case is illustrative:

> Everyone was in line for lunch except James and Richard who were in the back of the room, arms akimbo, posed unmistakably for a fight. James was dancing around Richard as Miss Jones, who had her hand on the doorknob, said, "James. Richard. You're holding us up. We're hungry and we'd like to go to lunch." She was echoed by a chorus of, "James, come on. Richard, come *on*. Cut it out you guys. We want to go to lunch." James and Richard dropped their hands to their sides and ambled over.

Probably no other way of handling the situation could have been more effective. While addressing James and Richard, Miss Jones was also communicating to the class that these boys were holding them up from lunch. This prevented the spread of the misbehavior and, at the same time, brought the pressure of the group to bear on the disrupters. It also stopped a fight before any blows were landed. Here the teacher was using the group dynamics model of discipline.

Avoiding Confrontations. Some teachers never seem to have blowups or fights in their classroom while others have them all the time. The difference is particularly striking when the teachers are next door to each other and have pupils of similar backgrounds and ability levels. The classroom management problems faced by these teachers are the same, it is the way that they are handled that makes the difference. A good classroom manager seldom has fights because he or she heads them off before the pupils are out of control. Being able to head off a fight requires that the teacher be aware that the trouble is brewing. The managerial ability that is central here is "withitness," the term coined by Kounin which means that a teacher knows what is going on in the classroom and has conveyed this knowledge to pupils.

The following case transpired some years ago at Continuation High School in San Francisco. As will be seen, the teacher did not have withitness. The story should be prefaced by explaining that continuation high schools aim to provide a program leading to graduation for the high school student who is unable to adjust to the mainstream high school and were among the first "alternative schools." (They have existed by law in California since 1919.)

It was a hot, still day in March. Some twenty or so students were in the class, carving designs on linoleum blocks for block prints. Elizabeth M, the intern teacher, was working closely with a group of five in what seemed to be a pleasant and serene situation. But she was oblivious to the nature of the conversation in progress in another part of the room. Jackie S was attempting to impress Frankie A and Eddie B with his famous relatives. So far they had remained unimpressed and even, it seemed, were growing a bit annoyed. "My cousin is Jackie Robinson," said Jackie. "And your mother is Jungle Jim," retorted Eddie. Jackie's response was explosive and uncontrolled. He raised his tool, poised to strike. At that instant, the room began to rock. An earthquake of considerable magnitude on the Richter scale was in progress. All was forgotten in the terrifying tremor.

Seemingly, natural forces were in league with Elizabeth. But since such forces cannot be depended upon, it is better for teachers to have withitness.

Teachers should avoid conflicts or power struggles with pupils. While dangerous aggression should be stopped immediately through protective restraint, rebellious behavior is another matter entirely. It is usually better to ignore short-lived rebellious behavior or try another tack than to make a threat that cannot be carried out.

Thus if a pupil says "I won't," or "Try and make me," when asked to take out the science book, a teacher's best strategy may be to ignore the remark as undeserving of a response. The pupil may have the book out the next time the teacher looks. Another approach might be to say "What was that? I didn't hear you." This gives the pupil a chance to back down without losing face with his or her peers. The pupil may say, "I didn't say anything," and take out the book. At this point teachers should congratulate themselves on a strategy that worked and *forget* the matter, getting on with the business of teaching.

If the pupil says, "I said, make me," the teacher may respond in several ways without getting in a corner. She might say for all to hear, "See me at 3:10" (dismissal time). Another response might be, "Well, the rest of us have to move on. We can't waste any more time." This last is perfectly true. The problems of one pupil should not be allowed to interfere with the right to learn of a whole class.

What must be remembered is that the really important test of whether a strategy works is the educative result, not who came out the victor. What we aim for is the pupils' involvement in their work. But whatever else teachers do, they should avoid "painting themselves into a corner" (making threats which they cannot deliver, or should not even *try* to deliver.) In a power struggle, there is always the chance that the teacher could lose.

The teachers' attitude should always be one of positive expectancy. The pupils should be expected to learn and to follow directions. If teachers sense trouble, then it may be necessary to use as a strategy one of their top skills, acting. In so doing they go to extremes to communicate a positive expectancy. Very often, the acting causes a shift in the attitude of pupils who refuse to do assigned work.

The Teacher as "Protector"

A problem which is within the teacher's scope of responsibility, yet one which many teachers all but ignore is the bullying of pupils by other pupils. Since most of the bullying and ganging up takes place before or after school, teachers are likely to feel that it does not concern them. They could not be more wrong. Children aggressing against children outside the classroom can affect what happens inside the classroom. Children who are terribly frightened cannot learn. The fear of a child who has been warned, "We'll get you after school," is all but paralyzing. All that youngster can think of is what might happen when it's time to go home.

In recent years, the problem has been complicated by the practice of extortion in some school. Pupils have been found to extort regular sums of money from their schoolmates with the promise that, if the money is forthcoming, they will leave them alone. Usually the victims are warned, "If you tell anyone, we'll get you."

Teachers must be concerned about the safety of their pupils. They must always be alert to scapegoating and threats made against pupils by pupils. When they feel that there is more than an idle threat involved they can lessen pupils' chances of being beaten up, persecuted, or robbed by asking older youngsters to escort them home or by making other arrangements for their safe conduct home.

Pupils should also be told not to flash money around in school or on the playground. They should always keep their money in their pockets until it's time to pay.

PUNISHMENT

When teachers think about punishment, they tend to think of physical "hurt" in the form of spanking or a ruler coming down on a pupil's knuckles. Thus teachers may say "I don't use punishment," when what they really mean is "I don't use one form of punishment, physical aversives." For there is more to punishment than corporal punishment. As MacMillan, Forness, and Trumbull note, punishment depends on the perception of the pupil, the recipient.[27] Thus a teacher frowns or shakes of the head could be punishment for some children, although many teachers would not perceive these behaviors as punishment.

On the other hand, what a teacher considers punishment may not be effective because it is not perceived as punishment by the pupil. Thus while a teacher may think that there is nothing worse than being scolded in class before their classmates, unless scolding in public is aversive (a noxious stimulus) to the pupils, the punishment will not be effective. As stated by MacMillan, Forness, and Trumbull, "no matter how noxious or aversive a particular consequence may seem to the punisher, it is the recipient's perception which determines the effect."[28] This point is enormously important for two reasons. First, teachers sometimes do things unknowingly that have punishing effects. Second, as these three researchers point out, there are no aversives which work in all cases except perhaps aversives such as spankings, which probably explains why corporal punishment so often comes up in teacher discussions about punishment.[29] Corporal punishment can have other noxious effects, as will be noted.

The only way teachers can tell whether the approach that they use is effective (aversive) is by the pupil's response. If the misbehavior decreases, it is aversive. But if the misbehavior increases, it is a positive reinforcer! Aversives include denial of privileges, verbal reprimand, scolding, social disapproval, and many other consequences, aside from those already mentioned. As might be expected, many teachers use aversives that are too harsh. When this happens the pupil's response could be avoidance of school and teachers.

[27] MacMillan, Forness, and Trumbull, op. cit., pp. 86-87.
[28] Ibid.
[29] Ibid., p. 87.

Effective Use of Punishment

Providing Alternatives.   Researchers have found that punishment is particularly effective if teachers inform pupils about alternatives to the antisocial behavior.[30] It is important that the alternatives be contrasting behaviors that are incompatible with the antisocial behavior. Say MacMillan, Forness, and Trumbull, "it is not enough that the teacher reprimand a child for grabbing a toy away from another child or scold him for fighting. One must also show the child how to share the toy or ask for it politely and must praise the child for doing so."[31]

This directive recalls the principle of consonance. In showing the pupils how to act, the teacher is helping them to move upward through the stages of discipline. Therefore the idea of providing prosocial alternatives for antisocial behavior is harmonious with the principle. Moreover, the suggestion that the desirable alternative be a contrasting behavior supports the strategy of substituting socially useful for destructive behavior (see Chapter 8).

By providing prosocial alternatives, the teacher is helping pupils to discriminate between acceptable and unacceptable behavior. Moreover, as Aronfreed points out, alternatives are reinforcing because they avoid punishment and lead to rewarding outcomes.[32]

Related to the foregoing discussion, researchers have found that providing a rationale along with punishment increases its effectiveness.[33] Giving a verbal explanation is also consonant with the developmental goal of understanding the basis for reasonable rules and procedures.

Timing of Punishment.   An important factor in the effectiveness of punishment is timing, the point at which the consequence follows the deviant behavior. In general, the earlier that punishment is administered during a deviant behavior, the more effective it is in suppressing the behavior. Researchers have found that punishment delivered after completion of the act is considerably less effective than punishment at the beginning of the act and that, further, the longer one waits between

[30] Ibid., p. 92.

[31] Ibid.

[32] Justin M. Aronfreed, "Aversive Control of Socialization," in W. J. Arnold (ed.), *Nebraska Symposium on Motivation 1968* (Lincoln, Nebr.: University of Nebraska Press, 1968).

[33] Ross D. Parke, "Effectiveness of Punishment as an Interaction of Intensity, Timing, Agent Nurturance, and Cognitive Structuring," *Child Development*, Vol. 49 (March 1969), pp. 213-235; and J. Allen Cheyne and Richard H. Walters, "Intensity of Punishment, Timing of Punishment, and Cognitive Structure as Determinants of Response Inhibition," *Journal of Experimental Child Psychology*, Vol. 7 (April 1969), pp. 231-244.

initiation of the misconduct and the administration of punishment, the less effective is punishment in inhibiting the behavior.[34]

In sum, as MacMillan, Forness, and Trumbull say:

> For the teacher these findings would indicate that the earlier in the response sequence one can administer punishment, the greater will be the punishing effect. In addition, instead of punishing a child after he has already committed a piece of misbehavior it is probably better to wait and punish him just as he begins to repeat the behavior, at which point the punishment will be more effective. The above evidence casts doubt on practices in which children are sent to the office for punishment "when the principal gets around to it" or in which a teacher watches a child complete an act of misbehavior, carefully waits for him to finish, and then punishes.[35]

Granted that early punishment is more effective, there may be times when it is impossible to punish early in the misbehavior. The evidence available suggests that the effects of delayed punishment can be increased if the teacher describes the misbehavior or has the child describe what he or she has done wrong before administering the punishment.[36]

Relationship between Teacher and Pupil.   Punishment is most effective when the child has formed a positive attachment to the parent (or teacher) serving as a socializing agent. The reason is that the withdrawal of affection is aversive to the pupil.[37] Hence teachers who have built up positive relationships with pupils and use punishment are in actuality using two kinds of punishment, while the teachers who lack this relationship use only the aversive because withdrawal of affection will cause little anxiety. The teachers who have formed positive relationships are also more likely to be able to use social rewards because their approval is valued.

Another Chance

Many teachers favor "giving the pupils another chance" when they misbehave instead of punishing the first time the deviant behavior occurs. A point of importance here is that consistency is crucial for the

[34] R. H. Walters, R. D. Parke, and V. A. Cane, "Timing of Punishment and the Observation of Consequences in Others as Determinants of Response Inhibition," *Journal of Experimental Child Psychology*, Vol. 2 (September 1965), pp. 10-34.

[35] MacMillan, Forness, and Trumbull, op. cit., p. 90.

[36] Ibid., p. 93.

[37] Ibid.

effective use of punishment. Teachers must follow through on any threats of punishment. The teacher should not ignore the misbehavior if it happens a second time, or the pupil may think, "I guess she didn't mean it." Other pupils who are aware of the situation may also make erroneous conclusions about their behavior. Steven may think, "Well, Larry got out of his seat again and she didn't say anything, so I guess it's okay for me to get out of my seat."

When teachers decide not to punish but to give a second chance, this should be part of a plan. Ott developed a four-step plan that he found particularly successful in dealing with discipline problems with normal as well as emotionally disturbed adolescents.[38] Step one involves restating the rule that was violated and explaining why the act is unacceptable. Step two occurs if the violation happens again. The pupil is given the choice between punishment now or returning to work with the understanding that the next time he or she will be a three-time loser and will automatically receive punishment and also told what the punishment will be. Step three is followed if the violation occurs again and the promised punishment is used. It is pointed out to the pupil that this was his or her choice. Step four is to consider the incident closed and not to mention it again.

Exclusion

A commonly used technique for suppressing defiant behavior is to exclude the pupil from the classroom. If used, exclusion should follow a plan. Hewett suggests five points to consider in exclusion.[39]

1. It should occur only after the pupil's behavior has exceeded previously stated limits.
2. It should occur matter-of-factly rather than as angry retaliation by a distraught teacher.
3. It should be explained to the pupil as an aid to learning rather than as arbitrary punishment.
4. The period of time for exclusion should be decided by the teacher, not the pupil.
5. When the time-out period has passed, the pupil should immediately return to class and the matter should be considered closed.

Suspension.   A commonly used technique for dealing with misconduct in some schools is exclusion from school for a specific period of time. In other schools suspension is rare or practically nonexistent. It

---

[38] John F. Ott, "Teaching the Emotionally Disturbed," *National Association of Secondary School Principals Bulletin*, No. 236 (March 1958), p. 181.

[39] Hewett, op. cit.

is doubtful whether pupils profit from being suspended. Indeed, for some pupils suspension may actually function as a positive reinforcer of misbehavior (reward) rather than as punishment. Keeping youngsters out of school probably will not help them unless something is also being done about their problems. Pupils who are suspended due to serious difficulties in school need help and they need it quickly. Some school systems do provide emergency assistance for pupils excluded from school. For example, the Emergency Evaluation Clinic of the San Francisco Unified School District attempts to provide an immediate assessment (within twenty-four hours) of the suspended pupil's abilities, emotional status, and academic achievement. Parental involvement is actively sought and recommendations for needed changes are made by the staff.[40]

Suspension is a complex issue, involving others besides the pupil in question. While it is easy to argue the case against suspension from the standpoint of the pupil's right to an education, in some instances the health and safety of other pupils may be involved. Suspension probably cannot be rejected out of hand when pupils terrify other pupils and teachers.

Corporal Punishment

"The message the paddle transmits to children is that superior physical size and strength is a powerful determinant of justice—a lesson they are likely to apply to their smaller and weaker contemporaries."[41] This comment by *The New York Times* on a judgment by the Supreme Court that teachers may resort to corporal punishment in disciplining pupils under state law neatly sums up a powerful argument against corporal punishment. For corporal punishment teaches that "justice" is determined by who is bigger and stronger and that primitive ways are best for dealing with problems. Needless to say, corporal punishment is inconsonant with long-range developmental goals.

Reutter and Hamilton point out that while many cases involving corporal punishment have reached the courts, "Corporal punishment per se is not a prohibited 'cruel and unusual punishment.' "[42] They go on to state, however, that many local school boards have rules forbidding corporal punishment or giving specified conditions under which it may be used.[43]

[40] Laurel N. Tanner and Daniel Tanner, "News Notes," *Educational Leadership,* Vol. 27 (February 1970), p. 553.

[41] *The New York Times,* October 22, 1975, p. 44.

[42] E. Edmund Reutter, Jr. and Robert R. Hamilton, *The Law of Public Education* (Mineola, N.Y.: The Foundation Press, 1976), p. 556.

[43] Ibid., p. 557.

In 1977, the Supreme Court, by a 5-to-4 majority, decided that school children are not protected by the Constitution against corporal punishment, no matter how severe or arbitrary. "The school child has little need for the protection of the Eighth Amendment," the Court argued, because state laws provide safeguards and the school is an "open institution" subject to community supervision.[44]

Yet corporal punishment can and does expose children to excessive physical force. In a survey of Dayton, Ohio, teachers, nearly half of the teachers were unable to define "reasonable corporal punishment" as permitted by state law. The 51 percent who gave the correct answer (paddling on the buttocks) varied widely on the amount and degree of severity. Principals had similar difficulties in answering the question.[45]

Other major findings of the study which was conducted jointly by the local chapter of the League of Women Voters and the American Association of University Women, are that corporal punishment is being used for a wide variety of reasons, often personal; that it is being applied in a variety of forms, often in anger and often without adult witnesses; and last, but not least, many teachers do not know other means for solving classroom problems.

The majority of teachers and principals agreed that they need training in alternatives to corporal punishment and that more guidance counselors could help both teachers and children.

It is of interest that a measure to abolish corporal punishment in Britain's schools was rejected by the House of Commons in 1976.[46] The caning of boys is permitted in the majority of schools. In other nations of the European Economic Community (of which Britain is a member) teachers would be liable to a charge of criminal assault if they struck their pupils. Eastern Europeans frequently cite the beating of youngsters in school as an illustration of Britain's unchanged Victorian cruelty.[47]

Corporal punishment can also leave psychological scars as the following reminiscence shows:

> I attended English Day and Boarding Schools where "six of the best" whacks on a child's rear or hand was common. I remember that many children would urinate or defecate in their pants from fear during or shortly before they were caned. Very few teachers retained self-control while administering a beating; I and other children developed blood blisters when the "brutes" thrashed us.
>
> The pain was excruciating, but short-lasting. The mental pain lasted for

[44] *Ingraham vs. Wright,* No. 75-6527 (U.S. 1977).

[45] Dayton Public Schools, "Corporal Punishment: Is It Needed?" *Schoolday,* Vol. 5 (May 7, 1973), pp. 1, 4.

[46] *The New York Times,* January 21, 1976, p. 39.

[47] Ibid.

many years, especially for children with inferiority complexes or lack of self-confidence. Children that had difficulty adjusting to the school environment found it harder to cope as time went on.[48]

It has long been recognized that children have some rights of their own, at least the right to be treated with loving care and decency. Some of the children in our classrooms have been brutalized elsewhere but there is nothing to be gained by further brutality. Indeed there is something to be lost, an educational and developmental opportunity. Moreover, making children learn or behave appropriately because they are afraid not to is incommensurate with the goal of making learning and appropriate behavior rewarding in and of itself. It is preferable to teach children to act for the pleasure of doing than to force them by the threat of punishment, physical or otherwise.

SUMMARY

In dealing with misbehavior we hope to end the misbehavior, engage pupils in their work, promote developmental goals, and maintain the flow of classroom activities. Disciplinary techniques should be consonant with developmental goals.

An incident might best be ignored when momentary, not serious or dangerous, and calling the incident to attention would interrupt the class, and the pupil is usually well-behaved. When misbehavior is dangerous, quick action must be taken and the pupils restrained from hurting themselves or others. This must be done on a "behavioral level" so that it is not confused by children with rejection or revenge.

Behavior modification can be effective in dealing with classroom behavior that is incompatible with learning (constant talking and vocalization, noisy inattention, getting out of the chair without permission, and the like). Most of these behaviors are characteristic of pupils below the basic disciplinary stage. Behavior modification can be a valuable tool for basic discipline and when properly used is not inconsonant with the development of self-direction.

Research has found that the use of soft reprimands (as opposed to loud reprimands) can cause disruptive behavior to decline. Soft reprimands, audible only to the pupils in question, do not bring their disruptive behavior to the notice of others. They provide a model of speaking softly and are less likely to trigger emotional reactions because they are different from the reprimands disruptive pupils usually receive.

[48] *The New York Times*, June 1, 1974, p. 28.

The permissive orientation of the psychodynamic approach makes it impractical for teachers and does not help pupils to discriminate between appropriate and inappropriate behavior. Life space interviewing, on the other hand, is a form of therapeutic first aid in which the teacher discusses the realities of a given problem with the pupil and a follow-through plan is developed. The life space interview can be a valuable technique for ending misbehavior and developing internal locus of control.

Classroom groups can be a powerful force for bringing misbehaving pupils to order. A good classroom manager heads fights off before pupils get out of control and avoids power struggles with pupils. The teacher's attitude should communicate the positive expectancy that pupils will learn and follow directions.

No matter how punishing a particular consequence may seem to a teacher, it is the pupil's perception which determines the effect. The only way a teacher can determine whether an approach is aversive (effective) is by the pupil's response. Aversives include verbal reprimand, scolding, social disapproval, denial of privileges, corporal punishment, and other consequences. Prosocial alternatives to punishment (showing the pupil how to act) are reinforcing because they avoid punishment and can have rewarding social outcomes.

Exclusion from the classroom should follow a plan with the time for exclusion determined by the teacher, not the pupil. [Although the courts have not found corporal punishment "a prohibited 'cruel and unusual punishment,' " many local school boards prohibit corporal punishment or specify the conditions under which it may be used. Corporal punishment teaches that primitive ways are best for dealing with problems and is inconsonant with long-range developmental goals. However a misbehavior is handled, by returning pupils to work as quickly as possible we are helping them to meet the goals of the school. This in itself is good behavioral insurance; it can prevent relapses into misbehavior.]

Experienced teachers of emotionally disturbed children have found improving the educational program the best approach for controlling pupils. This is important for all teachers since many disturbed and difficult children are in regular classrooms.

Problems and Activities

1. Is there a difference between the strategy of ignoring misbehavior and behavior modification? Explain your answer.
2. As discussed on page 15, the concept of locus of control has attracted wide educational interest. What, if any, are the implications of this concept for dealing with disruptive pupils?
3. In connection with problem 2, which of the strategies discussed in this chapter could help pupils to develop internal locus of control? Why?
4. Would you let a pupil who has been excluded from your class make the decision about how long his or her time-out period from class should be, or would you make the decision? Explain.
5. How would you deal with the following pupil behaviors? Support your answer in each case.
   (1) A ninth-grade girl in your French class quickly applies lipstick and puts it away.
   (2) Your fifth-grade class is working on a scenario which they have called "Great Moments in American History." Suddenly two youngsters working on props start to giggle rather loudly. They suppress it, going back to work.
   (3) A fourth grader in a small discussion group is continually shouting, "I know what we can do," before the group leader has a chance to call on group members for their suggestions.
6. Some teachers contend that corporal punishment should be used in cases in which "this is all the child understands." Do you support this prescription? Why or why not?
7. John, an only child in your first-grade class, does not know how to share materials with other children. Yesterday, he grabbed a crayon away from another boy at his table. You reprimanded him and demonstrated how he should ask for a crayon politely. Today as you walk by, he is politely asking another child for a yellow crayon. Would you praise him for doing so? Why?
8. How can teachers avoid a frequent criticism of punishment, namely, that it only tells the pupil what not to do?
9. Do you believe that there are times when punishment must be used in classrooms? Support your answer.
10. If your answer was affirmative, give examples of situations in which punishment might be a better alternative than ignoring misbehavior in order to end it.
11. Assume that you have caught a pupil in the act of defacing a classroom wall with graffitti. Select a strategy for dealing with the problem that is consonant with the personal-social growth model of discipline.

Discipline and the Needs and Rights of Children

10

No teacher can be in the classroom very long without becoming aware of the clear relationship between the problems and needs of children and classroom discipline. The attention of children whose basic needs are completely ignored or are only partially met is bound to wander. Although all of us have basic needs some needs are unique to children including parental care and protection and reasonable limits on conduct. Children who suffer physical abuse and do not have enough to eat or a secure place to sleep are not free to learn. These children are bound to fall short of their potential in school and in life.

We have long known this. In 1906 in *The Bitter Cry of the Children,* a book that shocked the nation, John Spargo showed how a large segment of the nation's children was unable to study or learn because they were underfed and improperly cared for.[1] Spargo correctly pointed out that aside from the obvious gap between our humanitarian social philosophy and reality, there were economic reasons for public concern. Since it was futile to try to teach hungry children, the money and energy expended were wasted. Moreover, these youngsters put a drain on the society when they grew up weak and incompetent and dependent on public support, not to mention the cost incurred by their presence in great numbers in our prisons and hospitals. Therefore apart from moral considerations and simply from the standpoint of enlightened

[1] John Spargo, *The Bitter Cry of the Children* (New York: Macmillan, 1906).

self-interest society had to care for children when they were not cared for by their parents. Spargo also argued that since society had agreed to provide an education for all of the children of all of the people, it should make certain that all children were healthy enough to profit from that education.

Although Spargo was writing about children at the turn of the century, his point about the futility of trying to teach hungry and neglected children is just as true today as it was then. But what gives us pause for thought is that the problem Spargo wrote about still exists. Society still does not care for many children who are uncared for by their parents. From time to time in our history, reformers have tried to arouse the public about this problem so that children's needs will be met. For teachers, however, the problem has been of enduring importance. Present concern for the "substantial segment of children whose basic needs are only partially met or totally ignored" began with the 1970 White House Conference on Children.[2] Since then interest in developing means for meeting the basic needs of children has not flagged. No one can face the deeper issues of discipline without knowledge of the theory of basic needs and the various proposals which seek to guarantee that the needs of children will be met. The area of children's rights is also of extreme importance for classroom discipline. We turn to these problems in this chapter.

THE REALM OF FEELING

Within the twentieth century, punitive methods of education and socialization have given way to a concept of helping an individual to develop. (It will be recalled that development refers to changes in a pupil that result from an interaction of maturation and learning.) Due to the influence of developmental psychological giants like Piaget, the conception of educational method as helping a pupil to develop seems to be building with increasing strength and impetus. What Piaget's "stage theory" means in terms of classroom method is that the teacher's role is to help the pupil to progress through the qualitatively different "cognitive stages." In this book we have taken a developmental view of discipline with teacher roles and pupil responsibilities delineated at each stage. The development of self-direction is seen as closely tied to cognitive development.

[2] U.S. White House Conference on Children (1970), *Report to the President* (Washington, D.C.: U.S. Government Printing Office, 1970), p. 389.

The mind is more than the substrate of intellective processes. Emotions and imagination are also involved. Indeed Piaget has been criticized for shying away from the realm of feeling in his studies of how the child's mind works. For example, psychologist Howard Gardner observes that in focusing on the forms of thinking involved in science and mathematics, Piaget has neglected the realms of imagination and emotion embodied in literature, art, and music.[3]

Gardner's point is an important one because theoretical knowledge in psychology influences the curriculum. Interest in Piaget's monumental theories on how children's thinking develops in science, mathematics, and morality may have resulted in further neglect of literature, art, and music in the curriculum. (To say this is not to deny that these areas were already neglected in the United States before the recent heightened interest in Piagetian psychology.) Literature, art, and music are important for developing self-awareness. Schools should be concerned with this aspect of individual development as well as what we ordinarily think of as "cognitive development." Arthur W. Foshay sees the arts as part of a wider set of school experiences that can lead to self-discovery, provide a basis for self-respect, and find answers to the question, Who am I? "As things now stand," observes Foshay, "we deal with these questions only on a crash or crisis basis. When a student gets into enough trouble, somebody may sit with him long enough to help him carry on the process of self-discovery."[4]

Dealing with the realm of feeling in the curriculum is important for classroom discipline because, as Foshay intimates, self-awareness is only a short step away from awareness of personal actions. Yet teachers are also concerned about a somewhat different aspect of the realm of feeling: motivation. As any teacher knows, getting pupils to want to do their work lies at the heart of classroom discipline.

Generally psychologists see positive approaches as more motivating than negative approaches. Thus praise is preferred over punishment and success over failure. Yet praise and success are not the whole of motivation. Sometimes they just do not work, such as when a pupil is hungry or being physically abused at home. Needed is a theory of motivation which encompasses the biological aspects of motivation as well as the personal and social, such as Abraham Maslow's theory of basic needs. Maslow's theory is also a developmental theory.

[3] Howard Gardner, "Jean Piaget at 80 Continues To Learn about Children," *The New York Times Book Review*, August 1, 1976, p. 1.

[4] Arthur W. Foshay, *Curriculum for the 70's: An Agenda for Invention* (Washington, D.C.: National Education Association, 1970), p. 32.

BASIC NEEDS

Maslow's Theory

"Wants seem to arrange themselves in some sort of a hierarchy," wrote Abraham Maslow, as he put forward his theory.[5]

Maslow's hierarchy lists these basic needs.

1. *Physiological needs:* hunger, thirst, sex, the need to breathe, and so forth
2. *Safety needs:* the avoidance of and defense against forces which might produce injury (such as assault), pain, impairment, extremes of heat and cold, and so forth
3. *Love and belonging needs:* the need to be given love, warmth, and affection by someone
4. *Esteem needs:* the need to feel adequate, self-confident and of worth, to be appreciated and respected by others
5. *Need for self-actualization:* the need for self-fulfillment and self-expression, to use and develop one's talents, to become what one is capable of becoming.[6]

This set of needs constitutes a developmental series in that individuals are normally able to satisfy needs toward the end of the list more and more adequately as they grow and develop. Thus infants are concerned almost exclusively with the first three needs of the hierarchy because they are most essential for life and growth.

Implications for Discipline.   Maslow's theory of human motivation demonstrates that children's basic needs for food, safety, love, and self-esteem must be met if their needs to acquire skills and knowledge are to emerge. The implications for classroom discipline are important. Hunger and neglect may be primary factors in the inability of some children to behave properly and concentrate on their work. Their hunger for food and need for safety must be reasonably gratified before they can progress through the stages of discipline. Basic needs bear a close and irrevocable relationship to classroom discipline. Teachers can improve pupil behavior by doing what is within their power to see that pupils' basic needs are met. The relationship between lower-level basic needs and basic discipline is particularly striking and may be stated as a principle:

[5] Abraham H. Maslow, *Motivation and Personality* (New York: Harper & Row, 1954), p. 69.
[6] Ibid., pp. 80-106.

Twelfth Principle: *Basic discipline can be achieved only when basic needs, such as food and safety, are gratified.*

The following illustration, supplied by a first-year teacher in Philadelphia, shows this very clearly:

> Belinda was a pupil in one of the classes where I student taught. She was belligerent, irritable, and completely unmotivated—the kind of child that really tries a teacher's patience. Fortunately, she had a teacher who wanted to know why Belinda behaved this way. She found that Belinda lived with her two older brothers who did little to provide for her. Sometimes Belinda was left to roam the streets all night and would steal milk and bread from doorsteps in the early morning. The teacher reported the problem to the child abuse center at city hall. With some food in her stomach (provided by the school) there was some improvement in Belinda's behavior and work, although the problem was by no means solved. Eventually Belinda was placed in a foster family home.

Child Abuse.   While many teachers think of child abuse in terms of child battery (physical injury), severe neglect is one type of abuse and should be reported. Barton Schmitt, Pediatric Consultant for the National Center for the Prevention and Treatment of Child Abuse and Neglect, states that "the definition of child abuse and neglect has been expanded considerably to include more than just the beaten child" and that further, "any condition injurious to the child's physical or emotional health that has been inflicted by parents, guardians or other caretakers can fall under this definition."[7]

Classroom teachers, particularly those working with elementary grade pupils, are in a good position to detect and report child abuse and neglect. In most states it is mandatory to report suspected abuse. Moreover, every state grants immunity to reporting persons.

As Schmitt points out, the most likely place for teachers to notice physical abuse is on an exposed body surface such as children's faces, arms, or legs. Sometimes the bruises resemble a handprint, paddle, or strap marks. The teacher should find out whether pupils have been kicked, hit with a closed fist, or hit with a blunt instrument elsewhere than the buttocks. All of these are dangerous situations. A parent can punish a child and leave bruises and not be guilty of child abuse if there are one or two bruises on the back or buttocks that do not appear again. But as Schmitt cautions, "bruises that are great in number, recur re-

---

[7] Barton D. Schmitt, "What Teachers Need To Know about Child Abuse and Neglect," *Childhood Education*, Vol. 52 (November-December 1975), p. 58.

peatedly or appear on sites such as the face indicate that the parent has a misunderstanding of parental rights plus a loss of control." Schmitt goes on to say, "Even though the parent may be very self-righteous about his or her reason for leaving the child black and blue and, in addition, may be a very respectable person, this situation is unquestionably one of physical abuse."[8]

Some children who are undergoing physical abuse at home and have been bruised on an unexposed body surface are willing to talk about their problem. The following case, related by one of the author's graduate students, serves as an illustration.

> Gena is a pupil in my third-grade class. Until recently she was interested, enthusiastic, and motivated. Over the past month she has suddenly become listless, participating little in classroom activities, and stares wide-eyed into space. When I questioned her as to what was bothering her she told me that she was having trouble going to sleep at night. She said that she cried every night because she was afraid that she was going to die in her sleep. When she finally would go to sleep she would dream that her mother was stabbing her in the heart. Upon further questioning, I found that Gena's mother beats her hard and often, leaving a great number of bruises on her shoulders and back. I reported the case but even so, it has been a frustrating experience for me and I feel at the moment that my hands are tied.

Gena's problem was discovered because she was willing to relate the details and was seen later by her teacher in a private office. Some children are so afraid that they will not say anything. If abuse or neglect is suspected, there are several approaches that a teacher can take to substantiate the diagnosis. Schmitt suggests the following:

1. The teacher or counselor can talk to the child in a private setting. Although some children may lie about their injuries because they are afraid of repercussions at home, many children are willing to relate the details of an abusive incident.
2. The pupil can be checked by the school nurse or a school physician to see whether the injuries are accidental or inflicted.
3. If there is still doubt about the diagnosis a pediatrician assigned to the child protection team at a children's hospital or teaching hospital is usually more than willing to give a phone opinion.[9]

If child abuse is certain, the situation must be reported to the child protection agency. The agency must be able to make a full evaluation of the case and put a therapeutic program into effect including follow-

---

[8] Ibid.
[9] Ibid.

up of the case so that the pupil does not return with a more serious injury. In some cases, the youngsters have to be temporarily removed from their homes to guarantee their safety. Since schools are not able to provide this service, the child protection agency must be involved. Schmitt has found that when schools have tried to deal with the problem on their own by reprimanding parents, they have frequently brought about additional beatings of the child for "telling."[10]

On January 31, 1974, the Child Abuse Prevention and Treatment Act was signed into law, creating a National Center on Child Abuse and Neglect in the Office of Child Development of the U.S. Department of Health, Education, and Welfare. The Center administers grants to states and to agencies for programs connected with child abuse. Thus nearly seventy years after Spargo wrote his book on the plight of abused and neglected children, protection of children has become law.

Malnourished Children.   What of other measures for helping malnourished children? Teachers can check the following. First, the federal government has long provided financial assistance for feeding hungry children to state educational agencies, and needy children who are eligible can receive either free meals or meals at a reduced price. Some schools have a breakfast program as well as lunch program.

While no one must go hungry, providing food for pupils who need it is not the entire answer for overcoming inadequate nutrition. As emphasized by scientist Philip Abelson, people must choose to eat nourishing foods. Abelson finds "a real need for general education in the basic principles of nutrition and for continuing efforts to assure that no one, and especially no infant, fails to develop properly because of malnutrition."[11] A second approach for helping malnourished children is to make certain that this knowledge is provided in the curriculum.

Third, children can, at least in some measure, learn to help themselves. This is a part of personal growth. As the following case demonstrates, even first graders can learn responsibility for meeting their own physical needs.

> Five-year-old Manuel comes to school in a disheveled state and obviously hungry. He tells us that his father is not living at home and that his mother works to support the family. His mother does not get up in the morning to fix breakfast or prepare the children for school . . . .
> Crackers and milk will certainly help but we suggest an approach with Manuel which can help him help himself. Can he dress himself, tie his own

[10] Ibid., p. 62.
[11] Philip H. Abelson, "Malnutrition, Learning, and Behavior," *Science*, Vol. 164 (April 4, 1969), p. 4.

shoes, wash his own face, comb his own hair? Is there milk and cereal in the house? Can he fix his own breakfast? We think the teacher ought to help him to try.[12]

Teachers have a responsibility to protect pupils from the abuse and neglect of others. Yet they must not protect children and youth from learning to be responsible for their lives.

It is noteworthy that the 1970 White House Conference on Children and Youth gave attention to the problem of teaching children responsibility. Listed with children's needs (such as parental care, proper nutrition, and moral guidance) is the statement that "children should be helped to recognize and assume responsibilities commensurate with their age and maturity."[13]

The Teacher and Basic Needs

While the relationship between basic needs at the lower end of the scale and basic discipline is most apparent, the whole hierarchy of basic needs has bearing for pupil progress through the stages of discipline. Indeed, the hierarchy of basic needs closely parallels the stages of discipline.

Lower-Level Basic Needs.   While the range of possibilities for helping pupils meet psychological, safety, and love needs is wider than most of us might think, we cannot also ignore the fact that the teacher's sphere of responsibility is limited in these areas. Teachers can and must report abuse and neglect and help pupils to learn to help themselves. They can marshall all available resources to help children who are in trouble. While they cannot meet children's love needs, they can establish an affectionate tie with children. (As noted in the previous chapter, researchers tend to find such a tie important for socialization.) Nevertheless, the primary adult devoted to the child's care is usually a parent or guardian.

The Need for Self-Esteem.   In the area of self-esteem, the teacher can reach all of his or her pupils and make a difference in their motivation and achievement. In their research, Backman and Secord found a correlation between self-esteem and school performance. A positive self-image was associated with academic success and a low

---

[12] Donald W. Hardy, "Primary Reading: A Suggested Environment," *Elementary English*, Vol. 51 (September 1974), pp. 866-867.

[13] U.S. White House Conference on Children (1970), loc. cit.

self-image with academic failure.[14] This finding is in accord with Maslow's theory. As Carl Braun points out, "the low self-image child typically preoccupies himself with needs for love and belonging and esteem. This being the case, the child has no pressing need or energy to strive for the highest order in the hierarchy—self-actualization."[15] Braun suggests that certain pupil behaviors such as inattention, daydreaming, and low motivation be viewed as symptoms of a negative self-image and that teachers should concentrate on improving the pupil's self-image in view of the powerful relationship between this image and academic achievement. Teachers can do this by providing pupils with challenging but realistic activities and giving nonpatronizing encouragement. But teachers must also become more aware of the influence of their expectations of pupils as a powerful factor in the pupil's self-image. There are no magical or easy ways to transform the self-image, concludes Braun, "but when one recognizes that changes in self-concept are frequently associated with parallel changes in academic achievement, the challenge deserves the best efforts of the educational community."[16]

While we must remember that a reformed self-image can lead to better achievement, we must also keep in mind that better achievement can lead to more positive self-expectations and an improved self-image. In helping pupils to master academic material, teachers are fostering higher self-expectations, making it more possible for pupils to become self-actualizing. They are also fostering growth in discipline. Pupils who perform well academically (meet the school's expectations) are at least at the basic disciplinary stage.

Self-esteem is also a factor in the development of independence. Hence this basic need is of critical importance for upward progress through the stages of discipline. Teachers can foster the development of feelings of self-worth by listening to pupils, taking their ideas seriously, and involving them in planning and decision making.

Esteem needs are the social needs. We judge ourselves by the standards others use in appraising our behavior. A pupil's accomplishments, whether six completed arithmetic problems, a painting, or a piece of social service, must be recognized by teachers and peers if self-esteem is to be enhanced.

The Need for Self-Actualization. "So far as motivational status is concerned, healthy people have sufficiently gratified their basic needs

[14] Carl W. Backman and Paul F. Secord, *A Social Psychological View of Education* (New York: Harcourt Brace Jovanovich, 1968), p. 43.

[15] Carl Braun, "Teacher Expectation: Sociopsychological Dynamics," *Review of Educational Research*, Vol. 46 (Spring 1976), p. 208.

[16] Ibid., p. 209.

for safety, belonging, love, respect, and self-esteem so that they are motivated primarily by trends to self-actualization (defined as ongoing actualization of potentials, capacities, and talents)."[17] As this statement by Maslow suggests, self-actualization is more than a basic need—it is also a limitless goal. Even when we reach the limits of our talents in one field, there are always the new and unattained reaches of talent and experience. Gordon Allport points out that the central problem of adolescence is the search for self-identity which centers on the selection of an occupation or life goal. Adolescents know that the future must follow a plan and this adds to their self-image a dimension that is lacking in childhood. Although young children "want" to be firemen or nurses when they grow up, they have no sense of long-range purpose or integrated effort. "Until youth begins to plan," states Allport, "the sense of self is not complete."[18] A sense of purpose is an important feature of personal maturity.

While children or preadolescents normally do not strive toward a life goal or personal fulfillment in the same sense as adolescents or adults, they do have a need for self-actualization at their own level of maturity. Teachers can aid pupils in meeting their need for self-actualization by helping them to become aware of their abilities and talents and encouraging them to plan wholesomely for developing their talents and interests. While it is inappropriate for fifth or sixth graders to make long-range goals and commitments, they should become aware of those who have and their subsequent achievements. Illustrations of self-actualizing people (explorers, scientists, artists) can help youngsters understand the nature of self-actualization, particularly how individuals will persist in the face of obstacles in their style of life, that there is discipline involved in self-actualization.

Knowing what options and avenues are open to them is essential if adolescents are to select a life goal. Many educators believe that learning about careers should begin in elementary school. In the 1970s there was a national thrust for career education as a function of the curriculum from the elementary school through the secondary school and beyond.[19]

There are some striking commonalities between the stages of discipline and the hierarchy of basic needs. In both, individuals begin their development with the efforts of others and progress to acting on their

---

[17] Abraham H. Maslow, *Toward a Psychology of Being*, 2nd ed. (New York: Van Nostrand, 1968), p. 25.

[18] Gordon W. Allport, *Pattern and Growth in Personality* (New York: Holt, Rinehart and Winston, 1965), pp. 126-127.

[19] Daniel Tanner and Laurel N. Tanner, *Curriculum Development: Theory into Practice* (New York: Macmillan, 1975), pp. 568-569.

own. Both scales are based on the principle that self-direction is necessary for personal maturity and must be learned by the individual. Moreover, learning and socialization are central concepts in both scales. And, finally, implicit in the disciplinary stages and the hierarchy of basic needs is the concept of development as an endless process of growth.

THE RIGHTS OF CHILDREN

Recently, concern for children has been expressed in terms of children's rights: the right to an education, the right to adequate nutrition, health services, and child development services. Some of the discussion has been rhetorical, proclaiming the preconditions for children's development and seeing the way as clear and simple: the public must be aroused so that the conditions of life for large numbers of poor children will be improved. However, much of the discussion has been strategic, urging the formation of advocacy groups as a force in bringing about changes in the way that children are served by public or private institutions. We are concerned here briefly with the relation of children's rights to one institution, the school. Many of the issues involved impinge directly on classroom discipline.

Rights versus Needs

In recent discussions about the fundamental preconditions for normal development, the emphasis has been on "rights" rather than "needs." Thus as Rochelle Beck notes about the report of the 1970 White House Conference on Children: "Children's developmental, health, and educational 'needs' were transformed into their 'rights,' the foundations of which were the same inalienable rights of life, liberty, and the pursuit of happiness guaranteed to every adult citizen."[20]

While a philosophical and political justification can be given for children's rights, a danger is inherent in transforming "needs" to "rights" in discussions about the necessary conditions for children's development. What may be overlooked in such discussions is that there is a scientific basis for meeting children's needs. Children and youth simply cannot develop optimally unless their physical and psychological needs are met. Teachers know all too well the truth of the adage that "the whole child" comes to school. As noted earlier, we have known this

[20] Rochelle Beck, "White House Conferences on Children: An Historical Perspective," *Harvard Educational Review*, Vol. 43 (November 1973), p. 662.

since the time of John Spargo and even before. In changing needs to rights, certain problems arise. In discussions of children's rights we become involved in philosophical justification whereas children's needs are definitely based on scientific evidence. Also, transforming needs to rights could put children at a disadvantage because, as Rodham reminds us, claims based on physical and psychological needs are not considered legal rights by our system.[21]

Legitimacy of Children's Rights

Basic needs aside, the question of children's rights still remains. Do children have rights under the law? They do but the rights are those which the state determines are in the best interests of children. Rodham has observed that those favoring the extension of children's rights follow two approaches: calling for the granting of adult rights to children and attempting to develop a set of rights deriving from the special nature of childhood.[22] Those who sound the theme for children's rights are opposed by others who argue that while children have rights, so do parents, teachers, minority group members, and so on. The advocates of children's rights counter that while this is certainly the case, children are usually smaller and weaker than anyone else, need protection, and lack political clout. This is probably the most powerful claim of advocates for children's rights.

Child Advocacy.   In 1969, the Joint Commission on the Mental Health of Children proposed a national system of child advocacy.[23] According to Knitzer in her excellent review of the child advocacy movement, the term "child advocacy" was coined by the Joint Commission and may also be traced to Ralph Nader's form of advocacy.[24]

Knitzer finds that conceptually advocates have been split, some seeing the movement as a delivery system (advocates providing direct service to children and their families) and others as a force in bringing about change in how children are served by public and private institutions, including schools. Despite this split, and because of the growing political sophistication of advocates, Knitzer believes that child advocacy can be a significant force in reforming the conditions of life

---

[21] Hillary Rodham, "Children Under the Law," *Harvard Educational Review,* Vol. 43 (November 1973), p. 944.

[22] Ibid., pp. 495-496.

[23] Joint Commission on Mental Health of Children, *Crisis in Child Mental Health: Challenge for the 1970's* (New York: Harper & Row, 1970).

[24] Jane Knitzer, "Child Advocacy: A Perspective," *American Journal of Orthopsychiatry,* Vol. 46 (April 1976), p. 200.

for children, although she cautions that child advocacy is not a substitute for an effective social policy for children and their families.[25]

Children's Rights and Classroom Discipline

Classification of Pupils. In recent years courts have examined school practices such as exclusion of "ineducable children" (including behavioral problem children), ability grouping, and special education placement. (Special education refers to classes for pupils with particular and acute learning disabilities.) These practices are tied in clearly with classroom discipline. Sometimes teachers who cannot deal with an acting-out child propose that the child be assigned to a special education class. When schools cannot afford the educational services required by severely retarded or unmanageable children, they may try to label them ineducable. David Kirp has observed that it matters little for the pupil whether schools describe the process as a punitive or an educational decision: "exclusion, whether premised on incorrigibility or ineducability, results in absolute educational deprivation: suspension or special class assignment both diminish educational opportunities and stigmatize the affected student."[26]

Several courts have held that exclusion from school is unconstitutional. For example, in the settlement of a suit brought by parents of retarded children against the state of Pennsylvania, the court ordered the state to provide an appropriate education for all handicapped children.[27] In a second important case, *Mills v. Board of Education*, the district court ordered that the Washington, D.C., public schools readmit all excluded youngsters "regardless of the degree of the child's mental, physical, or emotional disability or impairment." The Mills court noted that "placement in a regular public school class with appropriate ancillary services is preferable to placement in a special public school class."[28]

In several cases, the courts have refused to allow grouping of pupils based on test scores, finding that such practices deprived some pupils of their constitutional right to equality of educational opportunity.[29] While

[25] Ibid., p. 215.

[26] David Kirp, "Student Classification, Public Policy, and the Courts," *Harvard Educational Review*, Vol. 44 (February 1974), p. 46.

[27] See E. Edmund Reutter, Jr., and Robert R. Hamilton, *The Law of Public Education* (Mineola, N.Y.: The Foundation Press, 1976), p. 132; and Leopold D. Lippman and I. Ignacy Goldberg, *Right to Education: Anatomy of the Pennsylvania Case and Its Implications for Exceptional Children* (New York: Teachers College Press, 1973).

[28] *Mills v. Board of Education*, 348 F. Supp. 866, 880 (D.D.C. 1972).

[29] Reutter and Hamilton, op. cit., pp. 142-143.

the courts acted to secure equal protection of the laws, their actions recall our earlier discussion on the detrimental effects of labeling and tracking on slow pupils.

Judicial intervention in the realm of school classification has important implications for the classroom teacher. The thrust of recent opinion (judicial and professional) has been toward educating behavioral problem children in the regular classroom while providing them with ancillary services (resource rooms, counseling, and the like), For example, the Mills court viewed placement in a regular classroom, supplemented by special help, as preferable to special classes. Such decisions place more, not fewer, demands on the classroom teacher. More than ever, teachers need to be able to identify disciplinary alternatives and employ them systematically. They also must work effectively with specialists.

Mainstreaming.   Known as mainstreaming, the concept of integrating handicapped children into regular classrooms to give them contact with normal pupils, is generally endorsed by teachers.[30] However, when special education pupils are placed in regular classrooms, support services must be provided and teachers must be given special training if mainstreaming is to be successful. Many teachers also feel that when regular classes include handicapped youngsters, these classes should be smaller than those without any handicapped pupils. As an elementary teacher in Los Angeles stated: "I voluntarily accepted two children with serious difficulties into a class that already had 36 students. It made for a long and tiring day. It made me short-tempered and less able to find time to work with other children."[31] As noted, court decisions have forced the schools to admit tens of thousands of handicapped children who were previously denied a right to education. This, in turn, has resulted in teachers being given added responsibilities without adequate preparation and, in many instances, without special support services. This has become a cause of concern, and rightly so, for elementary and secondary school teachers. Handicapped children should not be segregated into special classes with little or no contact with other children. Yet certain conditions must be met if mainstreaming is to increase, rather than reduce, educational opportunity.

Civil Liberties of Pupils.   As Reutter and Hamilton point out, "Any enforceable rule of conduct must be connected with the welfare of the schools."[32] Of great importance is that courts have found that pupils are legally entitled to act in ways that some teachers and principals may

---

[30] *The New York Times,* August 19, 1976.

[31] Ibid.

[32] Reutter and Hamilton, op. cit., p. 544.

find disruptive such as wearing buttons indicating political positions, criticizing school authorities in school newspapers, refusing to salute the flag and, in many cases, wearing long hair.[33] Doubtless there are other behaviors in which pupils have a right to engage that are distressing to some teachers and principals but on which the courts have not yet ruled.

Behavior Modification Drugs.   "Does giving hyperactive children drugs to improve their classroom behavior free them for the better pursuit of happiness? Or does it infringe on their liberty?"[34] So asks Edward Ladd in an article in which he notes that requiring pupils to take medication may constitute an infringement on their civil rights, despite the appeal such measures may have to school personnel in attempting to cope with disruptive behavior.[35]

There are, perhaps, more critical problems involved in drug therapy. To begin with, there is the problem of diagnosis of "hyperkinetic behavior disorder" or "minimal brain dysfunction" for which drug therapy is prescribed. Doctors themselves have been unable to precisely define and diagnose hyperkinesis.[36] Pediatrician Arnold Zukow states that "identifying hyperkinetic children presents a perplexing problem" and, further, that "unfortunately, the medical literature and lay press use the terms *hyperactive* and *hyperkinetic* interchangeably."[37] In Zukow's opinion they are not the same. Zukow describes hyperkinesis "as a treatable illness characterized by involuntary behavior and/or learning problems in a child whose brain maturation is delayed." He stresses that "children who have hyperkinesis and go untreated may simply outgrow the syndrome."[38]

To return to the problem of diagnosis, Zukow states that the difficulty arising in the use of *hyperactive* and *hyperkinesis* interchangeably is considerably more than semantic. "For instance, frustrated adults reacting to a child who does not meet their standards can easily exaggerate the significance of the child's occasional inattention or restlessness and label a youngster hyperkinetic."[39]

[33] Ibid., pp. 544-555.

[34] Edward T. Ladd, "Pills for Classroom Peace," *The National Elementary Principal*, Vol. 50 (April 1971), p. 42.

[35] Ibid., pp. 42-47.

[36] Lester Grinspoon and Susan B. Singer, "Amphetamines in the Treatment of Hyperkinetic Children," *Harvard Educational Review*, Vol. 43 (November 1973), pp. 515-550.

[37] Arnold H. Zukow, "Helping the Hyperkinetic Child," *Today's Education*, Vol. 64 (November-December 1975), pp. 39-40.

[38] Ibid., p. 39.

[39] Ibid.

There seems little doubt that many restless, disturbed, and inattentive pupils constituting problems for teachers and parents have been mislabeled hyperkinetic. Grinspoon and Singer find that "it is impossible to believe that the 200,000 or more school children who are now being routinely administered stimulants are all suffering from organic brain damage or deficiencies in crucial CNS (central nervous system) chemicals. In other words, there is no justification for the increasingly popular leap from the observation of disruptive or inattentive behavior to the supposition that this is a result of a specific disorder of the central nervous system."[40] Grinspoon and Singer conclude that "symptoms, not causes have become the focus of treatment, creating a significant potential for abuse."[41]

Another problem in the use of amphetamines is that although they may calm hyperactive children, their long-term effects are unknown.

The final problem has to do with the objective of classroom discipline, self-direction. Our goal is to help children learn to govern their own behavior. Pupils need instructional and disciplinary approaches designed to help them "come to grips with their natural disposition and learn to use what Philip Jackson at the University of Chicago has nicely called their own executive powers. Any form of intervention that relieves a restless or unruly child of the need, or deprives him of the opportunity, to use his executive powers deprives him to that extent of the chance to develop insight and skill in self-control."[42]

In their review of the research on hyperkinetic children, Grinspoon and Singer found only two follow-up studies on the long-term effects of amphetamines on hyperkinetic symptoms. The first, conducted on 64 children who had been diagnosed five years earlier as severely hyperactive and were adolescents at the time of follow-up, found that although restlessness had diminished, attentional problems remained. Moreover, "seventy percent of the children were emotionally immature and a significant number had no future goals and suffered from low self-esteem and feelings of hopelessness."[43] These pupils' basic need for self-esteem had not been met and they had no sense of purpose (perhaps because for five years they had been deprived of the chance to use their "executive powers").

The second study was equally discouraging. Over 75 percent of the 83 "hyperactive children as teenagers" studied still had problems with impulsivity, concentration, and defiance and the majority continued

---

[40] Grinspoon and Singer, op. cit., p. 546.
[41] Ibid., p. 549.
[42] Ladd, op. cit., p. 45.
[43] Grinspoon and Singer, op. cit., p. 548.

to have serious difficulties with schoolwork and to suffer from low self-esteem.[44]

While with only two studies it is not possible to draw well-founded conclusions about the effectiveness of drug therapy, the results of the studies can hardly be called promising for long-range developmental goals. There are no short-cuts to self-direction. It must be learned and experienced. Pupils must progress upward through the stages of discipline and teachers should view with great caution any tempting detours.

POSSIBILITIES, NOT LIMITATIONS

Whereas the traditional concept of discipline has been one of putting limitations on the learner, the point of view taken in this book is that discipline is positive. Discipline is for learning and self-direction; discipline should help learners—and teachers—realize their possibilities, not limitations. Looking at discipline as limitations can also put limitations on the learning process.

All of the approaches described in this book are positive (geared to possibilities, not limitations) and based on the conception of discipline as development toward self-direction. The concept of development is very positive! Although the subject of discipline is charged with emotional overtones, and attitudes and opinions vary widely, teachers can be assured that dealing with discipline developmentally is good for children. Moreover, it is good for teachers when they can consider discipline developmentally and act on that consideration.

The teacher who asks, "What can I do about discipline?" is asking the right question. I have tried to target the content of the book to that question. Teachers can do so much by viewing discipline developmentally, ecologically, and relatedly (inseparable from teaching and learning). Oddly, discipline has been rarely viewed as a ladder to self-direction with models of discipline as rungs of the ladder. Indeed, models of discipline are seldom even presented for the teacher's consideration as alternatives. Hopefully, these ideas and others in the book will help teachers to more fully realize their possibilities for effectiveness.

Finally, classroom discipline is a common problem facing all teachers. But other problems of the profession have been dealt with successfully. Our educational achievements of the past give hope that teachers can help learners realize their possibilities. An individual teacher following the principles of developmental discipline can suggest the way ahead to others.

[44] Ibid.

SUMMARY

A powerful and irrevocable relationship exists between classroom discipline and the problems and needs of children. A developmental approach to education and discipline is an enormous advance over punitive methods. Granted this, basic needs are important determinants of development. Pupils' needs for food and safety must be met if their needs to acquire skills and knowledge are to emerge and they are to progress through the stages of discipline. Lower-level basic needs (food and safety) are central to basic discipline.

While teachers are not pupils' primary caretakers, they can realize the possibilities open to them for helping to see that their basic needs are met. Reporting child abuse and neglect (mandatory in most states), making sure that knowledge about nutrition is provided in the curriculum, and helping pupils learn to meet their own physical needs (personal growth) are some of the possibilities. Teachers can do much to help pupils meet the need for self-esteem. An improved self-image is often associated with improvement in school performance. In helping pupils to meet the academic goals of the school, teachers are fostering higher self-expectations, making it possible for pupils to become self-actualizing. And they are fostering pupils' upward progress through the stages of discipline. In both the stages of discipline and the hierarchy of basic needs, individuals begin their development with the help of others and progress to doing things independently.

The legal rights of children are closely tied to classroom discipline. Several courts have held that exclusion from school is unconstitutional. Teachers have to teach all students, including those formerly excluded by physical, mental or emotional disabilities or impairments. In schools in which handicapped children who were previously denied a right to education are placed in regular classrooms, support services must be provided if mainstreaming is to increase educational opportunity.

Difficulty in diagnosing hyperkinesis presents a potential for abuse of amphetamines ("behavior modification drugs"). Our goal is to help pupils to become self-directing, to develop their own "executive powers." The use of amphetamines may deprive pupils of this opportunity.

The approach to classroom discipline taken in this book is that discipline should help children and teachers to realize their possibilities, not their limitations. Discipline problems will not vanish from our classrooms. But if we use the best knowledge, the best ideas available to us, we have the best guides to action. The approaches presented here should give hope to teachers who want to improve their effectiveness and are dedicated to the goal of self-direction.

Problems and Activities

1. What illustrations can you give of the relation between basic needs and classroom discipline? Do you think that Maslow's theory is useful for teachers? Why?

2. What are the limitations of a theory of motivation based only on praise and success?

3. Mary Lee M, a third-grade teacher writes:

   > Children who live in fear of getting beaten up on the way home from school are often so upset that they cannot do their work. (Not a day passes that I don't witness three or four fights as I leave the building.) I have found three things to be effective: contact the parent to meet the child after school, seek the help of an older child to escort him home, or escort him home myself. I have done this last many times with positive results: the child functions better in school knowing that he doesn't have to worry about getting home safely, he realizes that I care about his welfare, and it lets his parents know that I care.

   What basic need of pupils is Mary Lee helping to meet?

4. According to Gordon Allport, being able to establish goals and follow a plan for reaching those goals is an important part of development [Gordon W. Allport, Pattern and Growth in Personality (New York: Holt, Rinehart and Winston, 1965), pp. 126-127.] Are there teacher responsibilities for helping pupils reach the constructive and generative stages of discipline that can also foster the ability to make and follow a plan? If so, what are they?

5. The National Center on Child Abuse and Neglect has received comments suggesting that corporal punishment be included in the definition of child abuse. [Frank Ferro, "Protecting Children: The National Center on Child Abuse and Neglect," Childhood Education, Vol. 52 (November-December 1975), p. 64.] Would you favor the inclusion of corporal punishment in the definition of child abuse? Explain.

6. In the opinion of pediatrician Arnold Zukow, a pupil "does not suddenly at the age of six, become hyperkinetic. The signs are present very early in the child's life." [Arnold H. Zukow, "Helping the Hyperkinetic Child," Today's Education, Vol. 64 (November-December 1975), p. 40.] In your opinion, is this helpful for teachers in dealing with short attention span, restlessness, and impulsiveness? Support your answer.

7. Do you favor the point of view taken in this book that discipline is positive and should help teachers and learners realize their possibilities, not their limitations? Why?

8. Do you believe that a developmental approach to discipline can help

teachers to face their classroom problems more effectively in the future than they have in the past? Explain.
9. Discuss the role of the individual teacher in bringing about better programs of developmental discipline.

Selected References

Allport, Gordon W. *Pattern and Growth in Personality*. New York: Holt, Rinehart and Winston, 1965.

Backman, Carl W. and Paul F. Secord. *A Social Psychological View of Education*. New York: Harcourt, 1968.

Bandura, Albert. *Principles of Behavior Modification*. New York: Holt, Rinehart and Winston, 1969.

Bany, Mary A. and Lois V. Johnson. *Classroom Group Behavior*. New York: Macmillan, 1964.

Berkowitz, Leonard. *Development of Motives and Values in the Child*. New York: Basic Books, 1964.

Birch, Herbert G. and Joan D. Gussow. *Disadvantaged Children: Health, Nutrition and School Failure*. New York: Harcourt, 1970.

Bloom, Benjamin S. *Human Characteristics and School Learning*. New York: McGraw-Hill, 1976.

Cremin, Lawrence A. *Public Education*. New York: Basic Books, 1976.

Cremin, Lawrence A. *The Transformation of the School*. New York: Knopf, 1961.

Dewey, John. *Democracy and Education*. New York: Macmillan, 1916.

Dewey, John. *Moral Principles in Education*. Carbondale, Ill.: Southern Illinois University Press, 1975 (originally published by Houghton Mifflin in 1909).

Durkheim, Émile. *Moral Education*. New York: The Free Press, 1973.

Gnagey, William J. *The Psychology of Discipline in the Classroom*. New York: Macmillan, 1968.

Good, Thomas L., Bruce J. Biddle, and Jere E. Brophy. *Teachers Make a Difference*. New York: Holt, Rinehart and Winston, 1975.

Good, Thomas L. and Jere E. Brophy. *Educational Psychology: A Realistic Approach*. New York: Holt, Rinehart and Winston, 1977.

Good, Thomas L. and Jere E. Brophy. *Looking in Classrooms*. New York: Harper & Row, 1973.

Hartshorne, Hugh and Mark A. May. *Studies in the Nature of Character*. Vol. 1. Studies in Deceit. Vol. 2. Studies in Service and Self-Control. New York: Macmillan, 1929-1930.

Havighurst, Robert J. *Developmental Tasks and Education,* 3rd ed. New York: McKay, 1972.

Hewett, Frank M. *The Emotionally Disturbed Child in the Classroom*. Boston: Allyn and Bacon, 1968.

Jackson, Philip W. *Life in Classrooms*. New York: Holt, Rinehart and Winston, 1968.

Jessup, Michael H. and Margaret A. Kiley. *Discipline: Positive Attitudes for Learning*. Englewood Cliffs, N.J.: Prentice-Hall, 1971.

Joyce, Bruce and Marsha Weil. *Models of Teaching*. Englewood Cliffs, N.J.: Prentice-Hall, 1972.

Kay, William, *Moral Education*. London: Allen and Unwin, 1975.

Kohlberg, Lawrence. "Education for Justice: A Modern Statement of the Platonic View," *Moral Education*. Cambridge, Mass: Harvard University Press, 1970.

Kohlberg, Lawrence. "Stage and Sequence: The Cognitive-Developmental Approach to Socialization," in David Goslin (ed.), *Handbook of Socialization Theory and Research*. Skokie, Ill.: Rand McNally, 1969.

Kounin, Jacob S. *Discipline and Group Management in Classrooms*. New York: Holt, Rinehart and Winston, 1970.

Liebert, Robert M. "Television and Social Learning: Some Relationships between Viewing Violence and Behaving Aggressively (Overview)," in *Television and Social Behavior*, A Technical Report to the Surgeon General's Scientific Advisory Committee on Television and Social Behavior. Washington, D.C.: U. S. Government Printing Office, 1972.

Long, Nicholas J., William C. Morse, and Ruth G. Newman (eds.). *Conflict in the Classroom: The Education of Children with Problems*. Belmont, Calif.: Wadsworth, 1971.

MacMillan, Donald L., Steven R. Forness, and Barbara M. Trumbull. "The Role of Punishment in the Classroom," *Exceptional Children*, Vol. 40, October 1973, pp. 85-96.

Madsen, Charles H., Jr. and Clifford K. Madsen. *Teaching/Discipline*. Boston: Allyn and Bacon, 1974.

Martin, Jane. *Explaining, Understanding, and Teaching*. New York: McGraw-Hill, 1970.

Maslow, Abraham H. *Motivation and Personality.* New York: Harper & Row, 1954.

Maslow, Abraham H. *Motivation and Personality,* 2nd ed. New York: Harper & Row, 1970.

Maslow, Abraham H. *Toward a Psychology of Being,* 2nd ed. New York: Van Nostrand, 1968.

Mussen, Paul. *The Psychological Development of the Child.* Englewood Cliffs, N.J.: Prentice-Hall, 1973.

National Society for the Study of Education. *The Psychology of Teaching Methods.* Seventy-fifth Yearbook, Part I. Chicago: The University of Chicago Press, 1976.

National Society for the Study of Education. *Teacher Education.* Seventy-fourth Yearbook, Part II. Chicago: University of Chicago Press, 1975.

Piaget, Jean. *The Moral Judgment of the Child.* London: Routledge, 1932.

Piaget, Jean. *The Psychology of Intelligence.* New York: Harcourt, 1950.

Redl, Fritz and David Wineman. *Controls from Within.* New York: Free Press, 1952.

Reutter, E. Edmund, Jr. and Robert R. Hamilton. *The Law of Public Education.* Mineola, N.Y.: The Foundation Press, 1976.

Rosenthal, Robert and Lenore Jacobson. *Pygmalion in the Classroom.* New York: Holt, Rinehart and Winston, 1968.

Sheviakov, George V. and Fritz Redl. *Discipline for Today's Children and Youth.* Washington, D.C.: Association for Supervision and Curriculum Development, 1956.

Silberman, Charles E. *Crisis in the Classroom.* New York: Random House, 1970.

Silberman, Charles E. (ed.). *The Open Classroom Reader.* New York: Vintage Books, 1973.

Skinner, B. F. *The Technology of Teaching.* New York: Appleton, 1968.

Sommer, Robert. *Personal Space: The Behavioral Basis of Design.* Englewood Cliffs, N.J.: Prentice-Hall, 1969.

Spargo, John. *The Bitter Cry of the Children.* New York: Macmillan, 1906.

Taba, Hilda and Deborah Elkins. *Teaching Strategies for the Culturally Disadvantaged.* Skokie, Ill.: Rand McNally, 1968.

Tanner, Daniel and Laurel N. Tanner. *Curriculum Development: Theory Into Practice.* New York: Macmillan, 1975.

Travers, Robert M. W. (ed.). *Second Handbook of Research on Teaching.* Skokie, Ill.: Rand McNally, 1973.

Younie, William J. *Instructional Approaches to Slow Learners.* New York: Teachers College Press, 1967.

NAME INDEX

Abelson, Philip H., 187
Adams, Gerald R., 92
Allport, Gordon W., 33n., 190, 199, 201n.
Arnold, W. J., 141n., 173n.
Aronfreed, Justin M., 141n., 173
Artuso, Alfred A., 10n., 12
Ausubel, David P., 1-2

Backman, Carl W., 188-189, 201n.
Bandura, Albert, 201n.
Bany, Mary A., 201n.
Baron, Robert A., 131n.
Beck, Rochelle, 191
Berkowitz, Leonard, 201n.
Berlak, Ann C., 86n.
Biddle, Bruce J., 105, 202n.
Bidwell, Charles E., 35-36
Birch, Herbert G., 201n.
Blake, Phillip R., 9n., 166-167
Blom, Gaston E., 157, 159
Bloom, Benjamin S., 201n.
Boguslaw, Robert, 5
Bown, Oliver H., 83
Braun, Carl, 93, 189
Brookover, Wilbur B., 10, 125n.
Brophy, Jere E., 105, 135, 202n.
Button, Christine, 46n.
Butts, R. Freeman, 5n.

Cane, V. A., 174n.
Carberry, Hugh H., 123-124
Cheyne, J. Allen, 173n.
Clifford, Margaret M., 92
Coates, Thomas J., 2n., 83n.
Coleman, James S., 15
Cornbleth, Catherine, 46n.

Cremin, Lawrence A., 5n., 11n., 63n., 73, 119, 132, 201n.
Culbertson, Frances M., 10n.
Cutler, Richard L., 160

Davis, O. L., Jr., 46n.
Dewey, John, 15, 36, 38, 47-48, 59, 140, 201n.
Dion, Karen K., 92
Dominick, J. R., 131
Drabman, Ronald S., 162n., 165n.
Dreeben, Robert, 100n.
Durkheim, Émile, 45, 201n.

Elkins, Deborah, 55, 63, 203n.
Ellson, Douglas G., 80n.
Enzer, Norman B., 9

Ferrow, Frank, 199
Fink, Albert H., 160
Forness, Steven R., 163, 172-174, 202n.
Foshay, Arthur W., 183
Freud, Sigmund, 11
Friesen, Wallace V., 159n.
Fuller, Frances F., 2n., 83

Gardner, Howard, 183
Garner, Howard S., 163
Gnagey, William J., 158-159, 201n.
Goldberg, I. Ignacy, 193n.
Good, Thomas L., 90, 105, 135, 202n.
Gordon, Thomas F., 132n.
Greenberg, Bradley S., 131, 132n.
Grinspoon, Lester, 195-197
Gump, Paul V., 141n., 157
Gussow, Joan D., 201n.

Hamilton, Robert R., 176, 193-195, 203n.

Hardy, Donald W., 188n.
Hartshorne, Hugh, 202n.
Havighurst, Robert J., 39n., 86, 147n., 202n.
Henry, Jules, 161
Hewett, Frank M., 9n., 10n., 12, 166-167, 175, 202n.

Jackson, Philip W., 12, 71, 90, 202n.
Jacobson, Lenore, 89-90, 203n.
Jarolimek, John, 147n.
Jessup, Michael H., 202n.
Johnson, Lois V., 201n.
Jones, F., 162-163
Joyce, Bruce, 106, 202n.

Kaltsounis, Theodore, 86
Kass, Ruth E., 162n., 165n.
Kaufman, Kenneth F., 162n., 165n.
Kay, William, 202n.
Kiley, Margaret A., 202n.
Kirp, David, 193
Kirsch, Dorothy, 57n.
Knitzer, Jane, 192-193
Kohl, Herbert R., 99, 116
Kohlberg, Lawrence, 20, 35, 202n.
Kounin, Jacob S., 13-14, 67-71, 77-79, 141n., 157-159, 202n.

Ladd, Edward T., 195-196
Lahaderne, Henrietta M., 90
Lavatelli, Celia S., 86
LaVoie, Joseph C., 92
Lawrence, Elizabeth A., 163
Liebert, Robert M., 129, 131n., 202n.
Liefer, Aimee, 130n.
Lippman, Leopold D., 193n.
Long, Nicholas J., 202n.

MacMillan, Donald L., 163, 172-174, 202n.
Madsen, Charles H., Jr., 202n.
Madsen, Clifford K., 202n.
Martin, Jane, 87, 202n.
Maslow, Abraham H., 183-184, 189-190, 199, 203n.
May, Mark A., 202n.

Miller, W. H., 162-163
Moore, Walter J., 86
Morse, William C., 160, 168, 202n.
Mussen, Paul, 30n., 203n.

Newman, Ruth G., 202n.
Norton, A. Evangeline, 159n.

O'Leary, K. Daniel, 162, 165
Ott, John F., 175

Packard, Robert G., 104n.
Parke, Ross D., 173n., 174n.
Piaget, Jean, 20-27, 41, 182-183, 203n.

Redl, Fritz, 88, 162, 167-168, 203n.
Reutter, E. Edmund, Jr., 176, 193-195, 203n.
Roberts, Donald F., 130n.
Rodham, Hillary, 192
Rosenthal, Robert, 89-90, 91n., 96, 203n.
Rotter, Julian B., 15
Ryans, David G., 67

Saeli, Joseph A., 128n.
St. John, Walter D., 126
Schmitt, Barton D., 185-187
Seaver, W. B., 46n.
Secord, Paul F., 201n.
Sheviakov, George V., 88, 203n.
Silberman, Charles E., 49, 203n.
Singer, Susan B., 195-197
Skinner, B. F., 105, 203n.
Sommer, Robert, 102-103, 203n.
Spargo, John, 181-182, 192, 203n.
Stodolsky, Susan S., 100n.

Taba, Hilda, 55, 63, 203n.
Tanner, Daniel, 2n., 11n., 48n., 86n., 147n., 176n., 190n., 203n.
Tanner, Laurel N., 2n., 11n., 48n., 86n., 147n., 176n., 190n., 203n.
Taylor, Frank D., 10n., 12
Thomas, Susan Christie, 100n.
Thompson, Marion, 8n.
Thoresen, Carl E., 2n., 83n.

Thorndike, Robert L., 89
Travers, Robert M. W., 9n., 100n., 203n.
Trumbull, Barbara M., 163, 172-174, 202n.
Turiel, Elliot, 35
Tyler, Ralph W., 136

Walberg, Herbert J., 100n.
Walster, Elaine, 92

Walters, Richard H., 173n., 174n.
Weil, Marsha, 202n.
Wilcox, Mary A., 34n.
Wineman, David, 162, 167n., 203n.
Winschel, James F., 163

Younie, William J., 53n., 203n.

Zukow, Arnold H., 195, 199

Mount Saint Mary's College
Emmitsburg, MD 21727

SUBJECT INDEX

Ability grouping, 133-135, 193
See also Teacher expectations, pupil behavior and
Accountability, 99
Activities
compatible vs. conflicting, 101-102, 114
engaging pupils in, 53-56, 67-71, 97-107, 111-115
socially useful, 140-153
Activity, 49-50
See also Purposeful activity
Administrative factors, 119
Aggressive behavior, televised violence and, 129-131, 137
Alienated pupils, 147-149
Appropriate behavior (*see* Behavior)
Approved practices, 2, 8, 36-37
Asking questions, pupil responsibility for, 28, 30
See also Basic disciplinary stage
Attention
discipline as responsible, 84
interest and, 85-87
and opportunity to respond, 90-93
as survival factor, 83
teacher's expectation and, 88-96
Attitudes, 44-45
toward learning, 60
of respect, 61-62
social, 60-62
of teacher, 38-39, 89-93, 171
Attractive vs. unattractive pupils, 92-93
Authority (*see* Teacher authority)
Autonomy, 26
See also Self-direction
Aversives (*see* Punishment)

Avoidance of work, 83-99, 101, 107

Basic disciplinary stage, 28-32, 110, 112, 115, 155
See also Basic discipline
Basic discipline, 29, 32, 53, 71, 84, 103-104, 110, 162, 164, 166, 184-185
See also Basic disciplinary stage
Basic needs, 181-182
Behavior
acceptable vs. unacceptable, 156, 161, 173
guide for appropriate, 15-16, 23-24, 48-50
increasing appropriate, 7-8
learning to choose, 16, 21
rebellious, 170-171
redirecting negative, 15, 140-143, 157, 173
Behavior modification, 7-11, 161-164
as building block, 11
effectiveness of, 9-10
method, 7-10
motivation and, 10, 105-106
parental cooperation in, 9-10
research in, 9-10, 105
social policy and, 10
vs. training, 11
Behavior modification drugs, 195-197
Behavior modification model (*see* Behavior modification)
Behavior problems (*see* Discipline problems)
Behavioral competencies, 28-39
Behavioral standards (*see* Standards; Behavior; Rules)
Boredom, 53, 69, 71, 93, 108-109

Bullying, 171-172

Child abuse, 185, 188
Child-centered discipline, 11-12, 167
Classification of pupils, 193-194
Classroom
  design of, 97-98, 100-103, 108
  open (see Open classroom; Open education)
  self-contained, 69, 97-98, 102, 107-108
Classroom activities, flow of (see Momentum)
Classroom climate, 117, 136
Classroom control
  through curriculum improvement, 43-60
  as instruction, 6, 12-14, 65-71
  socialization and, 139-140
  See also Classroom management; Discipline; Discipline problems
Classroom government, 37
Classroom group, 12, 65-81, 97
  alliance between teacher and, 169
Classroom management, 1, 13-15, 66-71, 97-98, 100-103, 117, 159, 169-170
Classroom momentum (see Momentum)
Classroom routines, 5
  See also Routines, as means
Classroom society, 45, 101
Co-curricular clubs, 133
Compatible vs. conflicting activities, 101-102, 114
Confrontations, avoiding, 169-170
Consistency, 108, 174-175
Consonance, principle of, 158, 169, 173
Constructive stage of discipline, 28, 32-37
Continuing projects, 76-77
Contracts, 104-106
Control techniques, 158-178
  See also Discipline
Controlling aim, 6, 17
Cooperation, 33-34, 36-37

Cooperative activities, 33-37
Cooperative planning (see Planning)
Corporal punishment, 9, 172, 176-178
Counseling pupils, 160
  See also Life space interview
Courtesy, 61-62
Curriculum, 43-63, 66, 86, 91-92, 99-100, 133, 183, 187
  behavior in areas of, 48-50
  cooperative experiences in, 36-37
  discipline through the, 43-45, 51
  interrelation of elements in, 44
  mastery of the, 60-61, 84
  moral education, 35-36
  self-direction and, 45
  social responsibility and, 142, 145-149
Curriculum improvement, as disciplinary approach, 42-62, 117, 160

Democratic ideal, 3-4, 33, 73, 119, 163-164
Destructive behavior, redirecting, 141-153
Development
  building on, 21-25
  conditions for, 24
  desirable direction of, 20-21
  of intelligence, 22-26, 32
  moral, 22-27, 40, 116
  as positive concept, 38
  See also Stages of discipline
Developmental goal, 32, 37, 197
Developmental level, 103-104
  See also Development; Stages of discipline
Developmental psychology, 20, 27, 40-41, 182-184
Developmental stages of discipline (see Stages of discipline)
Directions (see Giving directions; Following directions)
Discipline
  academic achievement and, 60-61, 189
  alternative routes to, 5
  children's rights and, 193-197

Discipline (*cont.*)
  classification of pupils and, 193-194
  conception of, 3-5, 39, 197
  developmental approach to, 2, 16, 19-39
  developmental cues for, 19-22
  education and, 3-4
  factors in, 117-137
  ideals in, 6, 33, 197
  as instruction, 13-14, 16
  as learning force, 3
  learning problems and, 45-47
  mind-body dualism and, 4
  in open classrooms, 98-110
  through pupil responsibility, 50-51
  purpose of, 4, 160
  reading and, 45-47
  as responsible attention, 84-85
  stages of, 27-39, 134, 145
  teacher education and, 1-2, 97-98
  and teaching, 13, 65-80
  See also Models of discipline
Discipline problems, 141, 155-179
  strategies for dealing with, 160-178
Disruptive behavior (*see* Discipline problems)
Distractions, 87-88, 101-102
Drill (*see* Training)
Drug therapy, 195-197
Dynamic discipline, 3-4, 17

Ecological factors, 117-137
Educational opportunity, 10, 37-38, 65, 122, 134, 178, 193-194, 198
  as opportunity to respond, 90-92
  See also Equality of opportunity
Emergent models of discipline, 6, 14-15
Emergent situation, 5-6, 16-17, 34, 50-51, 83
  See also Established situation
Empathy, 33, 139, 144, 153
Environmental control, 15
Equality of opportunity, 10, 90-93, 119
Established situation, 5-7, 11, 17, 61-62
  See also Emergent situation

Evaluation, 117, 135-136
Exclusion, 160, 175
Expectancy phenomenon (*see* Teacher expectations, pupil behavior and)
External control, 10-11, 15, 61, 100

Family, 45, 119
Fate control, 15, 148
Fights, heading off, 169-170
Following directions, 29-32
Freudian model, 11-12, 166
Freudian pedagogy, 11-12

Generative stage of discipline, 28, 37-39
Giving directions, 31, 87
Group dynamics model, 6, 12-14, 169
Group situations, 33, 65-66
  See also Group dynamics model; Small group work
Grouping, 117, 119, 133-135
  See also Ability grouping; Teacher expectations, pupil behavior and
Habit formation (*see* Training)
Home, 45, 119-120, 122
Homogeneous grouping (*see* Ability grouping)
Hostile parents, 126
Hyperkinetic children, vs. hyperactive, 195-196

Ignoring misbehavior, 8, 156, 161
Impulsive pupils, 30
Inattention, 17, 83-89
  See also Attention
Independence, 73-76, 103-104, 113-115
  See also Stages of discipline
Independent study, 102, 106-107, 113-114
Interest, 50-53, 67, 104-105
  and attention, 85-87
  developing pupil, 53
  and discipline, 51-60, 73, 110
  and experience, 57-58
Interests
  developing new, 52-53, 60, 99-100
  following, 51-52, 59-60, 98-100, 107, 135

Interests (*cont.*)
  general, 58-60, 113
  identifying, 59-60
  nature of children's, 57-58
  personal, 58-60, 113
Internal control, 11, 15, 100, 153, 163-164

Junior high school, 143-144, 146, 148, 149
Justice, concept of, 20-21, 28, 33

Learners, view of, 5-6, 106
Learning, as social process, 14
Learning centers, 74-75
Learning problems, 10, 21, 45-47, 53-56, 110, 136, 196-197
Life goals, 190, 196
Life space interview, 164, 167-169, 179
Listening, 29-32
Locus of control, 15
  external vs. internal control, 15
  fostering internal control, 15, 153, 169
  self-responsibility and, 15
Low achievers, 21, 53-57, 90-92, 125, 135, 137
Mainstreaming, 194, 198
Means as behavior, 15-16, 48-50
Misbehavior (*see* Discipline problems)
Models of discipline, 5-17
Momentum, 69-70, 76, 109-110
Moral development, 22-27, 40, 116
Moral education, 34-39
Moral judgment (*see* Moral development)
Motivation, 10, 51-60, 67, 105-106, 120, 183-185, 188-190
Movement management, 69-70
Music, 36

National Center on Child Abuse and Neglect, 187, 199
Noise levels, 48-50, 101
Nonreaders (*see* Reading)
Nonreciters, involvement of, 77-81

Open classroom, 75-76, 85-86, 98-110
  management problems in, 100-108
Open education, 98-100, 103-104, 106, 108-110, 114, 116
  See *also* Open classroom
Operant conditioning (*see* Behavior modification)
Opportunities to respond, 90-93
Out-of-school factors, 118-119
Overlapping, 14, 68

Pace, learning, 106-107
Pace, teaching (*see* Momentum)
Parent participation, 121-123
Parent-teacher conferences, 123-128, 137
Parent-teacher relationships, 117, 119-128, 137
Parent-teacher-pupil conferences, 127-128
Parental interest, influence of, 121-122
Parents, 45-46
Peer tutoring, 135
Personal-social growth model, 15-17, 44, 98, 100, 114, 169
  internal control and, 15-17, 100, 116, 163
Piagetian theory, 21-27, 183
Planning, 68, 74-76, 78, 99-100, 102, 108, 141
  with pupils, 32, 39, 48-51, 76, 150
Possibilities vs. limitations, 197
Praise, 8-9, 142, 183
Preventing misbehavior, 66
Program, pupil knowledge of, 76, 81, 136
  See *also* Planning
Prompting, 91-92
Protective restraint, 162, 170
Proximity, control through, 166
Psychoanalytic theory, 12
Psychodynamic model, 11-12, 14, 17, 166, 179
Public libraries, 132
Punishment, 5, 8, 161, 164, 172-179, 183

Punishment (*cont.*)
corporal (*see* Corporal punishment
timing of, 173-174
Pupil accountability, 79-80
Pupil-teacher conference, 128, 137
Pupil-teacher contacts, inequality of, 90-93
Purposeful activity, 47-48
Pygmalion effect (*see* Teacher expectations)

Reading
creating interest in, 47, 54-57, 108-109, 132
helping problem readers, 46-47, 54-56
methods, 46-47, 54-57
to nonreaders, 1, 55-56
Reciprocity, 24-26, 139
characteristics of, 25
development of, 25
Recitation group, 70, 77-80
involvement vs. waiting, 77-81
Redirecting negative behavior, 15, 140-143, 157
Reinforcement, 7, 9, 163
See also Behavior modification
Reluctant parents, 122-123
Repetition (*see* Training)
Reprimands, 160, 172
soft vs. loud, 165-166
Respect for others, 61-62
place in the curriculum, 62
Responsibility, 28, 78-81, 84-85, 104, 136, 163-164, 187-188
See also Social responsibility; Socialization
Restitution, 24-25, 160, 168
vs. retribution, 25
Retribution, 25, 158
Rewards, 7, 11, 105
Rights vs. needs, 191-192
Ripple effect, 157-158, 159
Rote teaching, 72-73, 79
Routines, as means, 31
Rules, 23, 25-26, 30-31, 40, 49, 107-108, 111, 194-195

Rules (*cont.*)
understanding basis for reasonable, 28, 32, 173

School, aims of, 4, 33, 45
School assembly, 37
Science, 36, 48, 50, 134, 135
Seatwork, 73-74
Self-actualization, 184, 189-190
Self-contained classroom (*see* Classroom)
Self-direction, 3-4, 7, 10, 14-17, 26, 33, 37-38, 40, 44-45, 73, 81, 113, 140-142, 148, 164, 182, 196-197
vs. self-control, 3, 197
vs. submission, 4, 33
Self-discipline, 84
See also Self-direction
Self-esteem, 184, 188-189, 196-197
Self-fulfilling prophecy (*see* Teacher expectations)
Self-management (*see* Personal-social growth model; Self-direction)
Sharing, 30-31
Significant others, 120, 125
Skills, 44, 57, 61, 87, 99-100, 122, 152
application of, 86-87, 98
Small group work, 33-34, 102, 110-112
Social responsibility, 33-34, 36-39, 108, 133, 141-143
models and, 38-39
practice in assuming, 38, 50-51, 140-152
Social studies, 33, 36, 52, 134, 135, 147-148
Socialization, 25-26, 32-33, 37, 51, 139-141
of unsocialized children, 25, 112, 139-153
Space, use of, 98, 102-103
Special education placement, 193-194
Stages of discipline, 27-39, 134, 145, 169, 173, 188, 190-191, 197
Standards
behavioral, 48-50, 99-100
of work, 84-86, 100, 106-107
Static discipline, 3, 17

Mount Saint Mary's College
Emmitsburg, MD 21727

DEC 1 7 1980

Subgroups, 74, 134, 151
  See also Recitation group
Suspension, 175-176, 193

Teacher
  authority of, in classroom (*see*
    Teacher authority)
  basic needs of pupils and, 188-191
  child development and, 19-21
  ideal of, 6
  as protector, 171-172
  pupil behavior and, 67-68
  role of, 28-29, 32-33, 37-40, 65, 97,
    100-101, 117, 171
  as role model, 25, 28, 31-32, 38-39
  as socializing agent, 174
Teacher authority, 12-14, 140
  vs. authoritarian behavior, 66
  classroom management and, 67-68
  as a quality, 66-69
  teaching effectiveness and, 67
Teacher behavior, pupil behavior and,
    66-68
Teacher expectations, pupil behavior
    and, 89-96, 189
Teacher, support for, 80-81
Teachers' unions, 80, 119
Teaching, 13, 17-18, 32, 42, 65-81, 88,
    97-100, 108-115, 117, 132, 136,
    147-148, 151, 197
  survival stage of, 1-2, 83

Team teaching, 102
Television, countering harmful effects
    of violence on, 132-133
  pupil behavior and, 128-132
Time out procedure, 8
Training, 6-7, 30, 45, 61-62, 164
  vs. behavior modification, 11
  as building block, 11
  vs. education, 7
  function of, 7
Training model (*see* Training)

Understanding (*see* Psychodynamic
    model)
Uninterested pupils (*see* Interest)
Unsocialized children (*see* Socializa-
    tion)
Urban vs. suburban discipline, 10

Values, 44
  individual vs. social, 33
  respect for others, 62
Vandalism, 37, 144
Verbal control, 164-166
Voice
  as conveyor of teacher's expecta-
    tion, 93, 96
  soft vs. loud reprimands, 165-166

Waiting, problem of, 71-79
Withitness, 13-14, 68, 170
Worksheets, 54, 86, 108-109